Critical Approaches to Six Major English Works:

Beowulf through *Paradise Lost*

edited by

R. M. Lumiansky

and

Herschel Baker

UNIVERSITY OF PENNSYLVANIA PRESS

PHILADELPHIA

PREFACE

The essays in this book treat six literary works—perhaps the six greatest literary accomplishments—which have come down to us from medieval and renaissance England. They are also probably the early English writings most widely read and studied in the United States. All six essays here presented have the same purpose and use the same method. In each, the writer is concerned with *the literary work as a whole*. First he surveys the critical approaches to it during the past twenty or thirty years. Then he presents in some detail that approach which in his opinion most nearly does it and its author full justice. The two editors and the six essayists believe that students, teachers, and general readers should find this collection interesting and helpful in their consideration of the six outstanding literary pieces.

The plan for this book developed in connection with the 1967 Program for English Section I of the Modern Language Association of America. The concern of that Section is English Literature from the Beginnings to 1660. Robert Lumiansky, as Section chairman, and Herschel Baker, as Section secretary, agreed early in 1966 upon the plan for the Program. They then selected the six books to be treated, and invited the six specialists to participate. By October, 1967, the six essays were in hand. At the Section meeting in Chicago, December 29, 1967, each of the six scholars presented a twenty-minute oral summary of his essay to an audience of several hundred persons. The editors are now pleased to make the essays available in full to a wider audience by means of this book.

CONTENTS

Critical Approaches to
Six Major English Works:
Beowulf through *Paradise Lost*

BEOWULF

R. E. Kaske

I

At the beginning of his famous paper on the thematic coherence of *Beowulf*,[1] now more than thirty years old, J. R. R. Tolkien remarks that the existing scholarship on the poem "is poor in criticism, criticism that is directed to the understanding of a poem as a poem" (p. 3). Though it is obvious that the past three decades have witnessed a spectacular improvement in our general intentions toward the poem *Beowulf*—in great part the result of Tolkien's essay itself—a survey of such attempts as have been made to interpret the poem *as a whole* leaves one with the impression that his comment is not altogether outdated. Let me add immediately that I do not intend to minimize the considerable progress which has in fact been made during this period toward a convincing interpretation of *Beowulf*. On the one hand, we have had countless interpretative studies of particular aspects or parts of the poem, many of them sensitive and well informed. Outstanding examples are a monograph by Anton Pirkhofer on the portrayal of characters in *Beowulf*;[2] and Adrien Bonjour's analyses of the digressions and other specific passages, which, while producing no overall interpretation beyond that of Tolkien, have made important contributions to our understanding of the poem.[3] On the other hand, there have been a number of

major works which bear upon the interpretation of *Beowulf*
with varying degrees of directness, though they cannot be
thought of as primarily attempts to interpret it. Obvious examples are the metrical studies of John C. Pope, A. J. Bliss, and
others; [4] the introduction and notes in the edition of C. L.
Wrenn (London, 1953); Dorothy Whitelock's valuable exploration of the poem's intellectual background in *The Audience of Beowulf* (Oxford, 1951); and Kenneth Sisam's *The
Structure of Beowulf* (Oxford, 1965), in large part a reaction
against the strenuous critical effort of the past thirty-odd years.
Another example, perhaps less obvious, is Arthur G. Brodeur's
admirable study *The Art of Beowulf* (Berkeley, 1959), which
—despite keen individual analyses like those of the role of
Unferþ (pp. 143–57), the passage on Freawaru and Ingeld
(pp. 157–81), and the "subplot" depending on the fall of
Hygelac (pp. 75–87)—is on the whole, as its title indicates,
a descriptive treatment of various aspects of the poem rather
than a comprehensive interpretation of it. We may notice in
passing that any relation of the prolonged controversy concerning oral formulas to the interpretation of *Beowulf* seems
thus far to be undefined and tentative, pending the development of a distinctive interpretative approach which can be
convincingly applied to the poem as we have it.

Studies devoted to the interpretation of *Beowulf* as a whole
during the past thirty years are, as I have suggested, fewer and
in many cases less substantial than might be expected in an era
enthusiastically committed to the intensive analysis of literary
texts. Any account of them must of course begin with Tolkien's *"Beowulf:* The Monsters and the Critics" (note 1,
above). As everyone now knows, Tolkien proposes that the
monsters are at the center of the action precisely because their
universality of meaning transcends what could be expressed
through specific human antagonists, and that the resulting
poem is "essentially a balance, an opposition of ends and

beginnings . . . a contrasted description of two moments in a great life, rising and setting" (p. 29). Despite sporadic and, in my opinion, quite unsuccessful attacks,[5] this basic view of the poem seems to have gained for itself something like a core of general acceptance, and most subsequent interpretations will be found to rest on it in one way or another. To this deserved encomium, one should add that Tolkien's analysis is limited to the poem's broadest and simplest design, and makes no attempt to clarify its complex lesser patterns: the relation of episode to episode, the relevance of the digressive passages, and so on. To this extent his essay is not so much a comprehensive interpretation of *Beowulf,* as a brilliant indication of the direction in which such an interpretation is to be looked for. The same sort of distinction applies much more completely to another valuable pioneering study, Marie Padgett Hamilton's "The Religious Principle in *Beowulf*"[6]—which, though hardly offering a unified interpretation of the poem, has increased radically our awareness of the possibilities for reading it in the light of patristic thought.

Let us glance next at a few brief articles presenting more or less summary opinions about the governing theme of *Beowulf.* B. J. Timmer's *"Beowulf:* The Poem and Its Poet,"[7] after stressing the importance of the number three in the structure of the poem, reaches a conclusion in many ways reminiscent of Tolkien:

> *Beowulf* . . . was written for the purpose of strengthening the Christian faith of the readers, rather than as a "speculum principum." Although *not* an allegory, it depicts the powers of Utgarðr invading the happiness of man as the evil powers that beset any man in this world and Beowulf as the representative of what is good. The battle of good and evil is the poet's theme, but he embroidered it upon a pagan background. But the poet knows

—and that is why the poem is not an allegory—that man is mortal and that the powers of evil remain: Beowulf is doomed to die and evil wins in spite of the slaying of the monsters. He chose a theme which would appeal to his readers and placed it against a background which would appeal even more, because it is the background of stories with which they were still familiar, representing an attitude to life which was not far removed from them—or from him—in time. It was his purpose to appeal to his readers and thus to strengthen them in their belief in the Christian faith. *Beowulf* is a compromise—an extremely clever and original one—made for religious-didactic purposes between heathendom and christianity [pp. 125–26].

Kemp Malone, in *"Beowulf,"* [8] maintains that the poet, "devout Christian though he is, finds much to admire in the pagan cultural tradition which, as an Englishman, he inherited from ancient Germania. It is his purpose to glorify this heroic heritage. . . . He accomplishes his purpose by laying stress upon those things in Germanic tradition which agree with Christianity or at any rate do not clash seriously with the Christian faith" (p. 162). Most of the episodes in the poem have the function of placing the hero in his historical setting; those in the first part place him within Germania at large, while those in the second part place him specifically within the Geatish tribe (p. 167). The first part of the poem is predominantly cheerful in tone, the second part melancholy; but "The hero is he who, like Beowulf, faces the worst without flinching and dies that others may live" (p. 172). In a later article, "Symbolism in 'Beowulf': Some Suggestions," [9] Malone proposes that the Danes in Heorot represent an ideal society preyed on by the murderous outlaw Grendel; for the dragon he suggests more hesitantly two early interpretations by Grundtvig, which identify him either with the destructive forces of nature or with greed (p. 90). J. L. N. O'Loughlin, in *"Beowulf*—Its Unity and Purpose,"[10] summarizes what strikes me as a totally inconclusive argument, ". . . we see, in the secular aspect of *Beowulf,* the Germanic ideal of placation and the settlement of feuds in conflict with kings and people who will not or cannot come to terms, and parallel with it, and reinforcing it, in the religious aspect, the Christian ethic in conflict with the inhuman powers of evil with whom no compromise is possible" (p. 13).

In "Beowulf's Three Great Fights,"[11] H. L. Rogers proposes to "examine the poet's attitude towards the material he used, in order to gain a better appreciation of why he made his poem as he did" (p. 339). Rogers' understanding of the poem, so far as I am able to discern it, seems most nearly expressed in the remarks, ". . . I do not believe that *Beowulf* can be regarded as an artistic unity in the modern sense, or that the poem has a higher theme than the life and death of its hero" (p. 341), and "The treatment in the three fights of the motives of weapons, treasure, and society implies a moral idea in which the poet believed: that a man should not trust in the things of this world, for they will fail him" (p. 342). His accompanying argument, however, is too scattered and lacking in point, and too dependent on summary of the action, to support even these rather unambitious judgments. The limitations of plot-summary as an approach to the interpretation of *Beowulf* are demonstrated afresh by John A. Nist in *The Structure and Texture of Beowulf,*[12] which emphasizes a tripartite structure in the poem supported by "a brilliant triad of variation: (1) The hero killed in the first act is Hondscio; in the second, Aeschere; in the third, Beowulf himself. (2) The enemy is progressively more justified throughout the three acts: viciousness in Grendel, vengeance in Grendel's dam, vengeance and self-preservation in the hoard-guarding dragon. (3) Beowulf's struggles become increasingly difficult" (pp. 20–22). Eight "basic intentions" of the poet provide ten major themes or motifs, the "cyclic linkage" of which is presented in a chart (pp. 22–24). Nist's support for this outline consists of an extended summary of the three major divisions of the poem (pp. 25–65), with the place of critical analysis filled largely by remarks like "excellent artistry," "brilliant pointillist description," and "truly magnificent movement."

Nearly all the more recent attempts to interpret the poem as a whole are distinctively "Christian," though differing widely in their emphases. Maurice B. McNamee, S.J., in *Honor and the Epic Hero* (New York, 1960), maintains that "the character of Beowulf is such a complete verification of the Christian notion of the heroic or the magnanimous that it would almost seem to have been created to exemplify the virtue as Saint Paul and the early church Fathers sketched it—limited by the virtues of humility and charity" (p. 109). In his article *"Beowulf*—An Allegory of Salvation?" [13] Father McNamee suggests that "as an allegory of the Christian story of salvation the *Beowulf* poem both echoes the liturgy and reflects New Testament theological dogma" (p. 191). Beowulf's three major combats allegorize various aspects of the Redemption: the fight with Grendel reflects the essential story of salvation; the descent to the mere echoes the regenerative symbolism of baptism, as well as the Harrowing of Hell; the fight with the dragon allegorizes the death of the Savior. Besides containing a number of curious errors—for example, a reference to Beowulf as "expiring, like Christ, at the ninth hour" ("Allegory of Salvation," p. 204)—these studies consistently lack both the detailed documentation and the disciplined literary analysis normally needed to support such an interpretation, and so produce no really close correspondences of the kind that might be expected to carry conviction. A somewhat similar interpretation—more extensively documented, and proposing a typological rather than an allegorical meaning—is offered by Lewis E. Nicholson in "The Literal Meaning and Symbolic Structure of *Beowulf*." [14] The setting of *Beowulf*, Nicholson argues, is antediluvian (pp. 156–66). The poem itself "contains a source of unity beyond simply the events in the literal, surface narrative, and this unity grows out of a consistent use of baptismal symbolism derived largely from the Easter vigil service of Holy Saturday" (p. 168); for example, Beowulf's seven-night swimming match with Breca reflects typologically the early Christian image of baptism as a struggle with a demon hidden in the waters, along with its symbolic relation to the seven world-ages (pp. 171–9). Nicholson concludes, "The *Beowulf*, then, *is* a glorification of Germania, but only insofar as Germania is in turn a glorification of the City of God" (p. 201). This last idea is in itself an exciting one, and several of Nicholson's proposed correspondences are individually attractive (e.g., pp. 183–84 and n. 68). In general, however, his interpretation suffers seriously from a tendency to ignore equally plausible alternative explanations for particular passages and motifs; from the apparent absence of a meaningful pattern in his proposed series of typological correspondences; and particularly from the lack of a really convincing "cornerstone of argument"—that is, of a single detail or passage which would constitute a problem if *not* interpreted as he suggests.

A more persuasive typological approach is that of Charles Donahue in "*Beowulf* and Christian Tradition: A Reconsideration from a Celtic Stance." [15] For the theological background of the poem, Donahue proposes an "Insular Mode" of Christianity peculiar to Ireland and Britain—a way of thought doctrinally less rigorous than its Augustinian counterpart, and allowing for a greater importance of the *lex naturæ* along with a greater reverence toward the pagan past (pp. 59–74). His interpretation is summarized as follows:

In arriving at his view of the theological stratum of Beowulf's personality, I believe, the poet found his first
paradigm in the account of Abraham in Genesis as interpreted by St. Paul. The first part of the poem deals with
the moment where the hero arrives at a faith and hope, a
trust, in God like that of Abraham. In the second part,
the account of the hero's death, the paradigm shifts to
Job as the hero, though tempted to despair, persists in
hope despite the fact that God is withdrawing His gifts.
At the same time he attains to a charity such as that
described by St. John and hence, like the other moral
heroes under the natural law, Job for example in the
passage just cited, he becomes a *figura* of Christ [p. 85].

Donahue's suggestion concerning the "Insular Mode" of
Christianity strikes me as the most plausible historical explanation yet proposed for the theological peculiarities of *Beowulf*. His typological interpretation of the poem itself points in
what seems to me a promising direction, and could well be
essentially correct—though here again I would like to see a
greater closeness in the proposed correspondences, and one or
more specific cornerstones of evidence on which the rest of his
analysis could be convincingly based.

A Christian poem of a different sort emerges from three
articles by Margaret E. Goldsmith: "The Christian Theme of
Beowulf," "The Christian Perspective in *Beowulf*," and "The
Choice in *Beowulf*." [16] Central in all these studies (though it
seems to become progressively milder and more qualified) is
the view of Beowulf himself as less than an ideal figure—a
noble though pagan hero, inevitably touched by the pride and
avarice warned against in Hroðgar's sermon:

. . . Beowulf is celebrated and yet, in a sense, found
wanting, by the Christian poet. The hero, knowing nothing of Christ, is unregenerate man at his mightiest and

most magnanimous. He conforms to the laws of his human nature, not to the laws of the Church. . . . In the first half of the poem the Christian ideal of loving service fuses with the Germanic ideal of love and loyalty to the lord. In the second part, the two ethics are in conflict in the person of the king, and here, by a subtle use of contrastive Christian allusion, the poet shows not only human strength and courage at their highest, but at the same time the weakness of unregenerate man alone in face of the Enemy ["Choice," pp. 63, 70].

A similar though more cogent distinction between the worthiness of Beowulf's actions in the two parts of the poem is drawn by John Leyerle in "Beowulf the Hero and the King." [17] According to Leyerle, the major theme of *Beowulf* is

the fatal contradiction at the core of heroic society. The hero follows a code that exalts indomitable will and valour in the individual, but society requires a king who acts for the common good, not for his own glory. The greater the hero, the more likely his tendency to imprudent action as king. The three battles with the monsters, the central episodes in the poem, reveal a pattern in which Beowulf's pre-eminence as a hero leads to the destruction of the Geats when he becomes king. . . . All turns on the figure of Beowulf, a man of magnificence, whose understandable, almost inevitable pride commits him to individual, heroic action and leads to a national calamity by leaving his race without mature leadership at a time of extreme crisis, facing human enemies much more destructive than the dragon [pp. 89, 101–02].

The studies of Goldsmith and Leyerle are full of illuminating points,[18] and their general thesis concerning the hero—particu-

larly as formulated by Leyerle—deserves serious consideration. My own opinion is that their arguments (especially that
of Goldsmith) suffer continually from small distortions of
emphasis, thus producing interpretations which, while difficult
to "disprove," manage to be basically at odds with what will
impress most readers as the governing attitude of the poem.

Most recently Charles Moorman, in "The Essential Paganism of *Beowulf*," [19] has reacted against the dominance of such
interpretations, maintaining instead that "the whole of *Beowulf*, despite its Christian elements, is strongly and most un-
Christianly pessimistic in its view of life and history" (p. 5).
The essence of Moorman's argument, however, seems based
on a confusion between an unequivocally pagan outlook and
what might more accurately be called a "secular emphasis";
the final pessimism of the poem, which he explains as a legacy
from Nordic mythology, seems to me at least equally plausible
as the traditional "pessimism" of the Christian contemplating
the transience of worldly effects.

From the preceding survey, it is evident that during the past
twenty years or so the richest and most informative interpretations of *Beowulf* (apart from the question of their ultimate
credibility) have been those employing Christian material and
ways of thought. One reason, of course, is the comparative
general neglect of Latin Christianity by earlier interpreters of
medieval vernacular literature, and its recent enthusiastic re-
discovery; another is the plethora of Christian writing which
survives from the early Middle Ages, as against the almost
complete lack of everything else; still another, I suspect, is the
fact that any Christianity which can be convincingly revealed
in *Beowulf*, with its pagan setting and essentially secular story,
is likely to be present in unusually complex and interesting
ways. Within the various Christian interpretations, the most
important single critical question at the moment seems to be

that of the poet's attitude toward Beowulf himself: to what extent is he an ideal heroic figure (possibly bearing some relation to Christ), and to what extent a somber portrayal of the inevitable doom that attends even the noblest of non-Christians? One possible answer will be suggested in my own interpretation of the poem, to which let us now turn.

II

The most profitable approach to *Beowulf* that I have found so far is by way of the old, widely recognized heroic ideal whose Latin formulation is *sapientia et fortitudo* ("wisdom and prowess").[20] In using this ideal as a basis for analyzing *Beowulf,* I do not of course mean to deny the existence or importance of other major themes and organizing principles in the poem. Interpretation of a work as early and isolated as *Beowulf* must of necessity be highly empirical; and the assumption that *sapientia et fortitudo* operates somehow as its thematic center seems to me to explain more about the poem —both its central narrative and its digressions—than any other theory I know of. In itself, of course, a series of direct references to such a formula, even at crucial points in the action, might be understood plausibly enough as an incidental interest of the poet; while, on the other hand, an apparent consciousness of it in the poem's larger patterns might in itself be reasonably discounted as inevitable. (In how many epics, for example, is the hero *not* depicted as wise and brave?) In *Beowulf,* however, the continual prominence of *sapientia et fortitudo* in both these ways seems to me to speak strongly for its being the governing theme.

Ernst Curtius has shown clearly the currency of this heroic ideal in authors possibly contributing to or reflecting aspects of the culture that produced *Beowulf:* Statius, "Dares" and "Dictys," Fulgentius, Alcuin, the *Waltharius,* the

Chanson de Roland, and perhaps most explicitly Isidore's
Etymologiae: "Nam heroes appellantur viri quasi aerii et
caelo digni propter sapientiam et fortitudinem." * [21] Similar
dichotomies occur frequently in the Old Testament, and occasionally in the *Disticha Catonis* and the Irish *Instructions
of Cormac.* In the Germanic tradition as we have it, the ideal
appears several times in the poems of the *Edda* as well as
in Old English poems like *Widsiþ* (138–41) and the *Gifts of
Men* (39–43, 76–77). There seems small room for doubt,
then, that *sapientia et fortitudo* as a heroic ideal was familiar
in the literature and the ways of thought most likely to have
been available to the poet of *Beowulf,* and that there is no *a
priori* unlikelihood about his having known and used the
theme.

But if so, what did it mean to him? As the quality of a
hero, *fortitudo* implies physical might and courage consistently enough. With regard to *sapientia,* we seem to have
in *Beowulf* a general, eclectic concept including such diverse
qualities as practical cleverness, skill in words and works,
knowledge of the past, ability to predict accurately, and
ability to choose rightly in matters of conduct. But there is a
further, partly overlapping problem: Christian *sapientia* or
pagan Germanic *sapientia?* I believe that in the theme of
sapientia et fortitudo itself we may find (to misapply a remark of Tolkien's) "the precise point at which an imagination, pondering old and new, was kindled" [22]—that the poet
has used this old ideal as an area of synthesis between
Christianity and Germanic paganism. In a broad way, he
seems first to draw on both traditions primarily as they relate to aspects of *sapientia et fortitudo;* and secondly, within

* For men are called "heroes" [*heroes*] as if to say that they are
"aerial" [*aerii*], and worthy of heaven on account of wisdom and
prowess.

this circumscribed area he seems to emphasize those parts of each tradition that can be made reasonably compatible with the other. We may notice that a core of this kind in the poem helps also to account for some of its apparent large ambiguities, like for example the co-existence of eternal salvation and earthly glory as the goals of human life; if Beowulf is deliberately made to behave wisely and bravely according to both codes, then the very ambiguity of both the *soðfæstra dom* and earthly *lof* is not only relevant but in a way demanded.

In Part I (1–2199), we find five key allusions to the *sapientia et fortitudo* of Beowulf, arranged symmetrically within the poem and themselves following a pattern of increasing elaborateness. The first is the poet's summarizing description of him as "snotor ond swyðferhð" (826), immediately following the defeat of Grendel. The second is Wealhþeow's admonition, "cen þec mid cræfte ond þyssum cnyhtum wæs/ lara liðe" (1219–20), near the end of the festivities following Grendel's defeat. The third is Hroðgar's remark, "Eal þu hit geþyldum healdest,/ mægen mid modes snyttrum" (1705–06), following the defeat of Grendel's mother. The fourth is Hroðgar's similar remark, "þu eart mægenes strang ond on mode frod,/ wis wordcwida" (1844–45), near the end of the festivities following her defeat. So far, I trust the symmetry is clear: a reference to Beowulf's *sapientia et fortitudo* as the thematic climax of each battle and of each celebration following his battles. The fifth and most elaborate statement occurs at the end of Beowulf's reception at the court of Hygelac, and seems to serve as the thematic climax of Part I as a whole. After praising Beowulf's *fortitudo* (2177–78) and summarizing the *sapientia* of his career (2178–80), the poet adds what sounds like an exact confirmation of Hroðgar's comment following the fall of Grendel's mother:

næs him hreoh sefa,
ac he mancynnes   mæste cræfte
ginfæstan gife,   þe him god sealde,
heold hildedeor.   (2180–83)

These five important passages are supported by Beowulf's speeches and actions in Part I. His *fortitudo* is obvious. His *sapientia* is variously illustrated by his skill and prudence in battle and a wisdom and foresight in the ways of violence generally; his skill in speech; his ability to predict accurately in his own and others' affairs; his respect for the counsels of the wise; his diplomatic ability, apparently including a grasp of situation and innuendo (1826–39); his realization of his dependence on higher powers; and by pagan Germanic standards, his properly high evaluation of glory. As a specific example, we may notice Beowulf's successive encounters with the coastwarden, Wulfgar, Hroðgar, and Unferþ, which form a series of confrontations designed to illustrate his *sapientia* in handling different types of questioners, and a broad parallel to the test of his *fortitudo* in the monster fights. The first three questioners are legitimate and courteous, and the success of Beowulf's answers to them is evident; the last, Unferþ, provides a hostile test of his *sapientia,* and can perhaps be interpreted in accordance with Gregorian psychology as the speaker of *sapientia* who is himself no longer *sapiens.*[23] Unferþ's taunt accuses Beowulf of recklessness—a lack of *sapientia*—and of a *fortitudo* inferior to Breca's. Beowulf defends his *sapientia* by emphasizing the formal *beot* (536) with its implicit purpose of attaining glory; the fitness of the venture for boys (535–37); and their prudence in carrying weapons (539–41). To the reflection on his *fortitudo* he replies that he was not overcome; and that for him—unlike Breca—the exploit turned into an adventure worthy of a grown warrior: a fight against monsters, representing like Grendel the forces of external violence.

With this suggestion of how the ideal applies to Beowulf in Part I, I turn to Hroðgar. Like Nestor, he is a model of kingly *sapientia* no longer supported by *fortitudo*. His *sapientia* is of course different from that of *Beowulf*—a contemplative wisdom primarily of inner cultivation of self, rather than of external proficiency and accomplishment. It receives its greatest expression in his "sermon," introduced as a sort of typical case-history to explain the phenomenon of such a king as Heremod. The explanation itself is simply a psychological analysis—in terms of patristic psychology, chiefly that of Augustine and Gregory—of the loss of *sapientia* in the human mind.[24] *Sapientia* is bestowed by God (1724–27). The beginning of the man's downfall springs from absorption in worldly delights (1727–39). Pride, the beginning of all sin, springs up as the *weard,* the *sawele hyrde*—probably *sapientia* itself—falls asleep (1741–42); it is followed by avarice, in the Augustinian sense of inordinate desire generally (1748); other sins follow, and the final state of the man is one of *malitia*—the continuing perversion of the mind to evil, and the antithesis of *sapientia* (1749–52). Against such a course, Beowulf is advised to choose *þæt selre . . . ece rædas* (1759–60)—the lasting counsels of *sapientia.*

But if Hroðgar is a model of kingly *sapientia,* how does he make such mistakes as the marriage of Freawaru to Ingeld, and, apparently, the unwise toleration of Hroþulf at the Danish court? There are situations in which wise decision itself must include a reliance on physical courage and prowess; and Hroðgar's very *sapientia* has been circumscribed by his decline in *fortitudo.*[25] As we meet him in the poem, he is no longer at his best when facing decisions involving violence or the prospect of it—a weakness that seems further dramatized by his failure to foresee the likelihood of vengeance for Grendel, though he had known that there were a pair of monsters (1345–57); by the aimless and ineffectual (though richly poetic) quality of his long speech to Beowulf after the fresh violence (1322–82), contrasted with Beowulf's brief and purposeful reply (1384–96); and possibly by his leadership of the *witan* who form the mistaken judgment about the violent action beneath the mere (1591–1602). This development in Hroðgar is paralleled in the Danish nation at large. *Sapientia* is there in great variety: Hroðgar, Wealhþeow, in a sense Unferþ, the scop, Æschere (2122–23), and the *witan* who are mentioned so often. But except for the early references to the coastwarden and Wulfgar, who play no further part in the story, we hear nothing about present Danish *fortitudo* and a good deal about its absence; and *sapientia* alone is at a loss against the brute violence of Grendel, as is shown dramatically by the Danes' futile search for an effective *ræd* (171–74) and by a remark of Hroðgar after the combat:

> Nu scealc hafað
> þurh drihtnes miht   dæd gefremede
> ðe we ealle   ær ne meahton
> snyttrum besyrwan.   (939–42)

As the product of this situation comes Grendel, whom I take to be an embodiment of external evil, or violence—a perversion of *fortitudo,* completely freed from the restraints of *sapientia* and governed instead by *malitia.* This interpretation of Grendel is supported not only by his reckless savagery but also by his relation to Cain and the giants of the Old Testament, who are traditionally creatures of strife and violence lacking in *sapientia.*[26] Just as Beowulf is first mentioned with a comment on his *fortitudo* (196–98), so Grendel is introduced as *se ellengǣst* (86); and the succeeding epithets and brief descriptions of him and his actions seem to lay particular stress on violent brutality. His lack of *sapientia* is alluded to in Beowulf's *for his wonhydum* (434) and possibly also in the later variant explanation that Grendel does not know how to use weapons (681–82); his rash approach (723–26, 739–40) seems contrasted with the circumspection of Beowulf (736–38); there is a continual contrast between what Grendel hopes or expects and what actually happens (e.g., 712–13 vs. 718–19; 730–34 vs. 734–36); and in terms of patristic thought, an absence of *sapientia* seems clearly implied by descriptions like *ond no mearn fore . . . wæs to fæst on þam* (136–37), *godes yrre bær* (711), and *dreamum bedæled* (721). There is, then, the strongest of contrasts between Grendel, who is all action and no reflection, and Hroðgar and his Danes, who reflect a good deal more than they act. And the tragedy of the Danish situation lies in this very spectacle of a rich and varied *sapientia*— in broad terms, a culture—so completely at the mercy of the mindless force which in a sense it has invited into being, and the sole remedy for which is an extraordinary *fortitudo:*

> Swa ða mælceare   maga Healfdenes
> singala seað,   ne mihte snotor hæleð
> wean onwendan;   wæs þæt gewin to swyð,
> laþ ond longsum.   (189–92)

Ealdgewinna (1776) is Hroðgar's final word for Grendel, and for the strife, *ofer ealdgewin* (1781); he is the outer evil that waits forever on a diminishing *fortitudo.* For the apparent duplication of motif created by the introduction of Grendel's mother, there are several possible explanations; most important, I believe, is the fact that she represents violence motivated by the duty of vengeance as against the purely malicious violence of Grendel, and so provides an important comment on the power of even defeated violence to spawn further violence.

Let us now turn to Hygelac and the Geats. Hygelac himself is presented as a king of unblemished *fortitudo,* but lacking in the developed *sapientia* of an ideal hero-king. The failing is epitomized in the repeated mentions of his Frankish raid, first introduced with a direct mention of his recklessness: "syþðan he for wlenco wean ahsode . . ." (1206). But I think this view of Hygelac is supported also by such things as his previous underestimation of Beowulf (2185–88); his evident opposition to the judgment of the wise men who encouraged Beowulf's exploit (202–04, 415–20, 1987–88); and the absence of a single epithet for him expressing a variant of *sapiens,* though he is described repeatedly as *fortis.* Hygelac, then, forms a basic contrast to Hroðgar, and the contrast is sharpened by the typical motifs of vigorous youth and wise old age. Together, the two constitute a melancholy presentation of the ideal almost inevitably divided; rarely does there come a Hroþgar-Hygelac, a man enduringly apt for all occasions, a Beowulf.

Hygelac is also implicitly contrasted with his wise young queen, Hygd (1926–28)—a contrast which gives new pertinence to the "þryð-Offa" episode which follows it. Offa is explicitly characterized by the ideal of *sapientia et fortitudo* (1957–60); his queen behaved unwisely before her marriage but changed under Offa's rule. Of the Geatish royal pair it is evidently the queen who is wise and the king who is less so; and Hygelac is not brought to kingly *sapientia* but dies through his own audacity, leaving queen and people without the protection of his *fortitudo.* The point of the contrast seems to be that while a wise and powerful king can control unwise tendencies in his queen, a wise queen in heroic times—even Hygd or Wealhþeow—can do little about a fatal lack in her lord. The successful ruler must combine both heroic virtues in himself. The significance of this contrast between Hygelac and Hygd seems supported also by a play on the meanings latent in the two names themselves, with "Hygd" carrying its obvious meaning "mind *or* thought," and "Hygelac" a meaning like "instability of mind." [27]

Just as the Danish nation resembles Hroðgar, so the Geats—particularly the Geatish rulers—share in various ways the failing of Hygelac. The Geatish *fortitudo* and lack of *sapientia* are elaborated most fully in the historical accounts of Part II, which I interpret as forming a sort of catalogue of persistent unwisdom in the Geatish royal house—the fatal *tristitia* of Hreþel, the audacity at the Ravenswood (2926–27), Hygelac's raid, the unwise royal hospitality of Heardred, and all their far-reaching consequences [28]—in contrast to the sober conduct of Beowulf himself where he appears in these affairs. As Danish lack of *fortitudo* invites Grendel, so Geatish lack of *sapientia* (as we shall see) partly accounts for the dragon. And as Danish lack of *fortitudo* circumscribes *sapientia* and results ultimately in disaster, so Geatish lack of *sapientia* exhausts *fortitudo*—witness Beowulf's retainers—and at the end leaves the Geat nation helpless before the very enemies made in earlier days through lack of *sapientia*.

We are now confronted by the difficult second part of the poem. Like Part I, it is governed by the ideal of *sapientia et fortitudo,* though less obviously and with an important difference: Beowulf has progressed from hero to hero-king, and the ideal accordingly exists in relation to a different set of responsibilities and goals. Again, however, we find a somewhat symmetrical pattern of three major statements of the theme, all more elaborate than those in Part I, and all bearing a direct relation to Beowulf's kingship. The first occurs at his real entry into Part II, following the announcement that his own hall has been burned. His *sapientia,* particularly his freedom from the pride warned against by Hroðgar, is illustrated by his wholesome fear of having transgressed the *ealde riht* (2327–32); [29] his *fortitudo,* by his determina-

tion to meet the dragon (2335–36, 2345ff.). The dichot-
omy is sharpened by the introductory epithets *se wisa* (2329)
for the first part, and *guðkyning* (2335) for the second. The
second major statement is Beowulf's own summary, following
the fatal battle, of his career as king—emphasizing first his
fortitudo by his protection of the realm (2732–36), then his
sapientia by his avoidance of the major forms of Germanic
wrongdoing (2736–43), all of them Christian sins as well. The
third statement is in the concluding fourteen lines of the poem,
where Beowulf is first praised for *fortitudo* (3169–74), then
said to have been

> *m*anna mildust   ond mon[ðw]ærust,
> leodum liðost   ond lofgeornost.
> (3181–82)

The first three adjectives describe traits traditionally associated
with *sapientia*—as for example in the Vulgate Old Testament,
and in patristic statements of the ideal of kingly *sapientia*.[30]
Lofgeornost I would interpret as the highest manifestation of
Germanic wisdom, preserving a final and meaningful balance
between Christian and pagan as well as between kingly and
individual *sapientia*.

Omitting several lesser statements of the theme, I approach
the interpretation of Part II with one important assumption:
that in view of the prominence given to Hroðgar's sermon in
Part I, and the fact that it is addressed specifically to Beowulf,
we may expect Part II to be in some way an account of how
Beowulf does or does not live up to its precepts. The latter
possibility—despite the recent arguments of Goldsmith, Leyerle, and others—seems to me to be contradicted by the total
emphasis of the poem. Now Hroðgar's advice has consisted,
briefly, of the admonition to cultivate *sapientia* and to combat
its opposite, *malitia,* by checking the initial inner growth of
pride and avarice. One notorious incitement to both pride and

avarice is of course wealth, and the dragon's hoard is quite literally wealth, fought for by Beowulf; this I take to be the most important significance of the curse that is on the treasure, at least that aspect of it that seems to threaten Christian damnation. There is, to be sure, a certain amount of suspense concerning Beowulf's attitude toward the treasure, which might at first be thought to show a final pathetic gleam of avarice (2535–36, 2747–51, 2764–66). Not until he is at the point of death does he reveal his motive fully: as a wise king he has desired not the gold itself, but the good of his people to which it may contribute (2794–2801). The reburial of the treasure with Beowulf I would interpret as a final recognition of his irreplaceable prowess and wisdom. Just as there has been no one else among the Geats strong enough to win the treasure and wise enough to avoid its dangers, so there is no one left among them with the *fortitudo* to hold it and the *sapientia* to use it blamelessly and well. The treasure is *unnyt* (3168) because the rare ability to wield it has perished. Even Wiglaf, who is clearly described by way of the heroic ideal (*hæle hildedior,* 3111; *se snotra sunu Wihstanes,* 3120), is a model young retainer rather than a king, and seems pointedly contrasted with Beowulf in this very respect.[31]

And now at last, what of the dragon? First of all he is a real dragon, by defending his people against whom Beowulf gives final proof of kingly *fortitudo*. But there is more. Just as Grendel is an embodiment of external evil, or violence, so the dragon represents the greatest of internal evils, the perversion of the mind and will, *malitia*. As Grendel is *se ellengǣst* (86), so the dragon is an *atol inwitgǣst* (2670); the roof of his lair is an *inwithrof* (3123), a detail so slenderly related to reality that it inevitably suggests allegorical intent; the identifications of both dragon and fire as *malitia* are patristic commonplaces;[32] and in a very real sense *malitia* does "sit on guard" over worldly treasure, in that the pursuer or possessor of it is subject to the constant initial dangers of pride and avarice. Grendel and the other perpetrators of violence in the poem must of course be thought of as themselves inwardly ridden by *malitia* (hence, I take it, Grendel's *glof* made of dragonskins, 2085–88); the dragon by contrast represents *malitia* itself, as a universal, and so comes a long step nearer to outright allegory than any other figure in the poem. As violence is the perversion of *fortitudo* and is combatted primarily by it, so *malitia* is the perversion or abandonment of *sapientia* and is combatted by it, as in Hroðgar's sermon. That some such idea of internal *malitia* and external violence as two great poles of evil did exist in the poet's scheme of things, seems evident from their mention by Hroðgar:

> ne him inwitsorh
> on sefan sweorceð, ne gesacu ohwær
> ecghete eoweð.   (1736–38)

The dragon fight, then, is a brilliant device for presenting in a single action not only Beowulf's final display of kingly *fortitudo,* but also his development and his ultimate preservation of personal and kingly *sapientia:* first in combatting the everpresent danger of *malitia* in himself as a human being, and so fulfilling the theme announced in Hroðgar's sermon; and secondly, as king, in combatting an apparent spread of *malitia* among his people, typified by the action of the goblet-stealer and the later defection of his own retainers.[33] But if all this is so, why is the dragon allowed to kill Beowulf? The answer, I suspect, lies less in any one compelling reason than in an overall fitness of this ending. For one thing, the theme of Beowulf's defending the Geat nation (against both *malitia* and the ravages of a literal monster) certainly gains added significance from his not only facing death, but undergoing it bravely and willingly for his people's sake. Again, in both Germanic and Christian terms the fact of physical extinction is inevitable and relatively unimportant; what *is* of desperate importance is having fought the good fight. And the dragon fight, as I have interpreted it, is not only the climax but also the summary of Beowulf's kingship and of his life—in a sense, he has always fought the dragon. One may reflect also that an ending in which Beowulf won a final victory over the dragon of *malitia* and yet remained alive would leave him in a condition rather like that of Adam before the Fall; for man, the permanent victory over evil can be realized only through death. And finally, there is about Beowulf's death an air of inevitability that tends to remove it from the cause-and-effect of even symbolic dragon's tusks. Poetically, it is perhaps less accurate to say that the dragon kills Beowulf, than that Beowulf dies fighting the dragon.

Seen in the light of this interpretation, the major digressive passages seem to have the general function of defining by example the relationship between *sapientia et fortitudo* and various important aspects of heroic life. The lay contrasting the careers of Sigemund and Heremod (874–915) and the later passage concerning Hama and Hygelac (1197–1214) center on the problems of fame and wealth respectively.[34] The thematic center of the Sigemund-Heremod passage is clearly the contrast between Sigemund's preservation of his fame through continuing deeds of prowess and courage (874–900), and Heremod's loss of fame through a decline in prowess and courage (901–15). In the Hama-Hygelac passage, the account of Hygelac's disastrous Frankish raid emphasizes the loss of treasure and life resulting from his rashness or lack of wisdom (1202–14); the cryptic allusions to how Hama bore away a famous necklace to *þære byrhtan byrig,* fled the *searoniðas . . . Eormenrices,* and *geceas ecne ræd* (1197–1201) seem understandable as a contrasting picture of the preservation of treasure and life through an exercise of wisdom (with *ecne ræd* as the counsel of wisdom itself, just as in Hroðgar's sermon [1760]). If this is so, both passages employ the device of a positive followed by a negative example, to dramatize two parallel but different themes: the preservation of fame through *fortitudo,* and the preservation of wealth and life through *sapientia.* These themes apparently dictate the appropriate device by which each of the two comparisons is introduced—a heroic lay for the Sigemund-Heremod passage on fame, and two necklaces for the Hama-Hygelac passage on wealth.

Now the Sigemund-Heremod passage follows immediately the first exuberant references to the sudden fame of Beowulf's prowess from his defeat of Grendel (856–61, 871–72); it is followed closely by Hroðgar's speech, with its praise of Beowulf's prowess (939–46) and its enthusiastic prediction of his enduring fame (953–55). The Hama-Hygelac passage is placed at the climactic point of the extended treasure-giving (1020–49, 1193–96) and Wealhþeow's references to it (1173–78) following the defeat of Grendel, and actually grows out of the final gift of the necklace (1195–96); it is immediately followed by Wealhþeow's speech, including a recognition of Beowulf's wisdom as well as his prowess (1219–20), and expressing repeatedly her promise and hope of his continuing prosperity (particularly 1224–26). I interpret the two passages, then, as a pair of thoughtful pauses in the narrative, in which the poet looks with questioning admonishment toward the future fame and prosperity of Beowulf. Behold a young warrior who has just achieved his first significant glory and material reward. Will he—like Sigemund and Hama, and unlike Heremod and Hygelac—keep them undiminished by maintaining or developing his *fortitudo* and his *sapientia?* In the one direction lie the triumphant epitaphs *wide mærost . . . ellendædum* (898–900) and *geceas ecne ræd* (1201); in the other, an inglorious or a wasteful death before the *eotenas* or the *Francan.* Let him take heed.

The notoriously difficult Finn Episode (1071–1159),[35] set with some appearance of symmetry between the Sigemund-Heremod and Hama-Hygelac passages, seems to me to dramatize in complex and inclusive form the relation between the ideal of *sapientia et fortitudo* and the great Germanic concept of *treow.* One important aspect of this relationship appears in the well-known dilemma of Hengest—who, I would suggest, is represented as painfully thinking his way to a wise decision in a problem involving *treow,* and having the strength and courage to carry it out. If so, his thematic relation to Beowulf himself is an important and interesting one. Hengest's predicament is of course one of those hardbitten ethical dilemmas so familiar in early Germanic literature, and the kind of decision it calls for would, in heroic terms, represent one important aspect of *sapientia;* in a poem so variously concerned with *sapientia* as *Beowulf* appears to be, it is not difficult to imagine the need for at least one such situation. The ideal character of Beowulf, however, seems to forbid his being faced with any such ethical conundrums; for him, as a more broadly symbolic figure than Hengest or the old Germanic heroes generally, there must be no laboring through an inherently ambiguous problem to at best a humanly imperfect conclusion. Hengest, then, is in this respect a device for embracing a wider range of situations that may actually confront human *sapientia,* without compromising the hero by a less than perfect choice. He is an extension, if not quite of Beowulf himself, of the ideal that Beowulf embodies.

In addition, the Finn Episode as a whole seems clearly designed as a tragedy of errors, paralleling certain failures of Danish *sapientia* to cope with the difficult problems created by *treow.* Finn's presumably unwise toleration of the prospective violence represented by Hengest reflects Hroðgar's similar blindness to latent violence—particularly that of Hroþulf and perhaps also Unferþ, which is alluded to by the poet immediately after the episode (1164–68) and a little later by Wealhþeow (1180–87). The plight of Hildeburh in the Finn Episode looks forward to the situation resulting from the unwise "peacemaking" of the Freawaru-Ingeld match (2024–69); if, as seems likely enough, we are to understand that Hildeburh was also married as a *frioðuwebbe,* the parallel becomes striking indeed. In a more general way, the episode may suggest the inevitable limitations of human *sapientia* which play so prominent a part in the poem as a whole, making harmony between tribes an imperfect, fragile, and temporary thing. If so, the violence within the episode seems to represent by specific example what Grendel and his mother embody in a more universal way; and the placing of the episode between Beowulf's two fights with the Grendel family allows the theme of renewed violence within the episode to foreshadow the renewed violence to the Danes from a source seemingly quelled. This significance, in turn, would be pointed by the curious passage almost immediately preceding the episode (1056–62), which can easily be read with emphasis on the contrast between human affairs, where *sapientia* cannot always foresee and *fortitudo* cannot always accomplish, and the *sapientia et fortitudo* of God which foresees and accomplishes all.

The reminiscence on the history of Wiglaf's sword (2610–25), introduced at a critical moment of the dragon fight, dramatizes the relation between *sapientia et fortitudo* and the ideal of good retainership.[36] The passage is closely bounded in the poem by the theme of retainership—preceded as it is by the flight of the retainers and the return of Wiglaf (2596–2610), and followed by an assurance of Wiglaf's steadfastness (2625–30), his exhortation to the other retainers with its clear account of what is expected of them (2633–60), his exhortation and promise of help to Beowulf (2663–68), and finally his heroic assistance (2669ff.). The mention of the sword provides the excuse first for an allusion to the killing of Eanmund through the hostility of his uncle Onela; but the central character in the little story is Weohstan, who throughout plays the part of ideal retainer in slaying the enemy of his lord, presenting the spoil to Onela, and receiving it again from Onela as the reward of loyal service. Now this slaying of a brother's son by a retainer of the uncle is evidently regarded by the poet as a serious matter in itself, no matter where the right lay (2619); but this very irregularity in the situation—whatever its implications for Onela—serves only to highlight Weohstan's wisdom in choosing a retainer's proper course regardless, and his courage and loyalty in following it. The relevance of the passage to its context, then, lies in the parallel between the good retainership of Weohstan and that of his son Wiglaf; and in the contrast between Weohstan and the other retainers, who in an unambiguous situation, involving no ethical peculiarities, abandon their lord in time of need. The contrast is sharpened by the prominent mention of Weohstan's well-earned war-gear (2620–24), set against Wiglaf's references to the equipment fruitlessly bestowed on Beowulf's retainers (2636–38, 2864–72).

And perhaps there is one further comparison. The Weohstan story provides an example not only of ideal retainership, but apparently also of some violation of the ties of kinship, most likely by Eanmund. In Wiglaf and the other retainers of Beowulf we have somewhat the reverse pattern; though Wiglaf is a retainer also, the poet chooses to motivate his right decision primarily by the claim of kinship (2600–01). It may be, then, that by the introduction of Weohstan we are being shown a four-cornered comparison rather than a two-poled one: the duties of retainership ideally observed by Weohstan and violated by Beowulf's retainers; the duties of kinship violated by Eanmund and ideally observed by Wiglaf. The two situations would thus combine to form a balanced dramatic portrayal of these two strong Germanic claims, each developed by the familiar juxtaposition of a positive and a negative example. In any case Weohstan, like Hengest, seems presented as having dealt successfully with an awkward situation requiring the exercise of *sapientia* as well as *fortitudo: sapientia* in deciding according to the demands of good retainership, *fortitudo* in performing the violent duty called for.

Much could of course be said about the significance of other specific passages and details in *Beowulf*. For example, the identity of Grendel's mother, the relevance of the mysterious passage concerning the Danes' idol-worship (175–88), and possibly even the meaning of the name "Grendel," can be explained by way of the apocryphal Book of Enoch, of which there is a fragment from a Latin translation originating in England during the eighth century.[37] Before concluding, however, let us glance briefly at the question of a possible figurative association between Beowulf and Christ, which has troubled the minds of scholars for generations. While an allegorical correspondence of this kind strikes me as virtually out of the question, there does seem to be a real possibility for some sort of conscious analogy between Beowulf and Christ—a connection, that is, by which Beowulf is made not to serve as a figurative representation of Christ, but to remind us significantly of him in certain respects.[38] There is, for example, the familiar parallel between Hroðgar's laudation of Beowulf—

> Hwæt, þæt secgan mæg
> efne swa hwylc mægþa   swa ðone magan cende
> æfter gumcynnum,   gyf heo gyt lyfað,
> þæt hyre ealdmetod   este wære
> bearngebyrdo   (942–46)

—and the remark of a woman to Christ in Luke 11:27: "Beatus venter qui te portavit, et ubera quæ suxisti." * I do

---

* Blessed is the womb that bore thee, and the breasts that thou hast sucked.

not think it has ever been pointed out that this speech occurs shortly after Christ has cast out a demon (11:14–18), while that of Hroðgar follows Beowulf's cleansing Heorot of the demonic Grendel. Again, Beowulf goes forth to fight the dragon accompanied by a band of twelve, one of whom is a culprit; during the fight the eleven retainers flee, and one (Wiglaf) returns. It would be difficult indeed to overlook the detailed parallel between this series of events on the one hand, and on the other the picture of Christ shortly before his death attended by the twelve Apostles; the treason of Judas; the flight of the eleven remaining Apostles; and the return of John at the crucifixion.[39]

In the light of my preceding interpretation, the most plausible thematic center for such an analogy between Beowulf and Christ would seem to be the ideal of *sapientia et fortitudo* itself. In accord with the familiar Pauline reference to "Christum Dei virtutem et Dei sapientiam" * (I Cor. 1:24), Christ is frequently represented by patristic writers as the *sapientia et fortitudo* of God—as for example in Gregory's exposition of Job 12:13: *"Apud ipsum est sapientia et fortitudo; ipse habet consilium et intelligentiam.* Hæc non incongrue de Unigenito summi Patris accipimus, ut ipsum esse Dei sapientiam et fortitudinem sentiamus. Nam Paulus quoque nostro intellectui attestatur, dicens: Christum Dei virtutem et Dei sapientiam." † [40] In Old English literature, Christ is credited more simply with the possession of *sapientia et fortitudo*. A Vercelli Homily, for example, remarks of his early life that "mæȝene 7 syntero he wæs ȝefylled

---

* Christ the power and the wisdom of God.

† *With him [God] is wisdom and might; he hath counsel and understanding.* Not unfitly do we accept these words as referring to the Only-Begotten Son of the supreme Father, so that we understand him to be himself the wisdom and might [*sapientia et fortitudo*] of God. For Paul also bears testimony to our understanding of this verse, when he says, *Christ the power of God and the wisdom of God.*

mid 3ode 7 mid mannum" * (cf. Luke 2:40, 52); and the poetic "Descent into Hell" describes him at the Resurrection as "modig . . . sigefæst ond snottor" † (22–23).[41] In addition, medieval interpretation of part of Ps. 90:13 (Vulgate), "et conculcabis leonem et draconem," ‡ produces an image of Christ triumphing over a pair of creatures whose exegetical meanings bear a strong resemblance to the violence and *malitia* that I have proposed for the Grendel family and the dragon respectively; witness a sermon by Caesarius of Arles, traditionally attributed to Augustine:

> Sed dictus diabolus leo et draco: leo propter impetum, draco propter insidias; leo aperte irascitur, draco occulte insidiatur. Pugnavit ecclesia prioribus temporibus adversus leonem; pugnat modo adversus draconem. Sed quomodo victus est leo, vincitur et draco. Quae fortitudo leonis contra illum leonem [*i.e.,* Christum] de quo scriptum est: *Vicit leo de tribu Iuda* [Apoc. 5:5]? Et quae fortitudo draconis contra mortem domini, qui serpentem suspendit in ligno? § [42]

The portrayal of a warlike and victorious Christ with his feet resting on a prostrate lion and dragon is also a commonplace in early medieval iconography.[43]

---

* he was filled with might and wisdom before God and before men
† brave . . . victorious and wise
‡ and thou shalt trample underfoot the lion and the dragon
§ But the devil is called a lion and a dragon: a lion because of his violence, a dragon because of his snares; as a lion he rages openly, as a dragon he lies secretly in wait. In earlier times the church did battle against the lion; now she fights against the dragon. But even as the lion was conquered, the dragon is conquered. What might of the lion can stand against that lion [*i.e.,* Christ] of whom it is written: *The lion of the tribe of Juda has prevailed* [Apoc. 5:5]? And what might of the dragon can stand against the death of the Lord, who hung the serpent upon a tree?

But if the poet has indeed seen fit to establish such an analogy on the basis of *sapientia et fortitudo,* to what purpose? And in particular, what are we to make of the apparently fatal objection that whereas mankind is saved by the death of Christ, the Geats are doomed by the death of Beowulf? I would suggest that in this final decisive difference we are to see the *raison d'être* of the entire analogy: the champion Beowulf, in life reminiscent of the champion Christ in various aspects of his wisdom and power, is in the end revealed to be not God-man but man, his death not a supernatural atonement but a calamitous natural phenomenon. We may notice in passing than an analogy of almost any kind between Beowulf and Christ might in itself account for the notorious absence of explicit references to Christ in the poem.

Whatever one may think of this proposed analogy, there remains for our consideration one great theme hovering over the poem rather than active in it: that of the infinite *sapientia et fortitudo* of God as the source of all finite human *sapientia et fortitudo.* The idea is a familiar one in the Old Testament, particularly in Job:

In antiquis est sapientia
et in multo tempore prudentia.
Apud ipsum [*i.e.,* Deum] est sapientia et fortitudo . . .
    (12:12–13).*

The frequency of similar brief allusions in *Beowulf* is obvious. Against this greater reality, the limited *sapientia et fortitudo* of the people in the poem are continually being projected, in a variety of ways. There are for example more or less explicit

* In ancient men is wisdom, and in length of days prudence. With him [*i.e.,* God] is wisdom and might . . .

references, like the poet's remarks on the Danes' idol-worship (175–88) and the passage preceding the Finn Episode (1056–62). By way of less explicit comparison, there is the whole texture of allusion to the giants and their works, the scop's unusual knowledge of the distant past, the forgotten past of which the treasure is a dim reminder, and so on—all suggesting the limitations of individual human *sapientia*. Its limitations are expressed again in what might be called the "men know not—" theme, usually though not always applied to the forces of evil (e.g., 50–52, 162–63). Still subtler contributions are the repeated mentions of the awe with which the people in the poem behold evidences of a mysterious evil imperfectly comprehended (e.g., 980–90).

Finally, there is a broader way in which the action of *Beowulf* is projected against this higher *sapientia et fortitudo*. Vital as human *sapientia et fortitudo* is for the very survival of peoples in the heroic age, the total impression left by the poem is that it is a rare enough combination in a world full of possibilities for error and weakness. Even the infrequent combinations of the two heroic virtues are not guaranteed to last; Hroðgar's decline in *fortitudo* invites Grendel, and Heremod's decay in *sapientia* as well as *fortitudo* brings on his own destruction and the dreaded lordless time. And finally, beyond his own control, man himself is mortal, as the elegy of the Last Survivor (2247–66) emphasizes to good purpose; even Beowulf, the persevering combination of both heroic virtues, must die at last, leaving to his people the unlikely chance of finding the ideal embodied in a new ruler. And above the imperfection, the mutability, and in any case the final impermanence of human *sapientia et fortitudo*—and heightening its poignancy—there towers the *sapientia et fortitudo* of God, perfect, unchanging, everlasting. In that contrast lies, at its deepest and most inclusive, the tragedy of *Beowulf*.

Notes

[1] *"Beowulf:* The Monsters and the Critics," *Proceedings of the British Academy,* XXII (1936), 245–95; references throughout are to the separate printing (Oxford, 1958). Reprinted in *An Anthology of Beowulf Criticism,* ed. Lewis E. Nicholson (Notre Dame, 1963; hereafter *ABC*), pp. 51–103.

[2] *Figurengestaltung im Beowulf-Epos* (Anglistische Forschungen, 87; Heidelberg, 1940).

[3] *The Digressions in Beowulf* (Medium Ævum Monographs, V; Oxford, 1950); *Twelve Beowulf Papers* (Université de Neuchâtel, Recueil de travaux publiés par la Faculté des Lettres, 30; Neuchâtel, 1962).

[4] Pope, *The Rhythm of Beowulf* (New Haven, 1942); Bliss, *The Metre of Beowulf* (Oxford, 1958).

[5] *E.g.,* T. M. Gang, "Approaches to *Beowulf,*" *Review of English Studies,* N.S. III (1952), 1–12; J. C. van Meurs, *"Beowulf* and Literary Criticism," *Neophilologus,* XXXIX (1955), 114–30; Sisam (above); and Rogers (n. 11 below).

[6] *Publications of the Modern Language Association,* LXI (1946), 309–31 (reprinted in *ABC,* pp. 105–35).

[7] *Neophilologus,* XXXII (1948), 122–26.

[8] *English Studies,* XXIX (1948), 161–72 (reprinted in *ABC,* pp. 137–54).

[9] *English Studies Today: Second Series,* ed. G. A. Bonnard (Bern, 1961), pp. 81–91.

[10] *Medium Ævum,* XXI (1952), 1–13.

[11] *Review of English Studies,* N.S. VI (1955), 339–55 (reprinted in *ABC,* pp. 233–56).

[12] Universidade de São Paulo, Faculdade de Filosofia, Ciéncias e Letras, Boletim 229, Lingua e literatura inglesa, 1 (São Paulo, Brazil, 1959). See also his earlier article, "The Structure of *Beowulf,*" *Papers of the Michigan Academy of Science, Arts, and Letters,* XLIII (1958), 307–14.

[13] *Journal of English and Germanic Philology,* LIX (1960), 190–207 (reprinted in *ABC,* pp. 331–52). This argument—along with those of Hamilton (n. 6 above) and Goldsmith (n. 16 below)—has been vigorously attacked by John Halverson, *"Beowulf* and the Pitfalls of Piety," *University of Toronto Quarterly,* XXXV (1965–66), 260–78, who suggests the possibility of an Arian background for the

poem. My own comment on Father McNamee's studies (below) applies even more strongly to another Christian interpretation by Raymond Carter Sutherland, *The Celibate Beowulf, the Gospels, and the Liturgy* (Georgia State College, School of Arts and Sciences Research Papers, 2; Atlanta, 1964).

[14] *Classica et Mediaevalia: Revue danoise de philologie et d'histoire,* XXV (1964), 151–201.

[15] *Traditio,* XXI (1965), 55–116; see also his *"Beowulf,* Ireland, and the Natural Good," *Traditio,* VII (1949–51), 263–77.

[16] *Medium Ævum,* XXIX (1960), 81–101; *Studies in Old English Literature in Honor of Arthur G. Brodeur,* ed. Stanley B. Greenfield (Eugene, Oregon, 1963), pp. 71–90 (abridged in *ABC,* pp. 373–86); *Neophilologus,* XLVIII (1964), 60–72. The first two articles are attacked by Bruce Mitchell, " 'Until the Dragon Comes . . .': Some Thoughts on *Beowulf,*" *Neophilologus,* XLVII (1963), 126–38.

[17] *Medium Ævum,* XXXIV (1965), 89–102. A less than ideal quality in Beowulf is suggested also by E. G. Stanley, "Hæthenra Hyht in *Beowulf,*" in *Brodeur Studies,* pp. 136–51, and *"Beowulf,"* in *Continuations and Beginnings: Studies in Old English Literature,* ed. E. G. Stanley (London, 1966), p. 139; and less distinctly by Tolkien, "Ofermod," *Essays and Studies,* N.S. VI (1953), 14–15.

[18] *E.g.,* Goldsmith's emphasis on echoes of the Psalms in *Beowulf* ("Christian Theme," p. 101); and Leyerle's quotation from Smaragdus on pride in kings (p. 98).

[19] *Modern Language Quarterly,* XXVIII (1967), 3–18. P. G. Buchloh, in "Unity and Intention in *Beowulf,*" *English Studies Today: Fourth Series* (Rome, 1966), pp. 99–120—a volume which became available only after the present study was in the hands of the editor—proposes that "the central theme [of *Beowulf*], which is varied time and again, is that of the futility of all human efforts and the almighty power of a good God. This unifying theme is to be found in the first part of the poem especially in allusions and digressions, and in the second part it dominates the narrative of the action as well as the moralizing parts" (p. 110). This opinion, however, receives little development or support in the rest of the paper, which is not primarily an attempt to interpret the poem. Edward B. Irving, Jr., *A Reading of Beowulf* (New Haven, 1968), appeared too late to be included in the present survey; see my forthcoming review of it in *The Journal of English and Germanic Philology.*

[20] For a fuller and more completely documented version of the interpretation which follows, see my article *"Sapientia et Fortitudo* as

the Controlling Theme of *Beowulf*," *Studies in Philology,* LV (1958), 423–56, hereafter *SF* (reprinted in *ABC*, pp. 269–310).

[21] I, xxxix, 9, ed. W. M. Lindsay (Oxford, 1911). Curtius (above), "Zur Literarästhetik des Mittelalters, II," *Zeitschrift für romanische Philologie,* LVIII (1938), 200–15, and *Europäische Literatur und lateinisches Mittelalter* (Bern, 1948), pp. 177–83. Documentation for the present paragraph is included in *SF*, pp. 424–25.

[22] "*Beowulf:* The Monsters and the Critics," p. 27.

[23] Gregory, *Moralia in Iob,* XXVII, xlvi, 75, on Job 37:24 (*PL* 76, col. 442): "Viri namque arrogantes et docti cum recte non vivunt, sed tamen recta dicere doctrinæ impulsionibus compelluntur, ipsi damnationis suæ aliquomodo præcones fiunt, quia dum ea quæ agere respuunt prædicantes insinuant, suis se vocibus damnatos clamant. . . .Unde summa cura providendum est ne accepta sapientia, cum ignorantiæ tenebras illuminat, lumen humilitatis tollat, et jam sapientia esse nequeat. Quæ etsi virtute locutionis fulgeat, elationis tamen velamine cor loquentis obscurat." *

[24] A fuller analysis, along with supporting documentation, is presented in *SF*, pp. 432–35. For *malitia* as the antithesis of *sapientia* (below), see particularly Jerome, *Epistola* C, 3 (*PL* 22, col. 815): "Pauci sunt, qui calcatis vitiis tramitem teneant veritatis, dum malitia innumeris nocendi utitur artibus, et vinci non potest, nisi sapientiæ desuper fulciamur auxilio. . . . Sapientia quippe in nobis operatur bonum: postquam ei mundum cordis præbuerimus habitaculum, et cogitationes in opera verterimus." †

[25] See Gregory, *Mor. in Iob,* I, xxxii, 45, on Job 1:4 (*PL* 75, col.

---

* For when men who are arrogant and learned do not live rightly, but are nevertheless compelled by the pressures of doctrine to say right things, they become in a way the heralds of their own damnation—because when they as preachers teach what they refuse to do, with their own voices they proclaim themselves damned. . . . Whence one must watch with the utmost care lest the wisdom that he has received, while it enlightens the darkness of ignorance, should take away the light of humility and no longer be able to exist as wisdom. Wisdom, although it shines by virtue of speech, nevertheless darkens the heart of its speaker with a covering of vainglory.

† So long as *malitia* employs its countless skills of doing harm and cannot be overcome, few there are who, trampling down their vices, would hold to the way of truth unless we were supported by the help of wisdom from above. . . . For wisdom works good in us, once we have

547); and Fulgentius, *Expositio Virgilianae continentiae,* ed. Rudolf
Helm, *Fabii Planciadis Fulgentii . . . opera* (Leipzig, 1898), p. 88, in
an analysis of "virtus et sapientia" in the opening line of the *Aeneid:*
"Defectus enim uirtutis egritudo est sapientiæ hoc uidelicet pacto, quia
quidquid sapientiæ consultatio agendum inuenerit, si ad subrogandum
posse uirtus deficiat, curtata in suis effectibus sapientiæ plenitudo
torpescit." *

²⁶ See particularly Baruch 3:26–28; and Augustine, *De civitate Dei,*
XV, xxiii, 4.

²⁷ See my suggestion in " 'Hygelac' and 'Hygd'," *Brodeur Studies,* pp.
200–06, with the important modification and further evidence presented by Fred C. Robinson, "The Significance of Names in Old
English Literature," *Anglia,* LXXXVI (1968), 52–57.

²⁸ For a fuller analysis of the references to Geatish history, see *SF,*
pp. 441–43.

²⁹ Gregory, *Mor. in Iob,* XV, xxxvi, 42, on Job 21:4 (*PL* 75, col.
1103): "Qui autem aut hominibus placens Deo displicet, aut simul Deo
et hominibus displicere se credit, si hunc tristitia non afficit, a virtute
sapientiæ alienus existit." † See also *SF,* pp. 445–46; I would now
incorporate, however, the convincing proposal of Morton W. Bloom-
field, "Patristics and Old English Literature: Notes on Some Poems,"
Brodeur Studies, pp. 39–41 (reprinted in *ABC,* pp. 369–72), that the
ealde riht is the *lex naturalis.*

³⁰ *E.g., Sap.* 7:22–23: "Est enim in illa [*i.e.,* sapientia] spiritus intelli-
gentiæ . . . benefaciens, humanus, benignus." ‡ Martin of Braga in the
Formula vitæ honestæ (*PL* 72, col. 26) admonishes the wise king:
"Cunctis esto benignus, nemini blandus, paucis familiaris, omnibus
æquus. Severior esto in judicio quam sermone, vita quam vultu: cultor
clementiæ, detestator sævitiæ, bonæ famæ neque tuæ seminator neque

offered it the clean dwelling-place of the heart and turned our thoughts
into deeds.

* For a lack of strength is an illness of wisdom in this sense: that
whatever the deliberation of wisdom has found is to be done, if
strength is not sufficient for it to be carried out, the fullness of wisdom,
curtailed in its proper ends, grows feeble.

† Whoever displeases God while pleasing men, or believes that he is
displeasing God and men together, lives a stranger to the virtue of
wisdom if sorrow does not afflict him.

‡ For in her [*i.e.,* wisdom] is the spirit of understanding . . . benefi-
cent, gentle, kindly.

alienæ invidus. . . . Ad iram tardus, ad misericordiam pronus." * See also Levin L. Schücking, "Das Königsideal im *Beowulf,*" *MHRA Bulletin,* III (1929), 143–54 (translated in *ABC,* pp. 35–49).

[31] For a fuller discussion of Wiglaf, see *SF,* p. 454.

[32] Gregory, *Mor. in Iob,* VII, xxviii, 36, on Job 6:18 (*PL* 75, col. 786): "Sed cum culpa culpæ adjungitur, quid aliud quam involutis semitis atque innodatis vinculis pravorum gressus ligantur? Unde bene contra perversam mentem sub Judææ specie per Isaiam dicitur: *Erit cubile draconum, et pascua struthionum, et occurrent doemonia ono-centauris, et pilosus clamabit alter ad alterum* [Is. 34:13–14]. Quid namque per dracones nisi malitia . . . designatur? . . . In perversa igitur mente draco cubat . . . quia et latens malitia callide tegitur." †
See also the further citations in *SF,* p. 451, nn. 79–80; Rabanus Maurus, *De universo,* VIII, vi (*PL* 111, col. 245); and the Old English *Andreas,* ll. 767–70. There are many others.

[33] For a fuller discussion of Geatish *malitia* in Part II, see *SF,* pp. 452–53.

[34] The interpretation which follows is presented more fully in my article, "The Sigemund-Heremod and Hama-Hygelac Passages in *Beowulf,*" *Publications of the Modern Language Association,* LXXIV (1959), 489–94.

[35] As to the vexed preliminary question of what actually goes on in the Finn Episode, I follow what might be called the traditional reconstruction—represented for example by Arthur G. Brodeur, "Design and Motive in the Finn Episode," *University of California Publications in English,* XIV (1943), 1–42. For the meaning of *eotena/eotenum,*

* Be kind to all, flattering to no one, familiar to few, just to all. Be more severe in judgment than in speech, in way of life than in appearance: a fosterer of clemency, a hater of ferocity, neither a sower of your own good fame nor an envier of another's. . . . Be slow to wrath, inclined to mercy.

† But when guilt is joined to guilt, what else is this than that the steps of the wicked are bound by involved paths and tangled chains? Whence it is well spoken by Isaias against the wrongly directed soul, under the likeness of Judæa: *And it shall be the habitation of dragons, and the pasture of ostriches, and demons shall meet with monsters, and the hairy ones shall cry out one to another* [Is. 34:13–14]. For what is signified by the dragons except *malitia?* . . . In the perverted soul, therefore, the dragon lies down . . . because lurking *malitia* is cunningly covered over.

repeated four times in the episode, see my article "The *Eotenas* in *Beowulf,*" in *Old English Poetry: Fifteen Essays,* ed. Robert P. Creed (Providence, R. I., 1967), pp. 285–310.

[36] The interpretation which follows is presented more fully in my article "Weohstan's Sword," *Modern Language Notes,* LXXV (1960), 465–68.

[37] Ed. M. R. James, *Apocrypha Anecdota: A Collection of Thirteen Apocryphal Books and Fragments* (Texts and Studies: Contributions to Biblical and Patristic Literature, II, 3; Cambridge, 1893), pp. 146–50. The complete text of the Book of Enoch survives only in Ethiopic; see the translation by R. H. Charles, *The Apocrypha and Pseudepigrapha of the Old Testament in English* (Oxford, 1913), II, 163–281. The probable contributions of some form of the Book of Enoch to *Beowulf* will be presented in a subsequent article.

[38] The distinction is essentially that drawn by Charles S. Singleton, "The Pattern at the Center," in *Dante Studies, 1: Commedia, Elements of Structure* (Cambridge, Mass., 1957), pp. 45–60. Note the similar remarks of Donahue, *"Beowulf* and Christian Tradition," p. 116, in proposing a typological or figural significance for Beowulf.

[39] Some further correspondences are suggested by Donahue, *"Beowulf* and Christian Tradition," pp. 107–08, 115–16.

[40] *Mor. in Iob,* XI, viii, 11 (*PL* 75, col. 958). See also patristic commentary on I Cor. 1:24 generally.

[41] Hom. VI, ed. Max Förster, *Die Vercelli-Homilien* (Bibl. der ags. Prosa, XII; Hamburg, 1932), p. 137. "Descent into Hell," ed. G. P. Krapp and E. V. K. Dobbie, *The Exeter Book* (Anglo-Saxon Poetic Records, III; New York, 1936), p. 219.

[42] Serm. LXIX, ed. G. Morin, *Sancti Caesarii Arelatensis sermones* (*CCL,* 103; Turnhout, 1953), I, 291–292. See also Augustine, *Enarrationes in Psalmos,* XXXIX, 1 (*CCL,* 38; Turnhout, 1956), I, 423.

[43] See for example a fifth- or sixth-century mosaic in the vestibule of the Cappella Arcivescovile at Ravenna; the ninth-century Utrecht Psalter, fols. 36^r and 53^v, ed. E. T. De Wald, *The Illustrations of the Utrecht Psalter* (Princeton, [1933]); an early eleventh-century psalter from Crowland, Lincolnshire (MS Oxford, Bodl. Douce 296, fol. 40^r); and an eleventh-century psalter from Bury St. Edmunds (MS Bibl. Vat. Reg. lat. 12, fol. 98^r), repr. Meyer Schapiro, "The Religious Meaning of the Ruthwell Cross," *Art Bulletin,* XXVI (1944), fig. 4 (at p. 233). The somewhat similar figures of Christ on the Ruthwell and Bewcastle Crosses seem less relevant for present purposes; see Schapiro, *ibid.,* pp. 232–36.

THE
CANTERBURY
TALES

Richard L. Hoffman

So real has been our modern "renaissance of interest in the literature of the Middle Ages," [1] that a bibliography of writings on Chaucer alone during the last quarter century or so would fill a very substantial volume, [2] and the greater part of this voluminous work has been devoted, quite naturally, to *The Canterbury Tales*. From such a brief survey as this, consequently, even much truly fine scholarship and sensitive criticism must be omitted. But this very fact of necessary omission may be viewed as a tribute to the zeal of modern Chaucerians.

It seems appropriate to begin our survey with the six-hundredth anniversary of Chaucer's birth, commemorated in 1940 by the publication, in Chicago, of John Matthews Manly and Edith Rickert's monumental study, *The Text of the Canterbury Tales*. The eight volumes of this exhaustive "critical edition" contain an indispensable body of textual information, patiently and accurately gleaned by a thorough examniation of "all known manuscripts" of the *Tales*. A single statistic will suffice to indicate the contribution of this epochal work of Chaucerian scholarship to the establishment of a reliable "standard text"—that primary duty of literary scholars: F. N. Robinson, who had himself collated the manuscripts for his edition of Chaucer's *Works* in 1933, made 167 changes in the text of the *Tales* for his second edition of 1957, and these "altered readings" were marked "chiefly in the light of the new evidence" provided by Manly and Rickert.[3] The statistic is rendered even weightier by the consideration that Robinson was, actually, quite conservative in admitting readings from Manly-Rickert.

Partly because it utilizes the Manly-Rickert evidence, but for a variety of other good reasons as well, this second edition of Robinson's remains, unquestionably, the most valuable single volume which any student of Chaucer can own. The text of *The Canterbury Tales* which it contains is the most accurate complete version available, superseding even the very estimable editions of Skeat and Pollard.

To maintain that Robinson's edition is uniquely excellent is not, of course, to claim perfection for it. Perhaps its major liability is retention of the Ellesmere order of the tales over the "Chaucerian" arrangement for which R. A. Pratt had argued so persuasively six years before in his essay on "The Order of the *Canterbury Tales*." [4] This reluctance on Robinson's part to adopt the so-called "Bradshaw shift" (which places Fragment VII directly after Fragment II, as in Skeat's Oxford Chaucer) is especially curious since Robinson himself admits, in his second edition (p. viii), that the "very reasonable" arguments of Pratt and others who had been stimulated by the researches of Manly and Rickert to re-open this important case "made it seem probable that Chaucer was on his way to the rectification of the inconsistencies in the traditional order."

The extent to which this "Chaucerian" order is conducive to a "rectification of the inconsistencies" and the numerous advantages, therefore, of reading and teaching the tales in that sequence may be discovered in two admirable critical editions of Chaucer published within the last five years: A. C. Baugh's *Chaucer's Major Poetry* (New York, 1963) and R. A. Pratt's *Selections from the Tales of Canterbury and Short Poems* (Boston, 1966). Unfortunately, neither provides a complete text of the *Tales*. Baugh, as part of the very design of his book, omits the two prose tales; and Pratt, from the spatial limitations of his Riverside Edition, gives only eighteen tales of the twenty-four.

E. T. Donaldson's widely used *Chaucer's Poetry: An Anthology for the Modern Reader* (New York, 1958) is not, properly speaking, an "edition," for here "the spelling of the manuscripts has been given internal consistency" in order "to improve the reader's recognition of recurrent words" (p. iii). It is perhaps true that this homogenized text will seem to the new reader of Chaucer slightly smoother than Robinson's. But surely any such advantage in reading speed or ease is overshadowed by the several dangers of acquainting students with a standardized brand of Middle English which neither Chaucer nor "any actual medieval English scribe" (Donaldson, p. iv) would have produced.

Like Baugh and Pratt, Donaldson selects from the *Tales* (thirteen complete); but unlike them he follows the Ellesmere order. The great merit of this book, and a very great merit indeed, is its "Commentary"—140 pages of thoughtful and lucid criticism, as valuable for the seasoned Chaucerian as for the novice.

That sexcentenary celebration of Chaucer's birth so worthily commemorated by Manly and Rickert was marked also by the completion of another work of major scholarship on the *Tales. Sources and Analogues of Chaucer's Canterbury Tales* (published, again in Chicago, in 1941) had been undertaken some years earlier under the aegis of the Chaucer Group of MLA. A collaborative project by more than twenty of our century's leading Chaucerians, its intention was to supplement and revise, rather than supplant, those *Originals and Analogues* published in London by the Chaucer Society from 1872 to 1888.

The essential difference between these two important source studies and the special value of *Sources and Analogues* are well expressed by general editor W. F. Bryan in his "Preface" to the new collection:

> *Sources and Analogues* treats all twenty-four of the tales, with additional sections on the general framework and on two prologues to tales, whereas *Originals and Analogues* was concerned with only thirteen tales; the present work, moreover, reproduces only twenty-two of the one hundred and eleven versions and duplicates only about one-fourth of the material presented in the earlier work. Further, in only two of the thirteen tales treated in *Originals and Analogues* does *Sources and Analogues* fail to make significant additions to those analogues which it reproduces from the older work. . . . The primary intent has been not to present a series of studies on Chaucer's sources but to present texts and thus to make readily accessible the material for the study of sources and influences (pp. vii–viii).

Of course, source studies have traditionally occupied a prominent place in Chaucerian scholarship, and there has been no abatement of activity whatever in recent decades. Since the sources of *The Canterbury Tales* are considerably more numerous and diverse even than the tales themselves, and since there are many more discernible influences upon most tales than clear sources for them, these investigations have dealt with a very wide variety of classical and medieval literary documents.

J. Burke Severs, who had prepared the chapter on the Clerk's Tale for *Sources and Analogues* (pp. 288–331), supplied the following year (1942) printed "proof of all generalizations" made there (p. 288), by publishing his full and comprehensive study, *The Literary Relationships of Chaucer's Clerkes Tale.*[5] Similarly, R. A. Pratt's chapter on the Knight's Tale in *Sources and Analogues* (p. 82–105) was confirmed and complemented six years later by his essay on "Chaucer's Use of the *Teseida.*"[6] His discussion of "Chaucer's Claudian," also published in 1947,[7] deals primarily with the influence of *De Raptu Proserpinae* on the Merchant's Tale. "Jankyn's Book of Wikked Wyves"[8] describes the medieval vogue of those authors and titles given in the Wife of Bath's Prologue as the contents of Jankyn's rather provocative anti-feminist anthology. And Pratt's most recent investigation of Chaucer's reading, "Chaucer and the Hand that Fed Him,"[9] provides strong evidence that Chaucer derived much of the "anecdotal and hortatory material" (p. 619) which appears throughout the *Tales,* and in his other works as well, from some such medieval manual or compendium as the *Communiloquium* of John of Wales.

Just twenty years ago, in his article on "Chaucer's Claudian," Pratt confessed that his primary aim there was "to redirect attention to the importance of studying Chaucer's sources as they appear in medieval manuscripts" (p. 429). Fortunately, that aim is being realized. Those of us who enjoy studying the complex and intriguing literary relationships of the tales have begun to open up the manuscripts that Chaucer himself would have read. We have voiced our concern not only to learn what Chaucer read but to know how and why he used his ancient and medieval sources as he did. This honest attempt to determine the nature as well as the extent of all literary influences on the tales has helped to change the very role and function of Chaucerian source study: no longer its own delightful excuse for being, it is playing an increasingly important part in literary criticism and interpretation.

As we should expect, it is in this wide, and sometimes bloody, arena of "literary criticism and interpretation" that activity has been most brisk. Scarcely a year has passed during the last thirty which has not brought forth several full-length critical approaches to Chaucer. Not all of these volumes, by any means, are devoted exclusively to *The Canterbury Tales,* but very few of them avoid the *Tales* entirely. Five rather different representatives from this large and distinguished assembly may serve to illustrate something of the quality and diversity of recent work.[10]

Muriel Bowden's *Commentary on the General Prologue to the Canterbury Tales* is one of the most widely read books on Chaucer ever produced. (Originally published in 1948, it reached its twelfth printing in 1964.) Some of the reasons for this almost universal popularity may be inferred from the author's Preface, where she explains her intentions and describes the audience for which she has written:

> This book is intended for three classes of readers. First, for those schooled in Chaucerian criticism I have attempted to collect and arrange the outstanding latest critical opinions on the *General Prologue* to the *Canterbury Tales,* and to point out the best of the known parallels between Chaucer's words and ideas and those of authors prior to or contemporaneous with him. Second, for the college students I have expanded the more important notes to be found in good editions of the *Canterbury Tales* with the hopes that the late fourteenth century will take on the colours of actuality, and that a reference which may suggest fields for further investigation will thus be provided. And third, for the general reader who

would like to become better acquainted with Chaucer I have striven to make clear what is obscure in the language, or in the ideas, customs, and institutions of Chaucer's England, so that the great poet will speak meaningfully and provocatively to him (p. vii).

In fact, the book has proved equally beneficial to all three of these classes: no teacher-critic, college student, or armchair reader of the *Tales* can quite afford to be without it, for in a very real sense these observations on the General Prologue form an essential introduction to all of *The Canterbury Tales*. As interesting as it is informative, the *Commentary* stands in many a Chaucer library as a worthy companion to the text itself.

Like Bowden's *Commentary*, R. M. Lumiansky's *Of Sondry Folk* (Austin, 1955) has enjoyed considerable, and understandable, vogue among teachers, students, and general readers of *The Canterbury Tales*. It differs from Bowden's book in technique by depending more heavily, for precept and example, upon the primary text than upon historical "background" materials, but once again the very subject of the study makes it a kind of general preface to the *Tales*. As Robinson observes in the notes to his edition (p. 650), "It has been the common practice of Chaucer critics now for two generations or more to emphasize the dramatic character of the *Canterbury Tales*. Their comment has ranged all the way from simple observations on the adaptation of the tales to tellers or to the situations on the pilgrimage to the comparison of Chaucer's art to that of Molière." Lumiansky's study, which summarizes and evaluates most of this earlier material, is not only the most comprehensive and practicable exposition of the very important "Dramatic Principle in the *Canterbury Tales*," but, by all counts, the most sensible and useful.

Ralph Baldwin's work on the unity of the *Tales*, originally prepared as a doctoral dissertation at Johns Hopkins, was published two years later (1955) in the monograph series *Anglistica* and has achieved even wider circulation in abridgement as an essay in the popular paperback anthology of *Chaucer Criticism* edited by Schoeck and Taylor.[11] By examining very carefully the opening lines of the General Prologue (1–42) and the pilgrim "portraits" which follow (43–714) in juxtaposition with the Parson's Prologue and Tale and Chaucer's Retractions, Baldwin discloses both the kind and the degree of artistic unity which Chaucer imposed on his work. The entire paper is well-documented, especially by evidence culled directly from the text, and the thesis is cogently and reasonably argued. Baldwin maintains that "an examination of the beginning and the ending of the *Tales* . . . reveals that they fulfill an architectonic function, hitherto overlooked, and that they sustain the story as they reinforce each other" (p. 15) so that "though the *Canterbury Tales* is incomplete, it cannot be properly called unfinished" since "the ending is as neatly calculated as the beginning" (p. 49). His argument provides a strong antidote to the still widely held and often preached theory that the *Tales* are, after all, an unpolished and rather uneven collection of heterogeneous and haphazardly arranged short stories.

It is probably no exaggeration to suggest that, in the long and spirited history of Chaucer scholarship, there has been no critical battle so fiercely fought as that which still rages between "Robertsonians" and "Anti-Robertsonians" over the "allegorical" or "theological" interpretation of "secular" medieval literature; and certainly no other Chaucerian controversy has been so widespread. Both sides—occasionally forgetting, as Robertson himself has sought to remind them,[12] that they are all Chaucerians—have sometimes betrayed a capacity for emotional involvement in academic debate so remarkable that the fiercest polemicists of the secular-regular controversy

might have learned from observation. Some unhappy consequences of this dispute have been that it has hardened the
ideas into dogmas and the disputants into propagandists. The
points of view have become fixed positions, marked "right"
and "wrong"; and the areas of disagreement, not always so
very wide, have been exaggerated to form the conviction that
"never the twain shall meet."

Robertson's own major statement is his *Preface to Chaucer*
(Princeton, 1962), which has been variously reviewed as a
great original study and "a strange hodgepodge . . . insulting
to the community of scholars and, indeed, to the Twentieth
Century itself." [13] At the very least, whatever its "doctrinal"
validity, it is a long work of impressive scholarship, erudition,
and thought by one of the most remarkable teachers of the
century. The impact of Robertson's mind upon modern Chaucer studies has already been strongly felt; and whatever subsequent generations may come to decide about this brand of
"historical criticism," his fresh and challenging ideas about
medieval literature cannot now be ignored or dismissed. It has
become the unequivocal duty of every Chaucerian to read and
assess the *Preface* itself, and not its reviews only.

Bernard Huppé, co-author with Robertson of *Piers Plowman and Scriptural Tradition* (Princeton, 1951) and *Fruyt
and Chaf,* published his *Reading of the Canterbury Tales*
(Albany, 1964) two years after *A Preface to Chaucer* first
appeared. While Huppé's book stands independent of Robertson's, both authors explain that their books began with "con-
versations about Chaucer" when they "were colleagues some
time ago." [14] These two scholars have long shared a common
methodological approach to Chaucer and other medieval literature, and in a sense Huppé's *Reading* represents a practical
application of the theoretical formulations in Robertson's
Preface. Huppé comments (p. vi), "My first chapter can
stand as an introduction to his *Preface,* and his *Preface* as an

indispensable introduction to my *Reading."* Huppé's book is dedicated to his Chaucer students at Princeton University and Harpur College and "is the direct product of lectures given annually for the last fifteen years" (p. v). Consequently, the interpretations offered in these eighteen chapters have all been "field-tested" many times, and the results are most rewarding, for Huppé's readings are uniformly thoughtful, refined, and engaging.

Any attempt to isolate here even the most extraordinary contributions among the many hundreds of critical notes and articles on the *Tales* published during these last three decades would be hopelessly futile. A fair sampling of the work before 1962 may be obtained from the very serviceable anthologies of critical essays collected by Wagenknecht, Schoeck-Taylor, and Owen.[15] The entire first half of the century is surveyed in Baugh's "Fifty Years of Chaucer Scholarship";[16] and a complete record of all modern work on Chaucer can be constructed from the bibliographies of Griffith (1908–1953) and Crawford (1954–1963),[17] supplemented by those published annually by MLA and MHRA.

The latest important development in Chaucer studies was the inauguration, in 1966, of *The Chaucer Review,* the first and now the only journal devoted exclusively to Chaucer. The first issue opened with a dedication to the memory of F. N. Robinson, who died the same year. Since the great editor himself had sacrificed chronology to fame by printing "Chaucer's most comprehensive work" first in his edition,[18] he would undoubtedly be gratified to discover that of the five articles contained in that first number of the *Review,* four are devoted to *The Canterbury Tales.*

Anyone who approaches *The Canterbury Tales,* especially for the first time, must be struck by its almost infinite variety in both form and substance. Some tales are told in heroic couplets; others in stanzas of six, seven, or eight lines, of varying meter and rime scheme; still others in prose. Of literary "forms," the following are eminently represented: the epyllion, the *fabliau,* the fairy story and folk tale, the anecdote, the romance, the Breton lay, the sermon and *exemplum,* the Saint's life, the ethical treatise or book of proverbs, the mock-heroic beast epic or animal fable, and the classical myth.

The stories, tragic and comic, treat of knighthood, chivalry, love, war, and death; cuckolding and adultery; gentility; marriage and "the battle of the sexes"; the swearing of oaths and the dangers of literalism; hypocrisy and anger; patience; spiritual blindness; honor and the fulfillment of promises; virginity and sacrifice; *cupiditas,* riotous living, and the plague; deception; martyrdom; prudence and morality; biblical, ancient, and modern tragedy; predestination, free-will, the interpretation of dreams, and the secular-regular controversy; alchemy; jangling; sin, contrition, confession, and penance; and scores of minor themes.

In the face of such incredible multifariousness—unequalled, surely, in any other English poem—the most natural and reasonable reaction to *The Canterbury Tales* is Dryden's response to the General Prologue alone: " 'Tis sufficient to say, according to the proverb, that *here is God's plenty.*" [19]

And yet, almost perversely it must seem to our students, one of the most persistent tendencies of Chaucerian scholarship and criticism has been to systematize the *Tales,* either in whole or in part, by emphasizing the artistic and thematic unity of the various groups and fragments or, more ambitiously, of the entire work. It is as if, even while demonstrating and praising the great diversity among the books of the Bible, we should hasten to add that the first thirty-nine of those books constitute an "Old Testament," the next twenty-seven a "New," and all sixty-six a "Bible." In literature, at any rate, the whole seems always greater than the sum of its parts—and properly so.

A large host of Chaucerians, counting Manly, Kittredge, Lowes, Root, and Legouis among their most articulate spokesmen, have viewed the *Tales* fundamentally as a kind of medieval tapestry, the "idea" or "purpose" of which is to depict panoramically "la comédie humaine." According to this very influential school of criticism, the *raison d'être* of Chaucer's work—its "relevance" for "us"—is its concern with those "passions and foibles" which are the constants of "human nature." [20] As Shannon put it, "Under the stimulus of this *idea* Chaucer's imagination conceived its greatest purpose—to make types of the various social groups of his own England troop into action for all succeeding generations to enjoy." Seen in this light, the very diversity of the poem imposes on it one species of unity: Chaucer's basic "commitment" to humanity, to his pilgrims and characters primarily as "real people," becomes his main organizational conception, and the Prologue "portraits" and pilgrim tales become variations on a single sociologically and psychologically realistic theme.

Lately, there has been increasing uneasiness about this representation of Chaucer as an early Balzac, and with the dissatisfaction have come some "new" approaches—theological and philosophical rather than psychological or "representational"—to *The Canterbury Tales*.

This paper will attempt to explore a few avenues of these "new" approaches, not from any desire to block up entirely the well-trodden older paths, but merely in the hope of showing that these newer ones may be profitably travelled. Chaucer's narrative skill, his poetic genius, his dramatic sense, and his love of nature and of people are all quite well established and were never really in dispute. But the quality and quantity of moral content in his verse (especially as an expression of his fundamental "world-view") and his use of theological and mythographical machinery to convey *moralitee* are very much disputed, as they should be. It is to these moot issues that we now must speak. [21]

It has been generally recognized for some time that the idea of pilgrimage itself lends some unity to the collection, and that at least two of the major themes which Chaucer treats are sin and love. Unfortunately, however, the structural and thematic significance of these three unifying factors has been weakened (1) by the refusal of most Chaucerians to consider the pilgrimage as a spiritual and theological concept rather than as a mere excursion through the English countryside, either realistically presented, or—as it has sometimes been argued—recalled by Chaucer from an actual personal experience,[22] and (2) by an inability to see "sin" and "love" as two aspects of a single theme.

Kittredge was able, in a now famous essay,[23] to isolate one group of tales (Wife of Bath, Clerk, Merchant, and Franklin) which are especially concerned with marital relationships. And Tupper, noting that love and marriage provide the theme for a number of other tales as well, attempted to extend Kittredge's "marriage group" to include all the tales, by proposing that the basic essential of Chaucer's entire collection is devotion to Venus.[24] But this theory has been criticized on the grounds that "while recognizing the obvious importance of love as a motif in the secular tales, [it] does not take sufficient account of the tales of religious, even of ascetic, spirit";[25] and the same charge of incomprehensiveness has been brought against Tupper's later suggestion [26] that *The Canterbury Tales* represents a systematic and methodical treatise on the seven deadly sins, with each pilgrim exemplifying the very sin which his own tale condemns. As Robinson observes (p. 650), "This holds true, without doubt, for the Pardoner, and perhaps for some of the other pilgrims. But the system breaks down when applied to the whole series of tales."

The point which Kittredge, Tupper, Robinson, and many others have failed to recognize is that love may be the theme of "tales of religious, even of ascetic, spirit" just as aptly as it may be "a motif in the secular tales." It is true that we are concerned here with two very different kinds of love and that only one of these involves the celebration of what we may call the rites of Venus, as Tupper conceived them; but in the Middle Ages, religious or ascetic devotion to God was love also.

These two kinds of love, which are everywhere present in *The Canterbury Tales,* were recognized by ancient authors, who associated both of them with Venus. In Plato's *Symposium* (180–181), Pausanias distinguishes between one Venus who pleases the body and another heavenly Venus who pleases the soul; and Lucretius implies the same kind of distinction in *De Rerum Natura* (I.1ff. and IV.1058ff.). But it is in Ovid that the Middle Ages would have found the formulation most concisely and memorably stated.

Ovid begins the fourth book of the *Fasti*—devoted to the month of April, when spring opens (*aperit*) the fertile earth —with an invocation to Venus: " 'Alma, fave,' dixi 'geminorum mater Amorum!' " ("Be favorable to me, gracious mother of the twin Loves," I said).[27] Since Ovid was strongly influenced by Neo-Pythagorean philosophy, it seems likely that he was indebted for his conception of the "twin Loves" to the Pythagorean system, evolved late in antiquity, whereby the conventional ancient deities were described as having two different natures, or as acting in two separate spheres—celestial and infernal.[28] Furthermore, Ovid's concept of two Loves, both sons of Venus, seems to imply also his understanding of the Pythagorean theory of a double Venus.[29]

In any case, the Pythagorean system of doubling deities was well known in the Middle Ages;[30] and despite the fact that Ovid actually mentions only one Venus as mother of the "twin Loves" in *Fasti* IV.1, medieval glosses on this line begin, sensibly enough, with a discussion of the two Venuses. The following anonymous gloss dates from the late eleventh or early twelfth century; but since the same description is given by Albericus of London (Mythographus Vaticanus III), who attributes it in turn to Remigius of Auxerre, it may in effect be as old as the ninth century: [31]

> Duae sunt ueneres. Vna casta et pudica que praeest honestis amoribus que etiam fertur uxor uulcani. Altera uoluptaria libidinum dea cui filius est hermafroditus. Sic etiam sunt duae amores. Alter bonus et pudicus quo uirtutes et sapientia armantur, alter impudicus et malus. Quare ad distinctionem boni amoris pluraliter amores dicuntur. Sed notandum quod hic una uenus quae apud romanos proprie genitrix uocatur quae mater utriusque amoris secundum ouidium nominator.* [32]

This interpretation of *Fasti* IV.1 is significant not only because it points up the importance of Ovid's line in the Middle Ages as a *locus classicus* for the concept of two Loves,[33] but also because it illustrates a typical technique of medieval mythography. That is, the ancient deities are conventionally regarded in the Middle Ages as two-sided coins, and their attributes and actions may be described both *in bono* and *in malo*. Venus *in bono,* as our gloss explains, is a chaste and modest goddess who presides over honorable love, is wife to Vulcan, and mother of the good Amor who strengthens wisdom and the virtues; Venus *in malo* is the voluptuous goddess of desire, and mother of that shameless wicked god, Hermaphroditus. In the same way, there is a good Mars, associated

* There are two Venuses: one, chaste and modest, who presides over honorable love and is said to be Vulcan's wife; the other, a voluptuous goddess of desires, whose son is Hermaphroditus. So also there are two Loves: the one, good and modest, by whom wisdom and the virtues are armed; the other, immodest and wicked. Hence, in order to distinguish this good Love from the other, one speaks of "Loves," in the plural. But note that this one Venus, whom the Romans properly term "mother," is said by Ovid to be mother of both Loves.

with just and virtuous warfare, and a wicked Mars, who is the father of violence, bloodshed, and murder.[34]

Since Ovid describes Venus in *Fasti* IV as "a cosmic force which governs the earth, the sea, and the heavens, causes plants and animals to perpetuate their species, inspires the arts among men, and, as Venus Verticordia, preserves the chastity of wives," this celestial Venus and Amor *in bono* came to be associated with "mundana musica," that universal concord which controls the elements, the seasons, and the stars and which joins people together in bonds of chaste and holy love.[35]

In Christian terms, this "mundana musica" or celestial Venus is divine love—that love by which God, the Prime Mover, preserves and regulates his physical universe and by which also he unites his children in charity and sacramental marriage. Chaucer's familiarity with this latter concept is shown by his translation of the *Consolatio Philosophiae,* where Boethius explains it, and by Theseus' speech in the Knight's Tale on "the faire cheyne of love":

> . . . al this accordaunce of thynges is bounde with love,
> that governeth erthe and see, and hath also comandement
> to the hevene. And yif this love slakede the bridelis, alle
> thynges that now loven hem togidres wolden make ba-
> tayle contynuely, and stryven to fordo the fassoun of this
> world, the which they now leden in accordable feith by
> fayre moevynges. This love halt togidres peples joyned
> with an holy boond, and knytteth sacrement of mariages
> of chaste loves; and love enditeth lawes to trewe felawes.
> O weleful were mankynde, yif thilke love that governeth
> hevene governede yowr corages. (*Boece,* II.m.8.13–26)

> The Firste Moevere of the cause above,
> Whan he first made the faire cheyne of love,
> Greet was th'effect, and heigh was his entente.

Wel wiste he why, and what thereof he mente;
For with that faire cheyne of love he bond
The fyr, the eyr, the water, and the lond
In certeyn boundes, that they may nat flee.
[I(A) 2987–93] [36]

The other Venus, designated as terrestrial or infernal in the
Pythagorean scheme, is, in the Middle Ages, "the shameful
Venus, the goddess of sensuality," and "concupiscence of the
flesh, which is the mother of all fornication"; she is identified
by John the Scot with man's original sin.[37] This Venus *in malo*
represents a kind of music, too: in the Knight's Tale, the walls
of her temple are painted with "Festes, instrumentz, caroles,
daunces,/ Lust and array, and alle the circumstaunces/ Of
Love" (lines 1931–33); and the statue of Venus there shows
a beautiful "naked" lady, holding a "citole in hir right hand,"
and standing near her "blynd" son, "Cupido," who bears his
"bowe" and "arwes brighte and kene" (lines 1955–66). It is,
fittingly, to this Venus that Palamon promises to "holden
werre alwey with chastitee" (line 2236).

The music of the lascivious Venus is theologically equivalent to the Old Song and the Old Dance which are traditionally
associated in the Middle Ages with that unregenerate Old Man
of whom the Apostle Paul speaks.[38] Among Chaucer's characters, the lustful devotees of this Venus include the Miller, who
leads the Canterbury pilgrims out of London playing upon a
bagpipe; "hende Nicholas" in the Miller's Tale, who makes
venereal "melodye" with Alisoun in the carpenter's bed; and
the Wife of Bath, who is described as expert at the "olde
daunce."

Those who are reborn in Christ and sing the New Song of
charity or divine love are typified by the "litel clergeon" in the
Prioress' Tale, who is martyred singing the "alma redemptoris
mater," and the Second Nun's St. Cecilia:

And whil the organs maden melodie,
To God allone in herte thus sang she:
"O Lord, my soul and eek my body gye
Unwemmed, lest that it confounded be."
                                        [VIII(G) 134–137]

Of much broader significance for our purpose, however, is
Robertson's observation that the distinction between charity
and cupidity, so basic to medieval Christian theology, "may be
thought of as a Christian fulfillment of Ovid's 'twin
loves' . . . ." [39] The Middle Ages understood that "good and
evil are fundamentally matters of love, and that love springs
like a fountain within the human breast which may turn either
in the stream of charity, a love which is the source of all good,
or in the stream of cupidity, a love which is the source of all
evil." [40] The standard medieval definitions of *caritas* and *cupiditas* are given by Augustine in his *De Doctrina Christiana:*
caritas is "the motion of the soul toward the enjoyment of God
for His own sake, and the enjoyment of one's self and of one's
neighbor for the sake of God"; *cupiditas* is "a motion of the
soul toward the enjoyment of one's self, one's neighbor, or any
corporal thing for the sake of something other than God"
(III.x.16). [41] The pattern of relationship between these two
kinds of love, like that between the Pythagorean celestial
Venus and infernal Venus, is hierarchical; that is, God-di-
rected love is superior to self-directed love. Love *in bono,*
obviously, is better than love *in malo,* for the first leads to
salvation and the second, to hell.

According to Augustine, these "twin Loves" constitute the
major theme of the entire Bible, for "Scripture teaches nothing
but charity, nor condemns anything except cupidity, and in
this way shapes the minds of men." Moreover, Augustine
cautions that whenever the Scriptures seem to promote cupidity or to condemn charity, our minds must be "subject to some

erroneous opinion" (III.x.15)—that is, we are reading and interpreting the Bible "incorrectly," as the Wife of Bath does.

Even this hasty discussion of the medieval tradition of double Venus and her two sons, Ovid's "twin Loves" (and, in a sense, Augustine's *caritas* and *cupiditas*), may serve to clarify certain issues concerning the setting and theme of *The Canterbury Tales*. The month of "Aprill" is mentioned in the very first line of the General Prologue, and we may question whether the whole reason for this is that medieval poems conventionally open in spring, that spring is the logical time for an English pilgrimage to begin, or that Chaucer was reconstructing a pilgrimage he had once undertaken in April. Chaucer's audience would have associated April mythologically with Venus,[42] Ovid's "geminorum mater Amorum," and theologically—as Baldwin has insisted [43]—with Easter, that time in the Christian year when the opening of the frozen earth and the rebirth of nature recall that other opening of the earth long ago when Christ arose and offered man the gifts of spiritual rebirth and eternal salvation.

In the Middle Ages, Robertson explains,

> Love moved the pilgrim's feet and determined the direction of his journey. The *Tales* are set in a framework which emphasizes this journey and its implications. The opening in April, the month of Venus, under the sign of Taurus, the house of Venus, with its showers and singing birds, suggests the love which may move the pilgrims to Canterbury toward either one spiritual city or the other. . . .[44]

The Parson's sermon on penitence points out, for the benefit of any pilgrim who "thurgh synne hath mysgoon fro the righte wey of Jerusalem celestial" [X(I) 80], one of the "weyes espirituels that leden folk to oure Lord Jhesu Crist, and to the regne of glorie" [X(I) 79]. And the Parson's words are rele-

vant to more "sondry folk" than the Canterbury pilgrims
alone, for the characters in their tales are, in the same measure
as the narrators themselves, conceived and depicted on one
basic level as "medieval people," making their pilgrimage
through life "toward either one spiritual city or the other." As
old Egeus observes in the Knight's Tale,

> This world nys but a thurghfare ful of wo,
> And we been pilgrymes, passynge to and fro.
> [I(A) 2847–48]

Perhaps Egeus' words may serve to remind us, once more,
that neither the older historical and realistic nor the newer
theological view of Chaucer's pilgrims and characters is *by
itself* wholly adequate. His "people" are, to be sure, in and of
"this world"—and, to this extent, they are real, even when
their attributes suggest types, concepts, and configurations.
But it is equally true that they are all pilgrims to the next
world; and it is, very largely, their attitude toward that next
world which is reflected in their behavior on the pilgrimage
through this one. To the medieval mind, as to the modern, this
attitude and all "behavior" may be measured and evaluated by
ascertaining *how* a man loves or *what* he loves, by inquiring
—in theological or "secular" psychological context—after his
"ultimate concerns." As the medieval mythographers realized,
much may be known of a man from the Venus he serves.

Chaucer's acquaintance with the two Venuses and his
Christian attitude toward divine and infernal love are nowhere
more clearly reflected than in the Knight's Tale, which for a
number of significant reasons—humanistic, philosophical, and
architectural—well deserves its undoubted pre-eminence as
the first of the tales. Its value in elucidating Chaucer's central
theme is scarcely less great than that which Kittredge, Tupper,
Baldwin, and Robertson have found, variously, in the "marriage group," with its treatment of human love relationships;

the Parson's Tale, with its exposition of sin and penitence; or the General Prologue, with its implications of spiritual pilgrimage and its theological significations of spring. In fact, the tale may be taken to represent Chaucer's "epic" or "high-style" treatment of the "love motif" in one of its more pervasive manifestations, that of the "sex problem."

Since the Knight's Tale is the most thoroughly "classical" in the entire book (even in genre, actually, more a "classical" epyllion than a medieval romance), its wealth of mythological detail provides a set of "clues" to interpretation quite as reliable and helpful as Boccaccio's own *chiose* on the *Teseida*.[45] Let us examine the very first of these mythological clues in the clear light of that most prolific writer of Latin epyllia, Ovid—Chaucer's favorite classical poet and usual mythological *auctoritee*—and the medieval commentators on him.

As the Knight's Tale opens, Theseus, "lord and governour" of Athens is returning from "Scithia," where "with his wysdom and his chivalrie,/ He conquered al the regne of Femenye" [I(A) 865–66] and wedded the Amazonian queen "Ypolita."

According to Ovid, it was another hero, Hercules, who had done battle with the Amazons and, as one of his twelve labors, won the girdle of Hippolyte.[46] Hercules bitterly recalls this feat in *Metamorphoses* IX, while dying in agony from the poison of the Lernaean hydra: "vestra virtute relatus/ Thermodontiaco caelatus balteus auro" (lines 188–189: [Was it for this, O hands, that] by your strength that girdle chased with Thermodonian gold was brought back?).[47]

Ovid's use of *virtus* in this context to mean "physical strength" or "prowess," with no apparent reference to moral virtue, represents one standard signification of the word in classical Latin. Lewis and Short, noting the derivation of *virtus* from *vir,* define *virtus* as "manliness, manhood, i.e. the sum of all the corporeal or mental excellences of man, *strength, vigor; bravery, courage; aptness, capacity; worth, excellence, virtue,* etc." [48] Since Hercules excelled in such qualities, it is not surprising that the first two hundred lines of *Metamorphoses* IX, where his heroic feats are related, contain four references to his *virtus.* In three of these usages, the word means "strength"; in the fourth, it represents "bravery," "courage," or "patience in adversity." [49]

Ovid's medieval commentators [50] understood this connection between *vir* and *virtus,* but to them the manly "virtue" of Hercules, upon which Ovid insists so strongly, was essentially a moral quality, implying more than mere physical strength and more even than courage.[51] In the Middle Ages, the *virtus* of such heroes as Hercules, Theseus, and Orpheus distinguishes them not so much from the weak or cowardly as from the vicious. Hence, Giovanni del Virgilio (p. 85) stresses the fact that the Amazons were conquered "ab Hercule i. a virtuoso" [52] (by Hercules; that is, by a "virtuous" man) and underscores his point by adding that it was *virtus* which brought down the "pride" of the Amazons. John of Garland's verses (p. 64: line 365) on the conquest of the Amazons describe Hercules as *"Vir vir*tute *vir*ens" [53] (a man flourishing in virtue); and the same poet (p. 60: lines 305–306) attributes to the "virtue" of Theseus his success in such exploits as the slaying of the giant-robbers who terrorized the road to Athens, the destruction of the walls of Thebes, and the killing of the Minotaur. Since the Athenian robbers, the walls of Thebes, and the Minotaur all symbolize wickedness rather than simple physical strength, their conquest by the *virtus* of Theseus represents the superiority of moral virtue over vice.[54]

The same tradition, rooted in classical Latin philology, which equated the manly and heroic with the virtuous quite naturally designated the vicious as effeminate; and the resulting moral distinction between those virtuous or manly persons who live "viriliter" and the vicious or effeminate, of either sex, who live "muliebriter," became a medieval commonplace.

Thus Arnulf of Orléans, commenting upon the metamorphosis of Iphis, a Cretan girl changed by Isis into a young man (*Met.* IX.666–797), observes (p. 221), "Iphis de femina in virum. Quod nichil aliud fuit nisi quod muliebriter se prius habens, postea viriliter fecit." (Iphis was changed from a woman into a man. This means simply that, first behaving "muliebriter," he later acted "viriliter.")

Arnulf (p. 222) furnishes a more extensive moralization for Ovid's tale of Orpheus and Eurydice (*Met.* X.1–85). Orpheus, having lost Eurydice for the second time, was not permitted to descend again to hell (i.e., to vices), but rather ascended a mountain (i.e., rose to virtues) where, with his singing (i.e., *praedicatio*), he tamed men and beasts. Henceforth his love was directed not toward women but toward men, and the reason given for this change is that women are more prone to lust and to other vices than men: "mulieres i. muliebriter viventes et viciosos vilipendit, sed amorem suum ad mares i. viriliter agentes transtulit. . . . Mulieres siquidem proniores sunt in libidem et vicia quam viri." (He despised women—that is, the vicious and those who live "muliebriter" —but he transferred his love to men—that is, to those who live "viriliter." Since, indeed, women are more prone to lust and the vices than men.) This explanation is consistent with Arnulf's later interpretation (p. 224) of the murder of Orpheus by the mad Ciconian women (*Met.* XI.1–43): "Mulieres i. luxuriosi Orpheum i. sapientem occidentes, re vera quia mares i. virtuosos amaverat, mutate sunt in diversas figuras. Quod ideo fingitur quia luxurie multe sunt species et in victu et in aliis rebus." (The women, that is the lecherous, who killed Orpheus, that is the wise, in fact because he had loved men, that is the virtuous, were changed into different forms. The reason for this is that there are many kinds of lechery, both in mode of living and in other things.)

There remains for consideration one final "Ovidian" contribution to the medieval concept of *virtus*. In his great commentary on the *Metamorphoses,* Berchorius not only provides the standard identification of *vir* and *virtuosus,* but also defines *vir* as *fidelis* and *mulier* as *infidelis,* thus revealing another moral facet of *virtus*. His theological exegesis (p. 113) of Ovid's legend of Tiresias in *Metamorphoses* III (323–331) affords a good example of this formulation: "Iste Tiresias michi signat populum iudaicum, qui pro certo in principio fuit vir i. virtuosus. . . . Vel aliter alii exponunt de Paulo qui primo fit factus mulier i. infidelis. . . . Tandem . . . in virum i. fidelem fuit mutatus." (This Tiresias signifies to me the Jewish people, who certainly, in the beginning, were "male"—that is, virtuous. Or others explain this differently, as concerning Paul, who first became a woman—that is, faithless. Finally, he was changed into a man—that is, he became faithful.) [55]

The foregoing evidence is sufficient to indicate that Ovid and his commentators must be held, to some considerable extent, responsible for what came to be a significant literary convention: the regular identification of manliness with moral virtue as well as physical strength, with fidelity or *pietas,* wisdom, and authority; and the concomitant association of effeminacy with vice (especially that of lechery), unfaithfulness, foolishness, and weakness—of character and not of body only.

The image and role of Theseus in the Knight's Tale (as well as in Boccaccio's *Teseida* and Shakespeare's *Midsummer Night's Dream*) depend in large measure upon the implications of this tradition—a tradition which, with Giovanni del Virgilio (p. 79), understood "in Theseus, a virtuous man" (per Theseum . . . hominem virtuosum). Just as it was, to the medieval Ovidians, *virtus* or true virility, with all its moral attributes, which had empowered Hercules to bring down the Amazons' pride and take Hippolyte's girdle, so it was by his "wysdom and his chivalrie," two aspects of manly virtue, that Theseus (according to Boccaccio and Chaucer) "conquered al the regne of Femenye" or, in the parlance of the Ovidian commentators, vanquished those who live "muliebriter." [56]

The wisdom of Theseus is consonant with his position of authority as "duc" of Athens, a city associated since antiquity with Athena, the Goddess of Wisdom; and the distinction between the virile and the muliebrous, already represented by Theseus' conquest of "Femenye" and his marriage to Ypolita, is further emphasized by Chaucer's allusion to "the grete bataille for the nones/ Bitwixen Atthenes and Amazones" [I(A) 879–80]. This mention of a war between Athenians and Amazons serves much the same purpose as Arnulf's contrast of the *sapientia* of Orpheus with the *luxuria* or lustfulness of the crazed Ciconian women who slew him because he had addressed his love to "mares i. virtuosos." Furthermore, the battle between Athenians and Amazons is later paralleled by Theseus' campaign against Thebes, the city of Bacchus and Venus, frequented by Jove in his search for amorous adventure, and therefore detested for its adultery by Juno Pronuba, the patroness of matrimony. It is no mere accident of plot that Theseus is an Athenian and that Palamon and Arcite are Thebans.

It is difficult to ignore the relevance of these several pairs of co-ordinates—wisdom and the "regne of Femenye," Theseus and Ypolita, Athenians and Amazons, Athens and Thebes, Theseus and Palamon-Arcite—to the central meaning of the Knight's Tale. As variant expressions of the fundamental concepts of wise, virtuous "manliness" and foolish, lustful "effeminacy," they suggest, early in the tale, the moral lesson or *sentence* which may be learned from the story of Palamon and Arcite.[57]

The conquest of the Queen of the Amazons by the "duc" of Athens and their subsequent marriage represent the rational and concordant subordination of the woman to the man, of the wife to the husband, of the flesh to the spirit, or of man's concupiscent appetite to his reason. Such a relationship is in accord with the precepts of Paul: "Wives, submit yourselves unto your own husbands, as unto the Lord. For the husband is the head of the wife, even as Christ is the head of the church: and he is the saviour of the body. Therefore as the church is subject unto Christ, so let the wives be to their own husbands in every thing" (Ephesians V.22–24).

Theseus himself admits, in his words to Palamon and Arcite after he has discovered them quarrelling in the grove, that he was not always so reasonable as this in his attitude toward love. Like these two hot and headstrong lovers, fighting for a "hare," he too once served the God of Love:

> A man moot ben a fool, or yong or oold,—
> I woot it by myself ful yore agon,
> For in my tyme a servant was I oon.
> And therfore, syn I knowe of loves peyne,
> And woot hou soore it kan a man distreyne,
> As he that hath ben caught ofte in his laas,
> I yow foryeve al hoolly this trespaas.
>
> [I(A) 1812–18]

At the time the narrative of the Knight's Tale begins, however, Theseus has already conquered the "regne of Femenye" in himself, subdued the Amazons of Scythia, and married their Queen. He has been wise enough to learn that marriage is the only proper condition of love, and he is presented as a model for the solution of the "sex problem" as it affects not only Palamon and Arcite but all the other foolish muliebrous lovers in the *Tales*.

The very fact that Palamon and Arcite are of Theban blood should lead us to suspect that they will not readily emulate the example of Theseus, but will be naturally more devoted to the lascivious Venus and her son Cupid than to Athena or Juno Pronuba; and their irrational reaction to Emelye fulfills our expectations. When Palamon first catches sight of Emelye in the garden outside his prison window, he sees her not as an Amazon to be conquered, but as Venus, a goddess to be adored:[58] "I noot wher she be womman or goddesse,/ But Venus is it soothly, as I gesse" [I(A) 1101–02]. Thereupon, he falls on his knees and prays to her—just as he will later pray to the real Venus to grant his petition that the girl whom he once confused with her may be made his. The arrow of Cupid which has entered in at Palamon's eye, bypassed his reason, and lodged in his heart at sight of Emelye in the garden, strikes Arcite with equal force.[59] He declares at once, with the unreasoning impetuosity characteristic of such lovers, that unless he is permitted at least to gaze upon Emelye, he must die:

> The fresshe beautee sleeth me sodeynly
> Of hire that rometh in the yonder place,
> And but I have hir mercy and hir grace,
> That I may seen hire atte leeste weye,
> I nam but deed; ther nis namoore to seye.
> [I(A) 1118–22]

If Arcite does not err quite so wildly as Palamon had in imagining Emelye to be Venus, his reaction to the girl differs from that of his fellow-prisoner only in degree of foolishness, for in a sense he too beholds Emelye with the eyes of a lustful idolator—and this is true despite his statement to Palamon concerning the distinction between their feelings for Emelye: "Thyn is affeccioun of hoolynesse,/ And myn is love, as to a creature" [I(A) 1158–59]. To Arcite's heated imagination, Emelye has already become his "paramour" (line 1155), whom he will love even at the cost of his sworn brotherhood with Palamon.

This kind of "love" which Arcite feels for a girl whom he has never seen before and does not yet even know, and his burning desire to contemplate her, in much the way a devotee adores his idol, are clear indications that his intention is not marriage—at least not of the order which Paul recommends —but rather an inverted relationship in which the man will submit himself to the woman, subordinating the spirit to the flesh, and allowing his concupiscence to subvert his reason.

Like Theseus, then, Palamon and Arcite meet the Amazon, but unlike the wise Athenian they are not sufficiently virtuous or manly to conquer her. Instead, being muliebrous and already subject to the "regne of Femenye" within themselves, they surrender easily to a woman. The discord which accompanies their irrational lust for Emelye destroys their friendship and results in the death of Arcite. In the end, it is Theseus who prescribes the proper remedy for this type of love by counselling Emelye to take Palamon "for housbonde and for lord" (line 3081) and by uniting the two, almost as a priest would, in that bond which "highte matrimoigne or mariage" (line 3095).

Of course, not every marriage in the *Tales* is so "proper" as that of Theseus and Ypolita—or, in the end, Palamon and Emelye. The Wife of Bath, that paragon of Amazonian muliebrity, is an unconquered Hippolyte, whose sermon-prologue and *exemplum*-tale are dedicated to the proposition (credited by "al hir secte") that what every woman most desires and ought always to achieve is "sovereynetee/ As wel over hir housbond as hir love,/ And for to been in maistrie hym above" [III(D) 1038–40]. But it is, surely, both historically and textually inaccurate to foist upon the *Tales* a "real" Hegelian dialectic, by claiming that the Wife of Bath's Prologue and Tale (thesis) interact dynamically with the Clerk's Tale (antithesis) to produce the Franklin's (synthesis), and that the Franklin's words on the marriage of Arviragus and Dorigen pronounce Chaucer's solution to the marital problem:

Heere may men seen an humble, wys accord;
Thus hath she take hir servant and hir lord,—
Servant in love, and lord in mariage.
Thanne was he bothe in lordshipe and servage.
Servage? nay, but in lordshipe above,
Sith he hath bothe his lady and his love;
His lady, certes, and his wyf also,
The which that lawe of love acordeth to.

[V(F) 791–98]

Some consequences of this ingenious compromise are illustrated in the tale which follows.[60] Dorigen takes "in pley" (line 988) an oath to commit adultery upon the fulfillment of certain conditions, interprets her oath seriously when those conditions seem fulfilled, determines to commit suicide rather than be unfaithful either to her oath or to her husband, but is persuaded by Arviragus that the "honorable" thing to do is keep her word. Happily, she is released from her "promise" by the would-be adulterer (Matthew might have suggested [V.28] that Aurelius had already committed adultery in his heart by having cast his eyes lustfully after another man's wife); and the Franklin, staggered by such magnanimity, concludes (lines 1621–22) by asking who has been most generous—Arviragus, for urging his wife to commit adultery rather than break a promise; Aurelius, for permitting her not to "do it" after all; or a magician from Orléans, who decides not to collect from Aurelius his fee for having done away with the rocks of Brittany (which, in fact, he has merely hidden beneath the tide, where they are not, perhaps, altogether innocuous).

If this tale is to be read as Chaucer's serious attempt to synthesize the Wife of Bath and the Clerk into a "golden mean" between two extremes, and if it does represent the poet's own last best word on marriage, then Chaucer must have been—among other surprising things—(1) "ahead" of his age in philosophy, (2) a "free-thinker" in religion, and (3) a rather dangerous man to know should he meet your wife in a mood to make outrageous bargains with her and then exact them ungenerously. (It is true, after all, that some golden means are gilded mediocrities.)

It is scarcely necessary to insist further upon the primacy of the Knight's Tale, both in introducing and "solving" this important kind of "love problem," than merely to suggest that Chaucer's "final word" on marriage may, very reasonably, be also his first, and that Theseus, or the Knight, seems a more likely "spokesman" for Chaucer in this matter than the Wife of Bath or the Franklin. We should not be misled by the fact that most of the pilgrims—in *The Canterbury Tales,* as in life— are, in fact, somewhat less "virtuous" than the Knight, or that the characters in their narratives are rather more "muliebrous" than Theseus. Many of the tales—especially those related by the Miller, the Reeve, the Cook, the Wife of Bath, the Merchant, the Squire, the Franklin, the Physician, the Shipman, the Nun's Priest, and the Manciple—are concerned, in varying degrees, with that lower form of love begotten by the lascivious Venus, "goddess of sensuality." In each of them, the terrestrial Venus has her devotees, her true servants making war on chastity; and some of them, like Damyan and Aurelius, she afflicts with a case of the "loveris maladye" as virulent as Arcite's. But to interpret such tales as representing Chaucer's acquiescence or delight in lecherous activity is, in Augustine's words, to be "subject to some erroneous opinion," and is somewhat like perverting the Bible so that it appears to promote cupidity and condemn charity. The spiritual dangers attendant upon just this kind of literal-mindedness are unmistakably illustrated in the Wife of Bath's Prologue.

To be sure cupidity, as Augustine defines it, embraces more deadly sins than lechery, or illicit carnal "love," alone. The tales of the Pardoner, the Friar, the Summoner, and the Canon's Yeoman all concern covetousness, or greed—that curse of postlapsarian man which Boethius (again, echoing Ovid) calls "amor habendi"—rendered in Chaucer's *Boece* as "anguysschous love of havynge" (II. m.5.30–31), and glossed by Nicholas Trivet in his commentary on the *Consolatio Philosophiae* as "cupiditas." [61]

The Nun's Priest's Tale represents the perils of pride or vainglory—the most basic kind of self-love, exposed by the Parson as the first of all the deadly sins, responsible for the fall of Lucifer from Heaven (as related in the Monk's Tale), and for the fall of man from grace.

A number of tales, naturally, involve more than one kind of terrestrial love. In the Manciple's Tale, for example, Phoebus' wife is an adulteress, while Phoebus himself is a jealous and possessive husband (like old John in the Miller's Tale and Januarie in the Merchant's) whose selfish "love" for his wife leads him, through that "ire recchelees" (line 279) which is the sin of anger, to murder her. And Chaucer's Tale of Melibee describes the plight of a man whose very name reveals his inordinate love of things temporal: he is too much concerned with "the hony of the goodes of the body" under which lies hidden "the venym that sleeth the soule" (VII.1415).

Enough has been said to show that, in effect, the theme of the Pardoner's Tale, "Radix malorum est Cupiditas," may be considered the message of many another Canterbury tale as well. But neither should we forget those other tales which show that "Radix bonorum est Caritas." The Physician's Virginia, the Prioress' "litel clergeon," and the Second Nun's St. Cecilia are all "virgin" martyrs, whose pure lives reflect the glory of divine love. And if the true gentility of Custance and the patience of Grisilde are rewarded in this life with blessings less resplendent than the martyr's crown of glory, they are none the less shining exemplars of Christian virtue in their steadfast devotion to God under the stings of adversity. That is, Chaucer looks, too, at the other side of the coin, and seeing both aspects of April's goddess and each of the Ovidian "twin Loves," writes also of the "virtuous" and of those who, reborn with the risen Christ of Easter, sing in their hearts that New Song of *caritas* which echoes the "mundana musica" of celestial Venus or divine love.

Finally, let us acknowledge (albeit too briefly) that Chaucer's ability to convey this *hy sentence* through the perennially charming medium of his narrative verse—laden with all the inexhaustible richness of his intellect, learning, and warm humanity—is a tribute to his essentially *poetic* genius. For the author of *The Canterbury Tales* is not primarily a philosopher, or theologian, or mythographer, but rather a true "maker," of that great class which Horace thought deserved all praise for combining in their poetry the useful and the sweet.[62]

Notes

[1] Dorothy Bethurum, ed. *Critical Approaches to Medieval Literature, Selected Papers from the English Institute, 1958–1959* (New York, 1960), p. v.

[2] William R. Crawford's newly published *Bibliography of Chaucer, 1954–63* (Seattle and London, 1967) contains 144 pages. Crawford notes (p. xiii) that "the number of entries recorded for this ten-year period is substantially larger than the total recorded for any similar period by Griffith [Dudley David Griffith, *Bibliography of Chaucer, 1908–1953* (Seattle, 1955), 398 pages] or, for that matter, by Eleanor Prescott Hammond [*Chaucer: A Bibliographical Manual* (New York, 1908), 597 pages]."

[3] *The Works of Geoffrey Chaucer,* 2nd ed. (Boston, 1957), p. 883. Robinson gives his "Table of Altered Readings" on pages 883–885 of the second edition.

[4] *PMLA,* LXVI (1951), 1141–67.

[5] Yale Studies in English, XCVI. The book had been Severs' doctoral dissertation (Yale, 1935).

[6] *PMLA*, LXII (1947), 598–621.

[7] *Speculum*, XXII, 419–29.

[8] *Annuale Mediaevale*, III (1962), 5–27.

[9] *Speculum*, XLI (1966), 619–42. The sound methodology of Severs, Pratt, and other Chaucerians like them who have devoted skill and patience to establishing "The Chaucer Library" and investigating the quality of Chaucer's learning is well reflected in three modern dissertations, each of which has yielded valuable published material. These are Richard Hazelton's "Two Texts of the 'Disticha Catonis' and Its Commentary" (Rutgers, 1956), summarized in *Speculum* (XXXV [1960], 357–80) as "Chaucer and Cato"; Paul Clogan's "Chaucer and the Medieval Statius" (Illinois, 1961), abstracted for *Studies in Philology* (LXI [1964], 599–615) as "Chaucer and the *Thebaid* Scholia"; and Robert Lewis' "Chaucer and Pope Innocent III's *De Miseria Humane Conditionis*" (Pennsylvania, 1965), represented by articles in *PMLA* (LXXXI [1966], 485–92) and *Chaucer Review* (II [1968], 139–58). Just as the chief value of Lewis' work for students of *The Canterbury Tales* is the light it sheds on the Man of Law's Prologue and Tale, so Hazelton focuses our attention on the tales of the Nun's Priest, the Miller, the Reeve, the Merchant, and the Manciple; and Clogan's major concern among the tales is the Knight's, which is, of course, rather heavily indebted to Statius.

[10] Crawford supplies, as an "Introduction" to his *Bibliography,* a brilliant essay on "New Directions in Chaucer Criticism" (pp. xiii–xl). I shall make no attempt here to rival his heroic feat of defining and synthesizing the major critical trends and systems of the last decade. Indeed, with the exception of Robertson's *Preface to Chaucer,* which is indispensable to my paper, I shall deliberately avoid discussion of those critics and works selected by Crawford, with the hope that my survey may, in some small measure, supplement his review rather than merely duplicate it.

Crawford's concern is essentially with those critical approaches which—like the "older historicism," the "new criticism," and the "new historicism"—endeavor either to recover or uncover Chaucer's "poetic," with such tools as medieval exegesis and rhetoric, or through the more modern interests of diction, syntax, structure, style, and tone. He marks out for special attention the following works, as having "added significantly to our critical understanding of Chaucer's accomplishment" (p. xxxix): John Speirs, *Chaucer the Maker* (London, 1951); Raymond Preston, *Chaucer* (New York, 1952); E. Talbot Donaldson, "Commentary" to *Chaucer's Poetry* (New York, 1958);

Charles Muscatine, *Chaucer and the French Tradition* (Berkeley, 1957); and Robert O. Payne, *The Key of Remembrance* (New Haven, 1963).

In addition to these five studies, and the five which I discuss below, the following modern works demand mention: P. V. D. Shelly, *The Living Chaucer* (Philadelphia, 1940); Nevill Coghill, *The Poet Chaucer* (Oxford, 1949); W. W. Lawrence, *Chaucer and the Canterbury Tales* (New York, 1950); J. S. P. Tatlock, *The Mind and Art of Chaucer* (Syracuse, 1950); Kemp Malone, *Chapters on Chaucer* (Baltimore, 1951); Gordon Hall Gerould, *Chaucerian Essays* (Princeton, 1952); D. S. Brewer, *Chaucer* (New York, 1953; 2nd ed., 1960) and *Chaucer in His Time* (London, 1963); Paull F. Baum, *Chaucer: A Critical Appreciation* (Durham, N.C., 1958) and *Chaucer's Verse* (Durham, 1961); B. H. Bronson, *In Search of Chaucer* (Toronto, 1960); Harold F. Brooks, *Chaucer's Pilgrims: The Artistic Order of the Portraits in the Prologue* (London and New York, 1962); T. W. Craik, *The Comic Tales of Chaucer* (London, 1964); Paul G. Ruggiers, *The Art of the Canterbury Tales* (Madison and Milwaukee, 1965); and George Williams, *A New View of Chaucer* (Durham, N.C., 1965).

[11] Richard J. Schoeck and Jerome Taylor, ed. *Chaucer Criticism: The Canterbury Tales* (Notre Dame, 1960), pp. 14–51. A portion of Baldwin's monograph is reprinted also in *Discussions of the Canterbury Tales,* ed. Charles A. Owen, Jr. (Boston, 1962).

[12] Bernard F. Huppé and D. W. Robertson, Jr., *Fruyt and Chaf* (Princeton, 1963), p. viii: "Chaucerians should do battle vigorously, but only that Chaucer's greater triumph may ensue. An interest in this goal unites us with all true Chaucerians, no matter how much they may disagree with what we have to say."

[13] See, respectively, R. E. Kaske, "Chaucer and Medieval Allegory," *ELH,* XXX (1963), 192 and F. L. Utley, "Robertsonianism Redivivus," *Romance Philology,* XIX (1965), 250.

[14] Huppé, p. vi. Cf. Robertson's *Preface,* p. x, and *Fruyt and Chaf,* p. vii.

[15] Edward Wagenknecht, ed. *Chaucer: Modern Essays in Criticism* (New York, 1959). For Schoeck-Taylor and Owen, see note 11, above. Some of the essays in these collections date from the earlier part of the century.

[16] *Speculum,* XXVI (1951), 659–72.

[17] See note 2, above. Much recent Chaucer scholarship which has not

dealt specifically—or sometimes even at all—with the text, the sources, or the meaning of *The Canterbury Tales* nonetheless deserves brief but grateful mention for supplying us with useful and often essential equipment in studying the *Tales*. Those patiently compiled bibliographies just mentioned constitute only one case in point. Other examples are such varied items as Marchette Chute's biography, *Geoffrey Chaucer of England* (New York, 1946; 2nd ed., 1962); T. F. Mustanoja's *Middle English Syntax* (Helsinki, 1960); F. P. Magoun's *Chaucer Gazetteer* (Chicago, 1961); Helge Kökeritz's *Guide to Chaucer's Pronunciation* (New York, 1962); Roger Sherman Loomis' *Mirror of Chaucer's World* (Princeton, 1965), containing nearly 180 illustrations; the Huntington Library's new brochure on the Ellesmere MS (San Marino, 1966), reproducing all the Ellesmere paintings of the Canterbury pilgrims; M. M. Crow and C. C. Olson's *Chaucer Life-Records* (Oxford, 1966); and H. Kurath and S. M. Kuhn's *Middle English Dictionary* (Ann Arbor, 1952–   ). There has been a second edition, within our period, of R. D. French's *Chaucer Handbook* (New York, 1947) and of W. C. Curry's *Chaucer and the Mediaeval Sciences* (New York and London, 1960). H. S. Bennett's *Chaucer and the Fifteenth Century* appeared as part of the Oxford History of English Literature in 1947, and the following year gave us J. Harvey's *Gothic England: A Survey of National Culture, 1300–1550* and the edition by Olson and Crow of Edith Rickert's *Chaucer's World*. Our knowledge of the political and social backgrounds of Chaucer's age has been much increased also by A. L. Poole's *Medieval England* (Oxford, 1958) and May McKisack's volume (1959) on the Fourteenth Century for the now complete Oxford History of England.

[18] *The Works of Geoffrey Chaucer* (2nd ed.), p. 1.

[19] *Preface to the Fables* (1700), in *Essays of John Dryden,* ed. W. P. Ker (Oxford, 1900), II, 262.

[20] For this and the following statement, see Edgar F. Shannon, *Chaucer and the Roman Poets,* Harvard Studies in Comparative Literature, 7 (Cambridge, Mass., 1929), p. 300. Italics mine.

[21] Much of what follows is taken from my book *Ovid and the Canterbury Tales* (Philadelphia, 1967). See pp. 11–20 ("Ovid and the Structure and Theme of *The Canterbury Tales*"), 41–48, and 102–103 ("Knight's Tale").

[22] Robinson's statement (*Works,* 2nd ed., p. 649) is typical: "The reason for Chaucer's choice of a pilgrimage as a setting for his stories is unknown. It has been commonly held that he described, at least in

part, a pilgrimage on which he himself was present, perhaps in 1387, and Skeat has shown (Oxford Chaucer, III, 373f.) that the dates mentioned in the narrative would fit well enough with the calendar of that year."

[23] George L. Kittredge, "Chaucer's Discussion of Marriage," *Modern Philology*, IX (1912), 435–67. Kittredge brought his proposal before a much wider audience in *Chaucer and his Poetry* (Cambridge, Mass., 1915), pp. 185–210.

[24] See Frederick Tupper, "Saint Venus and the Canterbury Pilgrims," (New York) *Nation*, XCVII (1913), 354–56.

[25] Robinson's 2nd ed., p. 650.

[26] "Chaucer and the Seven Deadly Sins," *PMLA*, XXIX (1914), 93–128.

[27] Citations from Ovid in my paper are to the Teubner *Editio Stereotypa*, 3 vols: I. *Amores, Epistulae [Heroides], Medic. Fac. Fem., Ars Amat., Remedia Amoris*, ed. R. Ehwald (Leipzig, 1907); II. *Metamorphoses*, ed. R. Merkel (1905); III. *Tristia, Ibis, Ex Ponto Libri, Fasti*, ed. R. Merkel (1904). Translations of Ovid—as of other Latin writers—in my text are my own.

[28] For a discussion of the late Pythagorean mythographical method, see Franz Cumont, *Recherches sur le symbolisme funéraire des Romains* (Paris, 1942), pp. 35ff. Ovid's familiarity with Pythagorean philosophy is mentioned by Hermann Fränkel, *Ovid: A Poet between Two Worlds* (Berkeley and Los Angeles, 1945), pp. 108–110.

[29] Some basis for this assumption may be found in the introduction to *Fasti* IV (8–12), where Ovid makes quite clear that the Venus whom he now invokes is very different from the lascivious mother of wanton Cupid who inspired those youthful love poems, the *Amores* and the *Ars Amatoria*. Later in Book IV (157–62) there is an allusion to Venus Verticordia (the "Heart-Turner"), who was known in the Middle Ages and the Renaissance as a "Third Venus besides the Celestial and Terrestrial," venerated because she "opposes and removes from the soul immodest desires and turns the mind of maidens and wives from carnal love to purity" (Erwin Panofsky, *Studies in Iconology* [New York, 1962], p. 168).

[30] See Robertson, *A Preface to Chaucer*, pp. 125–26; this entire section of my paper is much indebted to Robertson's study.

[31] See Robertson's "Chrétien's *Cligés* and the Ovidian Spirit," *Comparative Literature*, VII (1955), 35.

³² Cited from E. H. Alton, "The Mediaeval Commentators on Ovid's *Fasti*," *Hermathena*, XLIV (1926), 136.

³³ For a discussion ·of other ancient and medieval references to double Venus and the "twin Loves," see John P. McCall, "Classical Myth in Chaucer's *Troilus and Criseyde*" (unpub. Princeton diss., 1955), pp. 141–150.

³⁴ For medieval interpretations of Mars, see McCall, pp. 128–137.

³⁵ See Robertson, "Chrétien's *Cligés* and the Ovidian Spirit," pp. 35–36; cf. *A Preface to Chaucer*, pp. 124ff.

³⁶ Citations from Chaucer in my paper are to Robinson's 2nd edition. For convenience, but not from conviction, I have followed here his order (Ellesmere) of the tales.

³⁷ Robertson, *Preface*, p. 126.

³⁸ For discussion and illustration of this medieval iconographic convention, see Robertson, *Preface*, pp. 127–134. The Scriptural reference is Ephesians IV.22: "That ye put off concerning the former conversation the old man, which is corrupt according to the deceitful lusts."

³⁹ "Chrétien's *Cligés* and the Ovidian Spirit," p. 41.

⁴⁰ *Ibid.*, p. 36.

⁴¹ Saint Augustine, *On Christian Doctrine*, trans. D. W. Robertson, Jr. (New York, 1958), p. 88.

⁴² The usual medieval etymology of "April" is given by Isidore of Seville, *Etymologiarum Liber* V.xxxiii.7 (Migne, *PL*, LXXXII, 219): "Aprilis pro Venere dicitur, quasi *Aphrodis*. Graece enim 'Αφροδίτη *Venus* dicitur, vel quia hoc mense omnia aperiuntur in florem, quasi *aperilis*" (April is named for Venus [*Aphrodis*]. For in Greek Venus is called *Aphrodite*, because in that month all things "open up" in flower).

⁴³ Baldwin, "The Unity of *The Canterbury Tales*," in *Chaucer Criticism*, ed. Schoeck and Taylor, I, 17–19.

⁴⁴ *Preface*, p. 373.

⁴⁵ The *chiose* are printed in Aurelio Roncaglia's edition of the *Teseida* (Bari, 1941), pp. 371–465. It is not yet certain whether Chaucer knew these glosses; but a dissertation on "Boccaccio's *Chiose* to the *Teseide* and the *Knight's Tale*," undertaken by Robert Schlades at Ohio State University, should settle the issue.

⁴⁶ Chaucer, of course, follows Statius and Boccaccio in assigning this feat to Theseus. I use here the Ovidian reference to Hercules merely for convenience; that is, because there is a very large body of moral commentary on the *Metamorphoses*, and because, as we shall see, the

important point to the commentators is the moral implication of conquering "Femenye," whichever virtuous hero—Hercules or Theseus —makes the conquest. I do not pretend that any of the medieval concepts discussed below were derived exclusively from Ovid, but only that Ovid and his Christian interpreters of the Middle Ages constitute one very significant and easily traceable tributary stream—for Chaucer, certainly, the richest of all the classical streams which fed medieval literary tradition and iconological convention. I hope that I may demonstrate here, *minima ex parte,* the value of reading Chaucer's sources—whether Ovid, Dante, or the Bible—as the Middle Ages understood them.

[47] Ovid's one other similarly brief allusion to the girdle of Hippolyte is contained in Cydippe's answer to Acontius in the *Heroides:* "Nullus Amazonio caelatus balteus auro,/ Sicut ab Hippolyte, praeda relata tibist" (XXI.119–120—no girdle engraved with Amazonian gold was given you as booty [by me], as if by Hippolyte). Here again, Ovid does not explicitly associate Theseus with this exploit, although, according to the usual legend, Hippolyte was given by Hercules in marriage to Theseus for his assistance in securing the girdle.

[48] Charlton T. Lewis and Charles Short, *A Latin Dictionary* (Oxford, repr. 1958), p. 1997.

[49] For *virtus* as "strength," see *Met.* IX.62, 188 (quoted above), and 200–201; for the meaning "courage," see *Met.* IX.163 and cf. *patientia* in line 164. For Ovid's application of *virtus,* in these senses, to other manly heroes, cf. Ajax's boast (*Met.* XIII.21–22) that he is greater than Ulysses in nobility even if not in valor—"Atque ego, si virtus in me dubitabilis esset,/ Nobilitate potens essem"—and Theseus' statement (*Met.* VIII.407) that Ancaeus' bane was his rash courage (*temeraria virtus*).

[50] The texts of commentaries which I cite below are those edited by Fausto Ghisalberti, as follows: *Arnolfo d'Orléans, un cultore di Ovidio nel secolo XII* (Milan, 1932); Giovanni di Garlandia, *Integumenta Ovidii, poemetto inedito del secolo XIII* (Messina and Milan, 1933); "Giovanni del Virgilio espositore delle 'Metamorfosi,' " in *Il Giornale Dantesco,* XXXIV, N. S. IV (1933), 1–110; and "L' 'Ovidius Moralizatus' di Pierre Bersuire," in *Studj Romanzi,* XXIII (1933), 5–136. Ghisalberti's "Mediaeval Biographies of Ovid," in *Journal of the Warburg and Courtauld Institutes,* IX (1946), 10–59, is an invaluable study.

[51] Consider the etymology of the name "Hercules" given in MS Ambros. (*Integumenta Ovidii,* ed. Ghisalberti, p. 65): "Hercules per quem habemus virtuosum quia Hercules quasi hercleos dicitur i. vir sive per litem sive per laborem gloriosum" (Hercules, in whom we have the *vir*tuous man; for "Hercules" is to say "hercleos"—that is, a "man" [*vir*], either from strife or from glorious labor). And cf. this footnote in a manuscript of Garland's *Integumenta* (*ibid.*), interpreting Hercules as an exemplar of *virtus moralis* and a symbol of the soul of the just man: "Virtus enim quam habemus per Herculem in rei veritate moralis est. Hercules anima est iusti que deificata est et redditur suo creatori, corpus autem est terra" (For the virtue which we have in Hercules is, truly, *moral virtue*. Hercules is the soul of the just man, which is deified and returned to its creator; but his body is earth).

[52] Lewis and Short, *ibid.,* define *virtuosus* as a Late Latin word meaning "good" or "virtuous."

[53] Italics mine.

[54] Ovid mentions the *virtus* of Theseus in *Met.* VII.405: "[Theseus] qui virtute sua bimarem pacaverat Isthmon" (Theseus, who by his "virtue" had brought peace to the isthmus between the two seas).

[55] For this association of fidelity with manliness, Berchorius may have relied in part upon the authority of Ovid, who, in the *Epistolae ex Ponto,* had confessed to his friend Rufinus that even in exile he found love of his native land stronger than reason, adding, "Sive pium vis hoc, sive hoc muliebre vocari,/ Confiteor misero molle cor esse mihi" (I.iii.31–32—whether you wish to regard this as loyal or effeminate, I confess that my wretched breast contains a soft heart). Ovid's distinction here between what is "pium" and what is "muliebre" implies that true *pietas* is masculine and hence very different from mere soft-hearted effeminate sentimentality. The unreasonable *amor patriae* which Ovid felt in Pontus was not so much manly patriotism as a kind of uncontrollable nostalgia, which Ovid himself appears to have recognized as a symptom of weakness, arising from his "molle cor." It is in this sense that Philip of Harveng interprets Ovid's couplet, which he cities in his twelfth-century treatise "On the Silence of Clerks" to show that the exiled Ovid, having lost his virile authority, had become soft and effeminate: "et posita virili auctoritate velut in femineam mollitiem solvebatur" (Migne, *PL,* CCIII.1180).

[56] The Amazons are rather obvious examples of muliebrity—of "la femme par excellence." The fact that they exclude men from their

borders is merely a negative consideration, from which it does not follow that they are staunchly chaste. They are the enemies of men, and hence of the virtuous; warlike and proud, they are mannish in bearing without being manly in character. Amazons were, to be sure, renowned for physical strength, and it is only in this literal sense that they display any *virtus*. Thus, Ovid refers to Antiope (or possibly Hippolyte) as "Prima securigeras inter virtute puellas" (*Her.* IV.117 —first in strength among the axe-bearing girls).

[57] My discussion of the *sentence* of the Knight's Tale owes much to Robertson's treatment of that tale in his *Preface*, esp. pp. 260–66.

[58] It should be noted that Ovid himself declares, at the end of *Ars Amatoria* II, that his purpose in writing these books on the art of love has been to teach men how to conquer Amazons: "Sed quicumque meo superarit Amazona ferro,/ Inscribat spoliis 'Naso magister erat'" (II.743–44—but whoever shall conquer the Amazon with my sword, let him inscribe on his spoils, "Naso was my teacher"). It will be remembered that, in the Middle Ages, the *Ars Amatoria* was generally considered an ethical treatise "in quo [Ovidius] docuit iuvenes solum licitas amare puellas" (in which Ovid taught young men to love only honorable girls: Ghisalberti, "Mediaeval Biographies of Ovid." p. 39, n. 2; cf. pp. 12, 23, and 40). To the medieval Christian humanist, Ovid's exhortation to subdue the Amazon was an admonition to marry and hence escape submission to the wrong kind of love.

[59] See Robertson's explanation of John the Scot's theological account of the fall of man, *Preface*, pp. 69–72.

[60] The interpretation of the Franklin's Tale implied below is more fully elaborated by Robertson, in *Preface*, pp. 275–76 and 470–72.

[61] For the citation from Trivet, see Robertson, *Preface*, p. 27. I am indebted to my friend Professor Philip N. Lockhart of Dickinson College for pointing out to me the Ovidian original of Boethius' "amor habendi": "Insidiaeque et vis et *amor* sceleratus *habendi*" (Met. I.131 —deceit, force, and that cursed love of having).

[62] *De Arte Poetica*, 343–44.

should have attracted the respectful attention of a large number of distinguished critics and scholars. Yet in the nineteenth century Malory's name did not even appear in literary histories such as Taine's, nor in handbooks of literature such as Thomas Arnold's, and in the Ninth Edition of the *Britannica* Malory rated less than a dozen lines, in which he was identified only as a Welsh priest and minor translator; even as late as 1908, in the huge *Cambridge History of English Literature,* he is dismissed in a little over two pages (whereas Reginald Pecock rates almost twelve).

Certainly Malory's book was widely read in the nineteenth century, and poets often drew on its riches, but even those who owed their materials to Malory had a low opinion of his art. Tennyson, who did not like romance anyway and confessed that the *Morte Darthur* was the only one he had ever read all the way through, thought "it had many fine things in it, but all strung together without art." [2] Sir Walter Scott, who did like romance, was of the same opinion and considered the book thrown together "at hazard" and without "art and combination." [3]

The terms that critics used to characterize the work—"fragments" "strung together" "at hazard"—show that the main source of critical dissatisfaction was then, as it still is today, its form. Malory's work fitted into none of the familiar genres. A long prose narrative was expected to have the virtues of the fictional narrative the nineteenth century knew best, the novel. But *Le Morte Darthur* makes a very poor novel, as Mark Twain demonstrated in his *Connecticut Yankee,* in which the recitation of but two chapters from Malory puts the entire Round Table to sleep.[4] It makes an even more unsatisfactory epic. Edward Strachey argued vigorously that the book is epic in form,[5] but even so sympathetic a classicist as Andrew Lang found the work a "jumble," [6] and, as George Saintsbury pointed out, if we try to read the book as epic we find it "often difficult to say who is the hero and never very easy to say what contribution to the plot the occasionally inordinate episodes are making." [7] Even as a romance Malory's work—"Touch'd by the adulterous finger of a time/ That hover'd between war and wantonness" [8]—seemed unsatisfactory to an age that regarded romance as a more ethereal genre than this robust book would fit. Most important, *Le Morte Darthur* failed to show the organic unity that a successful work required. As Robert Southey, Malory's genuine admirer, had to admit, its aesthetic form is,

> Not like a tree, whose boughs and branches bearing a necessary relation and due proportion to each other, combine into one beautiful form, but resembling such plants as the prickly pear, where one joint grows upon the other, the whole making a formless and misshapen mass. [9]

It was not until the late 1890's, when George Saintsbury wrote about this work, that any critic questioned the assumptions on which these condemnations of Malory were based and argued instead for a sympathetic historical approach to the book. Saintsbury wrote,

> Criticisms have been made on Malory's manner of selecting and arranging his materials—criticisms which, like all unsuccessful exercises of the most difficult of arts, come from putting the wrong questions to the jury—from asking: "Has this man done what *I* wanted him to do?" or "Has he done it as *I* should have done it?" instead of "Has he done what *he* meant to do?" and "Has he done this well?" [10]

Saintsbury's considerable prestige helped win Malory his rightful place in literary studies, and scholarly and critical work on *Le Morte Darthur,* which had just begun when Saintsbury wrote that passage, has now continued for over seventy years. But the questions he raised have never been answered. Saintsbury himself, having decided what the book was not, never tried to say what it was, and he solved the problem of unity that had so bothered his predecessors by simple *fiat*—the flat assertion that the book is unified, that "Malory alone made of the diverse stories one story, one book." [11] This authority was enough to counter the earlier idea that the volume was simply a formless conglomeration of tales, but it did not change what seemed to be a fact: if *Le Morte Darthur* is one book, it is not a very satisfactory one. Even in recent years thoughtful critics have advised their readers that "Malory has no great skill . . . Much of the *Morte Darthur,* therefore, is best read for its individual scenes and not for its connected story." [12] The public has taken such critics at their word, and Malory's story of King Arthur is most often read in one of the many modern adaptations that began appearing in the 1880's and still find large audiences today.

Perhaps that lingering dissatisfaction with the *Morte Darthur* accounts for the rapid acceptance by many scholars of the revolutionary views set forth by Eugène Vinaver in the introduction to his *Works of Sir Thomas Malory*.[13] When that volume appeared in 1947 the study of Malory had still not developed much beyond where it began in the 1890's, for not until the 1920's and early 30's did any considerable number of studies of Malory begin to appear. Then in 1934 W. F. Oakeshott discovered the Winchester Manuscript,[14] which contained a version of Malory's work quite different from Caxton's edition yet probably quite similar to the exemplar from which Caxton worked. For the first time scholars could read what Malory wrote as distinct from what Caxton printed. But the exact contents of the manuscript were not generally known until Vinaver's edition appeared, and from 1934 to 1947 the study of Malory was suspended while students waited to see what the manuscript contained and "what theories it might refute or confirm." [15]

Astonishingly, it seemed to confirm the theory of those early critics, such as Scott, who regarded the book as a haphazard combination of tales. Instead of Caxton's twenty-one book divisions, the Winchester Manuscript contained seven "explicits" marking off eight separate tales. This showed, Vinaver concluded, that Malory had written not one but eight separate, unrelated works. Caxton had attempted to disguise this fact by suppressing the "explicits" and dividing the volume into twenty-one books in order to produce what would pass for a unified book "in the modern sense of that word." [16] Vinaver held that even the title we now use, *Le Morte Darthur,* was a subterfuge of the wily Caxton.[17] Critics had not been putting the wrong questions to the jury, as Saintsbury believed; they had simply been trying the wrong man: Caxton alone was guilty of the badly unified work we call *Le Morte Darthur;* Malory was the author of eight separate works that made no pretense of being parts of some ordered whole, and what we thought was a single book was actually a collection of books, *The Works of Sir Thomas Malory.*

Given the usual assumptions about what a book—"in the modern sense of the word"—should be like, this is a very attractive theory, and it was widely accepted, for it seemed to dispose of a number of problems that had bothered readers since the early nineteenth century. But, as we shall see, serious objections to the theory were soon raised, and the question of the "unity of the *Morte Darthur,*" so unsatisfactorily settled by Saintsbury, has become once again a dominant critical concern. In the debate that followed the publication of Vinaver's theory—and almost all the criticism of the past twenty years has been concerned with this debate—critics have modified or rejected most of Vinaver's views, and few today, including Vinaver himself, would accept without reservation his theory as it was presented in 1947.[18] But our debt to him is no less for all that. In criticism, as in most intellectual endeavors, the questions are often more important than the answers, and for the critical discussion of the past two decades Vinaver's theory posed the most basic and fruitful questions; after the publication of the *Works,* nothing could be taken for granted about *Le Morte Darthur,* and critics had to approach the book without being sure whether, so far as Malory was concerned, it even existed.

I

The text Vinaver produced made that discussion worthwhile, for the Winchester Manuscript revealed a Malory much different from the one we thought we knew from Caxton. Caxton, it now became apparent, had treated his exemplar very freely, especially in the section on the Roman Wars, where he not only modernized the language but considerably condensed his text, leaving out much of the poetic vocabulary of the Northern alliterative tradition that Malory had carried over into his work. The book was also better constructed than we had thought, since Caxton's rather pedantic division of the narrative into "books" had obscured the larger narrative movements that the eight-tale division revealed. Likewise, Caxton's obtrusive and often illogical chapter divisions had hidden from all but the most perceptive readers the skillfully varied pace of the narrative. To Caxton a chapter and a paragraph were usually co-terminal, and in his version the narrative plods at unvarying speed from one arbitrary pause to the next, with the sudden halts emphasized by those tiresome rubrics that nineteenth-century editors, following the authority not of Caxton but of Wynkyn de Worde, placed at the beginning of each chapter.[19] The absence of these divisions in the Winchester Manuscript allowed Vinaver to use modern paragraphing conventions, and his decision to allow the topic or the presence of direct quotation to determine the paragraphs was the most fortunate of his editorial acts. It revealed that the droning regularity, the "level Saharas of facts" of which Twain complained in Malory's style,[20] was largely the work of the Tudor printers whose paragraphing (or lack of it) had obscured the skillful variation in narrative speed and emphasis. I doubt that Twain would have been quite so hard on Malory if he could have read him in Vinaver's edition.

To some readers this new Malory came as a shock, and there has even been a slight reaction against Vinaver's text and in favor of Caxton's. C. S. Lewis, in an important review in *The Times Literary Supplement,* pointed out that the differences between Caxton's and Vinaver's texts are so great that we have not two editions but two distinct versions, and he made clear his preference for Caxton's. That Malory, he wrote, was like a great medieval cathedral, with its satisfying variety of styles and delightful surprises of unexpected crypts and chapels; Vinaver's edition, the Malory of the Winchester Manuscript, seemed to Lewis only an uninteresting "modern reconstruction." [21] Sally Shaw, in her contribution to the *Essays on Malory* edited by J. A. W. Bennett, argued that the Caxton version is even artistically superior to the Winchester.[22] Lewis agreed, and in his contribution to that volume he restated his preference for Caxton: "It is no misfortune that it has counted for so much in the English imagination. That is why I have quoted not only from Caxton but even from Caxton as edited by Pollard: the household book. I enjoy my cathedral as it has stood the test of time and demand no reconstruction." [23]

Lest others follow Lewis' example, perhaps my readers will allow me a brief bibliographical excursus: The idea that one can choose between Caxton's edition and Vinaver's is based on the assumption that these are the only two versions. A third appeared even before the fifteenth century had ended, when Wynkyn de Worde printed his edition in 1498 (reprinted

1529). De Worde not only corrected the errors in Caxton
(over 400) and completely modernized the spelling, he inserted several pages of his own composition, supplied rubrics
(taken from Caxton's table of contents) for the chapters, and
introduced some ten thousand other variants into the text.[24]
When Copland (1557) and East (two editions, 1585) produced their texts they reprinted not Caxton but de Worde.
These were the editions that the Elizabethans knew; indeed,
Copland's edition may have carried on its title page the original of Spenser's Red Cross Knight, labelled "Holiness." [25] A
new version of Malory appeared in 1634, in Richard Stansby's edition. Stansby used East's edition as his exemplar, but
by this time de Worde's language was too archaic and simple
for an age that preferred, as Stansby explained, "a more elo-
quent and ornate style in speech and writing." [26] He therefore
completely modernized the text, not only changing the words
and syntax and adding eloquence here and there but also
removing or rewriting whole passages in which "King *Arthur*
or some of his knights were declared in their communications
to swear prophane or use superstitious speeches." [27] The result
was a text that, leaving aside spelling changes, has over twenty
thousand variations from Caxton's version.[28] More important,
Stansby also changed the shape of the narrative. He rejected
Caxton's book-divisions and instead divided the whole work
into three parts, with the chapters numbered consecutively
throughout each part. The result is a volume as different from
Caxton as Caxton is from the Winchester, and one could
argue, using the same arguments that Sally Shaw advanced for
Caxton, that for modern readers Stansby's edition is superior.[29]

That was the opinion of nineteenth-century scholars, such
as Thomas Wright,[30] and of nineteenth-century publishers,
since until 1868 Stansby's version was the only version reprinted in popular editions.[31] In 1816 two separate and independent popular editions appeared, both modernized reprints

of Stansby's text. The next year Upcott's corrupt edition of Caxton was published, but it was expensive and its retention of Caxton's original spelling rendered it "useless to the general reader." [32] Consequently, as Strachey wrote in 1891, the 1816 editions of Stansby's version "were probably the volumes through which most of my own generation made their first acquaintance with King Arthur and his knights." [33] Certainly Tennyson first read Malory in this version; Leigh Hunt gave him a copy of the 1816 British Classics edition, and Tennyson kept and used that edition for the rest of his life. [34] A new generation of readers was supplied with Stansby's version by Thomas Wright in his edition of 1858 (reprinted 1865), and as late as 1886 when Ernest Rhys edited Malory for the Camelot Classics he too used Stansby's version. Not until Strachey published his edition of *Le Morte Darthur* in 1868 did English readers, aside from scholars, have a chance to read Malory in Caxton's version, and this only in a mercilessly bowdlerized edition. As Strachey explained, he omitted or rewrote any passage that might prove harmful to the morals of young boys, "From whom the chief demand for this volume will always come." [35] So tender were the morals of English boys in that age that Sommer characterized the resulting edition as "modernized and abridged," [36] and, in R. H. Wilson's words, "One can only speculate what use Twain might have made in his attack on medieval immorality and free language of an unexpurgated text." [37]

But there were no unexpurgated texts of Malory available. Not until after the publication of Sommers' edition of Caxton in 1889 were what we now think of as the standard popular editions produced: John Rhys' edition of 1893, which became the Everyman's edition, Israel Gollancz' edition for the Temple Classics in 1897, and finally Pollard's edition of 1900. The student interested in Malory's influence should therefore avoid Pollard unless he is concerned with the period from

1900 to 1947; for the last third of the nineteenth century he will have to consult Strachey's bowdlerized version; for the Tudor and Elizabethan periods de Worde's version must be used, and for the more than two centuries from 1634 to 1868 one must consult Stansby, whose version most nearly stood the "test of time." But for the study of Malory himself, apart from his later influence, the student must use Vinaver's edition.

Perhaps critics came to the defense of Caxton's edition partly out of a sense of fair play, for Vinaver, after the manner of editors, was very harsh toward his great predecessor. Vinaver was convinced that Caxton knowingly misrepresented Malory's collection of independent tales, that for the sake of commercial advantage he invented the title *Le Morte Darthur,* complete with its error in gender,[38] and suppressed the "explicits" in order to satisfy the damands of his public for a book "in the modern sense of that word." First for the misdemeanor, the title. As Vinaver himself argued in 1929, Caxton may have found this title in his exemplar.[39] The last few leaves of the Winchester Manuscript are missing, and the text may well have ended with the words, perhaps in a later scribal hand, *Explicit le Morte Darthur.* That is likely, since what we regard as Caxton's own colophon (the paragraph beginning "This boke is entitled le Morte Darthur") starts at exactly the point where we might expect such an "explicit." Furthermore, Caxton himself did not regard this as the title of his work; when he refers to this volume in a later preface he calls it not *Le Morte Darthur* but "the book of the noble & vyctoryous kyng Arthur." [40] Evidently Wynkyn de Worde called his version *The Booke of the Noble Kyng, Kyng Arthur* not, as Vinaver explains, because he saw through "Caxton's subterfuge" but because he was following his master's own usage. But this matter of the title is a minor offense; titles were not very important in this period, and when Caxton was working English books did not even have title pages.[41]

More felonious is the charge that Caxton misrepresented his volume in order to produce a "modern" book that would attract customers. This was not Caxton's practice; when he did produce composite works, such as his translation of *Charles the Grete* (of which the first and third books are from Vincent of Beauvais' history and the second—twice as long as the other two together—is an adaptation of a romance) he did not conceal this fact from his readers nor worry about the lack of "unity" that resulted, for his patrons were not interested in unified modern books. The noble gentlemen who asked him to print the book of King Arthur asked not for one story but for a collection of "histories," and throughout his preface and final colophon Caxton does all he can to assure these gentlemen that he is giving them what they wanted, "many wonderful hystories and adventures." Most likely Caxton's explanatory colophon—"This boke is entitled le Morte Darthur, Notwithstanding that it treateth of the birth, etc."—is not an "apology" but an advertisement, promising the potential reader not the modern pleasures of unity but the more typically medieval delights of copiousness and variety.

II

Vinaver was convinced that Caxton misrepresented Malory's work because of his belief that the seven "explicits" suppressed by Caxton proved that Malory had written eight separate and unrelated tales. Vinaver's new examination of Malory's use of his sources lent additional weight to this theory, since he found that Malory was not simply translating but was working consciously to disengage from his interlaced prose sources a series of independent tales. Moreover, the overall narrative contains serious contradictions and inconsistencies. Tristram appears as a mature knight in the first tale, though he is not born until the fifth; the knights Carados and Tarquin are dead in the third tale, but reappear, no worse for the experience, in the fourth. Finally, and perhaps most important, the whole book is badly proportioned, with an entire third of the narrative devoted to the apparently inconsequential adventures of Tristram. Such difficulties as these had convinced readers since the time of Scott that the book was indeed formless and thrown together without art; and all these problems disappear once one accepts the theory that Malory did not intend his eight tales to be read together as parts of a single work.

Despite its attractions, the difficulties in this theory soon became obvious. As R. H. Wilson pointed out, the volume contains more "explicits" than the eight Vinaver used as his tale-divisions.[42] What Malory called the Book or Tale of Balyn le Savage, for example, occurs within the limits of Vinaver's first tale, and it is set off by explicits as emphatic as those which set off the tale of Gareth. Likewise, the next internal division of that first tale is set off by an "explicit" ("Explicit the Weddyng of Kyng Arthur") as clear as that which ends what Vinaver considered the independent Tale of Sir Lancelot ("Explicit a Noble Tale of Sir Launcelot du Lake"). Similar divisions occur within the Book of Tristram. Vinaver himself recognized the difficulty when he singled out the "explicits" with an "air of finality," those after the first, fourth, fifth, and sixth tales, and observed that the others "may well have been inserted in the course of the writing." [43] If they were, we have not an eight-fold but a five-fold division, and all the advantages of the separate-tale theory disappear, since within those units we find all the contradictions, disproportions, and even the "explicits" the theory was designed to account for. Leaving that possibility aside (though a five-tale division deserves study), the presence of "explicits" even within the limits of what Vinaver regards as undoubtedly separate works, such as the first and fifth tales, shows us something about what Malory thought a "whole book" should be. Since he used "explicits" to mark off the units within what are considered his separate tales, there is no reason to assume he would not use them to mark off the next larger units in his whole book of King Arthur.

A number of critics, beginning with R. H. Wilson and Derek Brewer, have pointed out that the "explicits" themselves provide proof that this is exactly what Malory was doing.[44] At the end of the Book of Tristram, for example, we have one of the "explicits" that seems to Vinaver to have an "air of finality":

> Here endyth the secunde boke of Syr Trystram de Lyones, whyche drawyn was oute of Freynshe by Sir Thomas Malleorré, knyght, as Jesu be hys helpe. Amen.

But then Malory continues.

> But here ys no rehersall of the thirde booke.
> But here folowyth the Noble Tale off the Sankegreall, etc.

The second tale has the same sort of "explicit" ("And here folowyth affter many noble Talys of Sir Launcelot de Lake"), and so does that at the end of the seventh tale, where the naming of the author, the prayer and the "Amen" (which Vinaver calls the "medieval equivalent of THE END" [45]) actually come not in an "explicit" but in an "incipit," since it is not a conclusion to what goes before but an introduction to what follows:

> And here on the othir syde folowyth The Most Pyteous Tale of the Morte Arthure saunz Gwerdon par le Shyvalere Sir Thoman Malleorré, knight.
> Jesu, ayedé le pur voutre bone mercy! Amen.

Finally, as Derek Brewer emphasized by calling his essay on this problem "the hoole book," [46] the entire volume ends with a clear statement of the relation of the individual tales to the whole:

> Here is the ende of the hoole book of kyng Arthur and of his noble knyghts of the Rounde Table that when they were holé togyders there was ever an hondred and forty. And here is the ende of the Deth of Arthur.

Vinaver asked in a recent essay whether this "hoole book of kyng Arthur" is "a title or a description of a series." [47] But that is quibbling; whether title or description it clearly establishes the existence of a unifying frame within which the individual tales, such as the Deth of Arthur, exist.

One reason Vinaver gave less weight to the connections established by the "explicits" than to the separation they implied was that the first "explicit" seemed to him so unambiguously final:

> Here endyth this tale, as the Freynshe booke seyth, fro the maryage of kynge Uther unto kyng Arthure that regned aftir hym and ded many batayles.
> And this booke endyth whereas Sir Launcelot and Sir Trystrams com to courte. Who that woll make ony more lette hym seke other bookis of kynge Arthure or of Sir Launcelot or Syr Trystrams; for this was drawyn by a knight Presoner, Sir Thomas Malleorré, that God sende hym good recover. Amen.
>
> Explicit.

Here, Vinaver writes, "The author bids farewell to his work and disclaims any intention of writing another Arthurian romance." [48] However, T. C. Rumble points out that Malory here distinguishes between his own tale and the French book that was his source: [49] "Here endyth this *tale,* as the Freynshe *booke* seyth." The next mention of the book ("This booke endyth . . .") refers not to what Malory has written but to his source, and Malory invites whoever wishes to write more about this period of Arthurian history to seek other French books on the subject. In short, Rumble explains, this "explicit" is not Malory's farewell to Arthurian romance but his announcement that he has stopped following this particular French source.

Malory himself must have interpreted the passage in about that way, if not at the moment he wrote it, certainly at the moment he rewrote or recopied the tales to place them in the order in which they now stand. That Malory did so gather his tales together is a necessary consequence of the assumption that the tales were written in an order different from that in the Winchester Manuscript. Vinaver held that Malory's second tale, the Noble Tale of King Arthur and the Emperor Lucius, was actually first in order of composition; the evidence for this is very slight, and the important question of the order in which the tales were composed remains in need of further study.[50] But if we do accept Vinaver's assumption, as have most critics, then it follows that the "explicit" of the first tale must have survived the second stage of composition during which the tales were placed in their present order. Other revisions were made at that time (if we assume separate composition, the "links" discussed in the next paragraph were added then) and there is no reason why this "explicit" could not have been cancelled or revised. That it was allowed to stand as written is a strong indication that Malory did not intend his words as a farewell to Arthurian romance, since on the next leaf another Arthurian romance was to be written.

In addition to the evidence of the "explicits," the connectedness of the tales is established by the linking passages written into the bodies of the tales themselves.[51] The first tale ends, as its "explicit" emphasizes, when "Sir Lancelot and Syr Trys-

trams com to courte." In the first paragraph of the next tale
Malory has added, with no hint from his source, "Sone aftir
com sir Launcelot de Lake unto the courte and sir Trystrams
come that tyme also." Between the second and third tales there
is a similar link; the second tale ends with Arthur's return to
England from Rome, and the third begins "Sone aftir that
Kynge Arthure was com from Rome into Ingelonde." Likewise, the Tale of Tristram ends with the feast of Pentecost
during which Galahad comes to the court, and the following
Tale of the Sankgreall opens at the same feast, "At the vigyl of
Pentecoste." The next tale also begins with a linking sentence,
"So aftir the queste of the Sankgreall was fulfylled and all the
knyghtes that were leffte on lyve were com home agayne—as
the BOOKE OF THE SANKGREALL makith mencion," and
that tale in turn is so closely linked to the following that
Vinaver himself held that the two make a unit.[52] The only tale
that is not explicitly linked to what precedes and follows is the
tale of Gareth, and arguments have been made for less obvious
links even in that tale. But this is the only point at which the
links are not obvious, and one must conclude that Malory
intended these tales to be read in a connected order. The only
other explanation is wholesale scribal tampering; Vinaver first
thought that possible, though he now seems to concede that
they are Malory's work, and the idea is now almost universally
accepted that these tales exist in a connected series.[53]

Moreover, the series has a definite form. It begins with
Arthur's birth and ends with his death, and within these limits
the tales are in their proper order in relation to the generally
accepted course of Arthurian history. This has not been clear,
since critics have accepted Vinaver's assertion that the second
tale is out of order; he claimed that in none of the French
romances "is there anything resembling" Malory's placing
the adventures of Lancelot after the Roman Campaign, for

"the Roman Campaign invariably occurs at the very end, in the *Mort Artu,* long after the Lancelot proper." [54] This is completely untrue; perhaps Vinaver was thinking of the Huth *Merlin,* in which there is no Roman Campaign (though the Roman embassy appears). In the Vulgate Cycle these events are ordered in exactly the way they appear in Malory. The Vulgate *Merlin* has the account of the Roman Campaign at the same point in Arthur's career; it deals with the same events as we find in Malory, ending, like Malory's tale, with the death of the emperor and omitting the rest of the story as it appears in Wace (the probable source of the *Merlin* account) and the alliterative *Morte Arthure.*[55] Though Malory chose to use an English source for his tale of the Roman Wars, his knowledge of the *Merlin* probably determined the position of his tale and the shape of its narrative, and in his version he retains some details—such as the anger of Arthur's knights at the Roman messengers' words—that seem to have been suggested by the Vulgate *Merlin.*[56] Following the Roman Campaign, the *Merlin* tells of the birth of Lancelot; this is the last important event in the book and it provides a link between the Vulgate *Merlin* and the prose Lancelot, the next stage in the Vulgate Cycle. These facts make it very likely (*pace* Vinaver) that Malory wrote his tale of Arthur's Roman Wars after he wrote the tale of King Arthur, and they justify (*pace* many critics) his assertion at the beginning of his third tale that Lancelot "is the fyrste knyght that the Freynsh booke makyth mencion of aftir kynge Arthure com frome Rome." As Derek Brewer wrote, the tales may be strung together like beads, "but the string is a backbone and the beads are not interchangeable." [57]

This internal evidence—the order of the tales, the linking passages, the "explicits" themselves—shows only that *Le Morte Darthur* has what Brewer calls "cohesion," which could have been achieved by a few minor alterations after the tales themselves had been composed without any thought of a larger structure.[58] Vinaver's own examination of the sources had seemed to prove this. However, new studies of Malory's use of his sources have cast doubt on that conclusion. Mary Dich-mann's essay on Malory's use of the alliterative *Morte Arthure* demonstrated that Malory systematically changed the structure and characters of this story in order to fit it into the larger scheme of Arthurian history that he was already planning.[59] About the same time as Miss Dichmann's article appeared, a number of other scholars were at work on Malory's other sources, and the results of their investigations appeared in the volume edited by R. M. Lumiansky, *Malory's Originality.*[60]

This volume provides an excellent survey of our present knowledge of Malory's sources, and the essays it contains will probably remain the standard treatments for some time to come. They establish several important points. First, they show that Malory was indeed engaged in producing a unified work composed of smaller parts, for they show that his deviations from his sources not only produced shorter tales with simpler plots, as Vinaver emphasized, but also established unifying relations between the tales. I have already mentioned Miss Dichmann's study of the second tale, which appeared in a revised form in this volume. T. L. Wright's study of the first tale demonstrates that even in this apparently early composition there is an abundance of references to later tales, some of them carried over from the French source, others added by Malory himself, such as, to take the most obvious example, the reference to Mordred's future career—"As hit rehersith aftirward and towarde the ende of the MORTE ARTHURE." [61] The other contributors to this volume—W. L. Guerin, T. C. Rumble, Charles Moorman, and Lumiansky himself—found similar indications of a larger structure unifying each of the tales they studied.[62] Their work leaves no doubt that Malory intended his tales to be read as a unit and either thoroughly revised each tale for that purpose or, more likely, planned this unifying structure before he began to compose and carried out this plan as he adapted his sources.

The studies in this volume also cast an important new light on Malory's artistic techniques. They provide fresh confirmation for what Vinaver had already demonstrated—that Malory was a conscious literary artist. The idea that Malory had little control over his materials, that he was "at the mercy of his sources" is still widely accepted, as is the assumption that Malory simply passed on with few changes the stories as he found them—Lewis' idea that "whatever he does Malory's personal contribution cannot be very great." [63] But Malory knew what he was doing; his contribution to the *Morte Darthur* was at least as great as Chaucer's to the *Troilus,* and his art should receive as much respect as Chaucer's. It has not; much as Malory has been admired for his style, no one has ever studied it. [64] Perhaps the proof offered in *Malory's Originality* that Malory was a genuine literary artist (who need not be "inventive," which I think was what Lewis meant) should lead to a new interest in this as yet unexplored aspect of the book.

The larger features of Malory's art, his structural techniques, were also illuminated by these source studies. Vinaver had emphasized the differences between Malory's work and his French sources, and he showed that Malory's preference for a simpler and more concentrated story line did result in a work less dependent on *entrelacement* than we find in the French prose romances. [65] But that does not mean that Malory completely rejected the technique. As T. L. Wright demonstrated, to consider "each division (of the story) as a self-contained entity" can be very misleading: "Malory's narrative is by no means confined to the shorter unified episodes he constructs,

and to stress this aspect of his writing is to neglect some of the
most distinctive features of his work . . . . Far from casting off
the interweaving method of the cyclic romances, Malory uses
it to develop continuity between the individual stories and to
link the larger divisions of *Le Morte Darthur*." [66] This is a
significant fact. The concept of *entrelacement* did not enter the
criticism of French romance until the first decades of this
century,[67] too late to affect Malory-studies before the discovery
of the Winchester Manuscript suspended them for so many
years. Since the publication of the manuscript, the great authority of Vinaver, who understands *entrelacement* better than
any other student of English literature and yet is convinced
that Malory disliked the technique and was trying to escape it,
has discouraged critics from approaching *Le Morte Darthur*
from that standpoint. Yet an understanding of the workings of
this technique, which revealed the structural integrity of the
French prose romances that had seemed even more wildly
formless than Malory, remains a most promising approach to
Le Morte Darthur. As C. S. Lewis has pointed out, the "polyphonic technique" of composition survived Malory by at least
two centuries, "And to the present day no one enjoys Malory's
book who does not enjoy its *ambages,* its interweaving." [68]

Indeed, something like the "polyphonic technique" has been
used to explain those contradictions in the narrative of the
Morte Darthur that Vinaver had offered as proof for the theory of separate tales. Actually, there are not very many
contradictions,[69] and they are not very bothersome. As Derek
Brewer wrote, "We may question whether inconsistencies have
ever worried any genuine lover of Malory." [70] Homer nods,
and so may Malory in a work that contains around 425
characters [71] and has 883 pages even in Vinaver's second,
smaller-type edition.

Yet some of the lapses have bothered readers, and even
after we have allowed for the magnitude of Malory's task,

perhaps his lack of time for final revision, and the fact that he could have answered with Whitman, "Very well then I contradict myself/ (I am large, I contain multitudes)," we are still left with the major problem of an apparently confused chronology. Tales I through IV proceed with only minor difficulties, but the Tale V begins before the birth of Tristram, who had already appeared in the previous tales as a mature knight. R. H. Wilson was the first to point out that at the beginning of the Tristram Malory is "looping back" in time.[72] R. M. Lumiansky developed this idea of "retrospective narrative" and demonstrated that both the Tale of Gareth and most of the Tale of Tristram are such "backward loops." [73] Charles Moorman developed the idea even further and showed in detail the temporal scheme that underlies the shifting chronology of the narrative.[74] Lumiansky also pointed out the significant fact that the two tales beginning with these sudden shifts backward in time, the tales of Gareth and Tristram, are also the two tales that begin without any specific linking passages to connect them with what precedes; no such links are possible, since both tales begin at chronological points before the preceding tales.[75]

Such a method of arranging a narrative by theme rather than natural chronology, yet with a clear temporal scheme underlying the apparently confused whole, is obviously related to the technique of *entrelacement* that Malory found in his French sources. Even within the individual tales this technique is occasionally used. Charles Moorman has shown that this sort of interweaving is used within the Tale of Tristram, where the intercalated story of Alexander le Orphelin is a retrospective narrative, looping back in time to tell what happened at an earlier stage in Tristram's history.[76] T. L. Wright has found traces of the same technique within the Tale of Arthur.[77] In both the Tale of King Arthur and the Tale of Tristram, we should note, inconsistencies remain,[78] as they do in the *Morte Darthur* as a whole, but the major chronological difficulties and inconsistencies are solved by a recognition of Malory's narrative method.

All of the characteristics of the *Morte Darthur* that have been taken as indications of the independence of the tales— the existence of the "explicits," apparent confusions in the narration, the tendency toward self-contained episodes—can be applied with equal force to the longer tales within the book itself. Indeed, Vinaver himself has done so and argued for the independence of the Balin episode from the tale within which it is contained. But this shows only that the features that have been interpreted as proof of the separate existence of the tales are actually the characteristics of Malory's method of writing long narrative. We need not hesitate to agree with the majority of critics and assume that Malory did organize his tales into a single work. Indeed, it would be surprising if he had done otherwise, for his prose sources were already parts of those huge, yet integrated structures of interlocked tales that we now know as the Vulgate Cycle and the *Roman du Graal.*[79] The architects of these works provided solid precedent for Malory's decision that he in his turn would make "of the diverse stories one story, one book."

III

This does not solve the problem of the "unity" of the *Morte Darthur;* indeed, the restoration of the whole book of King Arthur, which has been the main accomplishment of criticism in the past twenty years, also restores all the prickly problems of that apparently formless, cactus-shaped narrative. As Lumiansky has pointed out, there are at least two kinds of unity involved here—"historical unity," the problem of the author's intentions, and "critical unity," the problem of what the author achieved whatever his intentions may have been.[80] Usually we know more about achievements than intentions, though in this case it is clear that our author intended his tales to be in some sense "successive chapters of a single narrative." [81] However, this only shows that the work has what Coleridge called "mechanical unity," which Coleridge explained occurs when

> each part is separately conceived and then by a succeeding act put together—not as watches are made for wholesale—for here each part presupposes a preconception of the whole in some mind—but as pictures on a motley screen. (N.B. I must seek for some happier illustration.) [82]

The question is whether the *Morte Darthur* might have made a happier illustration or whether Malory also intended and achieved "critical unity," which to most readers means "organic unity."

Most critics of Malory have seemed to identify "organic unity" with "unity of action," and arguments both for and against the integrity of the book have concerned themselves mainly with proving or disproving the proposition that the action is unified, though it is clear that whatever Malory aimed for it was not that sort of unity. As critics have recognized since the time of Stansby, the *Morte Darthur* does have a three-part structure corresponding roughly to the rise, flowering, and fall of the Round Table, and it does therefore have a beginning, middle, and end. But, judged by Aristotelian standards (which even the most recent critics apply to this work[83]), the middle is a failure; it becomes lost in what even Moorman, a determined proponent of the work's unity, calls its lapses into "digressive meanderings." [84] Some such disappointed expectation that the middle must accord with the beginning and end probably underlay E. K. Chambers' opinion that the *Morte Darthur* would have been better if the Tale of Tristram had been left out,[85] and certainly Vinaver invokes Aristotelian assumptions about unity of action when he argues that if the *Morte Darthur* had been intended as a single work Malory could have done "not only without the Tristram but without at least five of the eight romances." [86]

This is the assumption that leads Vinaver to insist upon the separability of the tales, as if the fact of separability destroyed the unity of the whole. Many of Vinaver's opponents share this position; Lumiansky, for example, objects that the desire of Brewer and Wilson "to have things both ways—to maintain that Malory's work is both one book and eight books—is reminiscent of the argument that the individual narratives in the *Canterbury Tales* are at the same time to be taken as independent tales and as sections of a unified book." [87] But of course they are; separate editions of Chaucer's tales, like Vinaver's separate editions of the tales in the *Morte Darthur*,[88] give pleasure in a way impossible to separated chapters of a novel. This is true of all cyclic compositions, even the Homeric poems—a fact which led that early dogmatist of unity of action, J. C. Scaliger, to point out that

> Aristotle laughs at those who think that either the Iliad or the Odyssey is a complete organism with one plot, for he says that one may draw several plots from either one, because there are many plots and many episodes. So it was that the ancients used to recite certain portions taken from the whole body, as for instance the battle and catalogue of ships, the summoning of the spirits, those things which happened on Circe's island, etc.[89]

Scaliger thought this a fault, and we now smile at him, for we recognize that Homer simply had an idea of unity less restricted than Scaliger's. So did Malory. As T. C. Rumble has shown, Malory's underlying time scheme provided a chronological slot for the wars against Claudius.[90] Had Malory included such a tale in his book, its structure would not have been much changed, and certainly it would not have been harmed. One can easily imagine the *Morte Darthur* with a tale of the wars against Claudius or without, say, the Tale of Gareth, for Malory is working in a more elastic form than neo-classical ideas of unity of action will allow.

Yet we have no alternative to these ideas. As Derek Brewer has written, "Our problem in discussing the form of the *Morte Darthur* is a lack of satisfactory descriptive and critical terms for the kind of experience Malory gives us." [91] We are at an impasse; we are not agreed on what sort of unity this book has beyond the merely "historical" and "mechanical" sorts because our ideas of narrative unity do not comprehend this form. We cannot even be positive that "unity" is a proper critical concept to apply to this work. As C. S. Lewis wrote, if we were to ask Malory whether his work had unity, he would not know what we were talking about. "The difficulty . . . would be not merely linguistic. We should by the very form of our questions be presupposing concepts with which his mind was not furnished." [92] We should, as Saintsbury said, be putting the wrong questions to the jury.

Of course, many literary works lack a strict unity of action, and since the sixteenth century, when Aristotelian categories first entered our tradition, critics have sought other criteria. The early eighteenth-century critic, de La Motte, proposed a "unity of interest," which "can give pleasure of itself" in place of "the three unities strictly observed." [93] Certainly Malory has "unity of interest"; that is the quality C. S. Lewis emphasized when he wrote, "Of course his matter was one—the same king, the same court. Of course his matter was many—they had many adventures." [94] But unity of interest is perhaps too vague a criterion to account for the effect of a work, and most critics in search of a substitute for the Aristotelian unities would probably follow Coleridge:

> Instead of unity of action I greatly prefer the more appropriate tho' scholastic and uncouth words—homogeneity, proportionateness, and totality of interest.[95]

That Malory's work has a totality of interest and some degree of homogeneity has been amply demonstrated. P. E. Tucker's and R. T. Davies' essays on chivalry and courtesy in the *Morte Darthur,* the studies of Charles Moorman and S. J. Miko on the tragic aspects of the book, and Vinaver's own introduction to the *Works* have shown the importance of some of the larger themes that move through the tales, as have a number of studies, such as F. Whitehead's, on the characters in the book.[96] Yet it is possible to grant the book "totality of interest" and even "homogeneity"—as Vinaver does [97]— without recognizing its unity, for we feel that a work must have some underlying structural principle that lends it "proportionateness."

On this Malory might well have agreed, for though he may never have heard about "unity" we can be sure he knew about "proportionateness," since the one piece of literary criticism that we know Malory read—a passage in the *Suite de Merlin,* which Malory used as the source of his first tale—is a discussion of the problems an author encounters in writing a cyclic work like the *Roman du Graal* or the *Morte Darthur* and a clear statement of this author's intention to achieve "proportionateness." The author states that he has divided his work into three parts (a *Merlin,* a Quest of the Grail, and a *Mort Artu*) and that he has taken care to maintain a proportion between the parts—" each part as large as the other—the first as large as the second, and the second as large as the third." In a later passage he remarks that he has removed the story of Lancelot from his book, "not because it does not belong to it and deal with its subject matter, but because it is necessary that the three parts of my book be equal in length. . . . if I added this long story the middle portion of my book would be three times as big as the other two." [98] Malory thus knew of the aesthetic value of "proportion," even though he did not try to achieve it in the manner of the *Roman du Graal.* His structural model seems rather to have been the Vulgate Cycle. But this does not mean that he rejected the principle of "proportion-ateness"; at least in the individual tales, he achieved that in the less obvious, though to him perhaps more familiar, manner of the English metrical romances.

IV

It is curious that Malory has never been studied as an English romancer. The historical study of the Morte Darthur has been limited to examining its relations to its earlier French sources, while the critical study of the work has generally been restricted to its effect on a modern reader. We see Malory in relation to the thirteenth century on the one hand, and to the twentieth century on the other, but we almost never try to see him in his own time, in England in the middle of the fifteenth century, and in relation to his chosen genre, romance.

When critics do consider Malory in the light of romance in his own time, they seem always to think he was trying to escape it, either moving backwards, as nineteenth-century crit-ics assumed, or far forward, as modern critics believe. Vinaver regards Malory as a leader in a revolt against romance, a general European movement that developed partly under the influence of Boccaccio's *Decameron* and "partly as a sponta-neous reaction against the technique of interlaced composition." [99] Malory, like the writers of the novella, is thus moving to "within sight of our modern idea of unity," and "in all his works he instinctively conformed to the principle of 'singleness' that underlies the rhythmical structure of any mod-ern work of fiction." [100] Whereas the older critics saw Malory as "out of the general line of progress," [101] Vinaver sees him as a pioneer in the progression toward the novel by way of the novella. Charles Moorman is Vinaver's most recent and out-spoken critic, but he accepts without question the assumption that Malory was aiming at our "modern idea of unity" and differs from Vinaver only in thinking that Malory has moved farther toward his supposed goal. He too sees Malory as rejecting the romances from which he "extracted his purer ore" and aiming instead at "a unified piece, one which should be neither digressive nor episodic but clearly manifesting a beginning, middle, and end"; we should therefore consider Malory's structural problems, Moorman believes, in relation to *"Tom Jones,* or *Emma,* or *Vanity Fair,* or, in a different form, the *Iliad."* [102]

The effect of both Moorman's and Vinaver's views is to move Malory out of his own time. Both quote the criticism of romances expressed by the Canon of Toledo in *Don Quixote,*[103] as if Cervantes and Malory were contemporaries engaged in a common revolt against romance. But when Malory was writing, the birth of Cervantes was still a hundred years in the future, and the romances the Canon objects to had not yet been written. Even Amadis of Gaul, which the Canon regards as the model of all the other romances of Knight-errantry, did not appear until 1508, a half-century after the *Morte Darthur* was written.

The general reaction against interlaced composition of which Vinaver writes had not yet taken place. *Orlando Furioso* had not yet been composed, and Tasso had not even been born. Even in France the old forms retained their popularity; the prose Tristan, so much abused by modern critics, went through nine editions between 1489 and 1586 (three more than Malory). And in England, where Boccaccio's *Decameron* would not appear in English until 1620,[104] the elaborate and digressive romances of Lord Berners were still far in the future, and Sidney's *Arcadia* would not appear for another one hundred and fifty years. As Arthur Ferguson has shown in his *Indian Summer of English Chivalry,* the old chivalric ideals were still strong,[105] and Rosamund Tuve's last book, *Allegorical Imagery,* demonstrated that romance was by no means dead in Malory's time and was not to die until well into the Elizabethan period.[106] Short fiction characterized by unity of action was developing, as it had been in exempla, fabliaux, and Breton lays since long before Boccaccio, but the recent studies by Margaret Schlauch demonstrate how slowly modern fiction developed and how far Malory was from that movement.[107]

There is therefore little reason to assume that Malory rejected the aesthetic of romance. Vinaver speaks of him as removed from his sources by a great gap in time, as a man who "at a distance of more than two centuries could still approach romance from within." [108] But Malory was not two centuries away from the age of romance, which was still flourishing all around him. The French works that he translated were still being recopied by both English and continental scribes;[109] English verse romances were still being composed; [110] English prose romance was just now beginning not only with Malory but with other skilled writers of this time, such as the author of the English prose *Merlin,* and the output of Caxton's press would bear witness to the coming popularity of this genre among his highly cultivated patrons.[111] Malory is in a sense an innovator, not because he rejected romance but because he helped develop the English prose romance, a genre that was to have considerable importance in the next hundred and fifty years.

There is a good deal of evidence that Malory was widely and deeply read in the romance tradition that flourished around him. Vinaver believed that Malory knew little of romance when he began to write, that when he wrote his first work he had no idea of what happened in the later stages of Authurian history.[112] That is like assuming that a writer would begin a sonnet cycle after having read only one poem. Malory not only knew the works he translated, he also knew other versions of the same events he narrates, and, as R. H. Wilson has shown, even in his earliest work he was able to supply the correct names to characters left anonymous in his sources.[113] The names show he was conversant with English as well as French romance, and in his recent *The Ill-Framed Knight* William Matthews offers extensive proof of how greatly Malory's style was affected by English romance.[114] Matthews shows that our author had read deeply in Northern English romance and had such a command of the difficult alliterative style that he was able to compose regular alliterative lines—an unlikely attainment, Matthews argues, for a Warwickshireman and a near impossibility for one who had not often read and enjoyed such romances.[115] Moreover, in his one seemingly independent composition, the Book of Gareth, Malory turned to a theme especially popular in English romance and used a large number of characters and situations from the English tradition. That he preferred the alliterative *Morte Arthure* to the account of the Roman Wars in the French *Merlin,* and turned again to an English source in the composition of his last book, seems to indicate that Malory never lost his admiration for the romances of the English tradition.

That tradition accounts for many of the characteristics of Malory's work that have been taken as evidence of its "modernity"—Malory's occasional "realism," his apparent lack of interest in the psychological subtleties of love, his relative disinterest in the supernatural, his preference for a simple plot line with less interweaving than in the French romances.[116] When we compare Malory's tales to their French sources, we can almost always note changes introduced to achieve these more "modern" effects. But the same is true of almost all English romances. The author of the metrical *Arthur and Merlin,* writing in the thirteenth century, and the author of *Ywain and Gawain,* writing in the fourteenth, handle their sources in about the same way Malory does.[117] I suspect that when Malory is studied from this point of view, it will become clear that his method of handling his sources is due in large part not to a desire to "modernize" them but to his attempt to "anglicize" them, to adapt them to the forms and conventions that he admired in English romance.

A full study of that aspect of Malory's art requires many more pages than I have at hand. My point is simply that Malory is essentially an English romancer and that his work can best be understood and appreciated in the light of that tradition. This is true especially of what has seemed the most difficult aspect of his work, its form. From the standpoint of other genres both *Le Morte Darthur* as a whole and its individual tales seem lacking in proportion and unity. This is because most narrative forms that we know are characterized by unity of action, with a cause and effect relation of the parts, whereas romance, as Vinaver has so convincingly argued in his discussion of French works, depends on a unity of theme. Certainly in a romance the action is a principal focus of interest, especially in Malory's English romances, which tend to be less concerned with psychological issues than their French sources. We rightly prize Malory's narrative skill. So, too, do we prize his occasional realism, his sometimes telling descriptions, and his often impressive psychological insights. But these are the "accidentals" of Malory's art. The theme is his essential concern.

Of course, critics have recognized and discussed some of Malory's themes, but they have tended to approach the theme from the standpoint of modern realistic fiction in which the sequence of actions is central. In such works the plot produces the theme and defines the shape of the work; in Malory's romances, the theme dominates the sequence of action and provides the narrative with its order and "proportionateness."

Perhaps a hasty discussion of one tale will make my meaning clear. The Tale of Gareth is a good test case. It probably

was written around the middle of the period during which the
Morte Darthur was composed, and it is therefore a mature
work. Though it is based on the tradition of the "Fair Unknown" romances and shares many features with them, it is
apparently Malory's own composition rather than a translation
or adaptation of some existing work,[118] and it thus reflects
Malory's own idea of what a narrative should be. Moreover, it
is one of the simplest tales in the *Morte Darthur* and therefore
seems to many, as it does to Vinaver, one of Malory's most
"modern" works, "a story which can serve as a genuine example of the technique of the modern tale applied to medieval
romance." [119] Yet, even in outline form, it is clear that from the
standpoint of modern fiction this tale is a failure, for its plot is
badly disunified:

A handsome young man who refuses to tell his name comes
to Arthur's court, where he serves for a year as a kitchen
knave, scorned by all save for Lancelot and Gawain. Then a
maiden appears and asks for a knight to free her lady from
the Red Knight of the Red Lands. The young man takes up
the quest. He is pursued by Kay, whom he fights and defeats, and then by Lancelot, whom he battles to a draw. He
reveals to Lancelot that he is Gareth, Gawain's younger
brother. Lancelot then knights him, and he departs with the
maiden, who ceaselessly mocks him for his employment in
the kitchen. After overcoming a series of opponents, Gareth
defeats the Red Knight, rescues the lady, and wins her love.

The two attempt to consummate their love but are prevented by a strange knight who attacks and wounds Gareth.
Meanwhile, the Queen of Orkney, Gareth's mother, arrives
at Camelot and reveals his true identity. Then Gareth has
his lady proclaim a tourney, with her hand as the prize.
Gareth enters this tournament in disguise and wins the hand

of his lady against all the Round Table. Then, when the heralds proclaim his identity, he rides away. He encounters and overcomes more opponents and then by chance he meets and battles Gawain until they discover one another's identity, whereupon they embrace and return to Camelot, where Gareth marries his lady.

So far as the action is concerned, the tale starts out well enough, and it seems tightly unified up to the point where Gareth defeats the Red Knight and wins the lady. But then, when it seems to us that the tale should end, Malory wanders off into "Arthur-land" at large with a series of apparently anti-climactic battles and disguises culminating in a chance meeting with Gawain that somehow serves to bring the story to an end. When Tennyson adapted this tale for the *Idylls of the King*, he was interested mainly in turning Malory's apparently simple tale into an allegory, but even for that purpose he felt that he needed a well-made plot. He achieved that simply by lopping off the last half of Malory's tale and ending his poem at the point where the hero defeats the Red Knight and wins the lady. This yields a self-contained action with a beginning (for clarity Tennyson adds an exposition in Orkney explaining why Gareth came to Camelot rather than leaving that until the Queen of Orkney's entrance, as Malory does), a middle consisting of the preliminary obstacles Gareth overcomes on his way to the lady's castle, and a climactic end in which Gareth defeats the besieger and wins the lady. Each part contributes to the main action, and we could not easily add or remove an episode without obscuring the relations of the events. The ease with which Tennyson accomplishes this might lead one to agree that Malory was indeed concentrating on single episodes that "drop away from the rest of the book as independent organisms." [120]

But Malory does not let the episode drop away; the marriage is delayed until the last lines of the tale, so that what seemed the plot of a single episode is stretched out to provide an overall framework for the action. Gareth's conquest of and marriage to his lady Lyones are thus used to provide a beginning and end for the action. But the middle of this tale—like that of the *Morte Darthur* as a whole—is characteristically formless, and the episodes have little relation to that overall plot and no tight cause-and-effect relation to one another. So far as the action is concerned, in this tale as in the whole book, we could omit some episodes, we could shift around others, and we could add another opponent or two if we wished. We could do all this without affecting the course of the overall plot, for this tale has that elasticity of form that is characteristic of romance narrative and that allows for the process of addition that is so often employed in the composition of romances, as in the *Morte Darthur,* with its added tales, such as the Tale of Gareth, that seem merely extraneous from the standpoint of the overall plot.

We can practically see Malory adding to the story of Gareth, for again and again the action comes to a logical conclusion and then for no apparent reason starts out afresh—after the conquest of the Red Knight of the Red Lands, for example, or after Gareth wins his lady's hand for the second time in the tournament, or even after his year of abasement as a kitchen knave culminates in his battles with Kay and Lancelot and his achievement of knighthood. At each point the demands of the action would have been satisfied if the tale had ended. But at each point the theme would have been left incomplete, and in this sort of work theme, not action, controls the structure. Therefore at each of these points a new episode is introduced, an episode selected not as the effect of any cause in the preceding action but as a means of expressing the major theme. In this tale that theme is the education and vindication of the "Fair Unknown." [121]

Even if we did not know that Malory was drawing on this traditional theme when he wrote this tale, we could recognize its presence by noting that at every major stage of the tale—at all those points where it seemed as if the story should end—Gareth's identity is revealed to someone. Malory's tale, like all the "Fair Unknown" romances, turns on the problem of identity and involves the use of false names, disguises, and the concealment and discovery of one's proper name. All this is common enough in other romance themes that Malory used, for his knights are constantly disguising themselves or refusing to reveal their names. But in the tradition of the "Fair Unknown" the matter of one's name is especially important; the hero of such a romance is unknown because he must earn his name, show that he is worthy of it and the state it implies before he reveals it to himself or to others.

The Tale of Gareth is built about the developing revelation and vindication of Gareth's identity, and the stages of that process mark the important stages of the narrative. When Gareth first arrives at the court he conceals his identity from everyone, and he is scorned by all save Lancelot, the knight whom he most admires, and Gawain, his eldest brother. There is no "prologue" such as Tennyson adds to explain why Gareth conceals his name in this fashion; but none is needed, for the theme of the "Fair Unknown" is a common one. Malory himself used it again in the story of Alexander le Orphelin, and his readers simply accepted the conventional situation of the mysterious young stranger who arrives at the court. When Gareth has served his year of abasement and rides off with the maiden, first Kay and then Lancelot ride after him. He defeats Kay and then fights Lancelot to a draw. He thus proves his worth to Lancelot and he can therefore reveal to him his name and receive knighthood from Lancelot's hands. When that happens, the first stage of the tale is completed.

In the next stage Gareth passes the test posed by the damsel's abuse of him—an extension of his humiliation as a kitchen knave. Simultaneously he is tested by the foes he must overcome on his way to the lady's castle. As usual in the "Fair Unknown" romances, the young man is undergoing an education at the same time he is proving his fighting abilities, for though he kills his first opponents he grants mercy to the last three at the request of the maiden who is his guide. He is learning noble manners, especially chivalric self-control, which he shows both in suffering the lady's abuse and in granting his opponents mercy.[122] He shows self-restraint too in the sexual temptation that occurs after the last of these preliminary duels. When Gareth spares the life of Sir Persaunte, he sends his daughter to Gareth's bed, and Gareth, in a line reminiscent of *Sir Gawain and the Green Knight,* gently refuses her offer: "I were a shameful knight and I wolde do your fader any disworship." [123] When Sir Persaunte hears this, he concludes that truly Gareth "is com of ful noble blod." Having proven this, Gareth now learns the name of the damsel who guided him, Lyonet, and of her besieged sister, Lyones. He in turn reveals his name to Lyonet and Sir Persaunte—those to whom he has proven himself at this stage of the tale.

Then he fights the Red Knight of the Red Lands and, reluctantly, spares his life, thus putting into practice the lessons he has learned on his way to this battle. He thereby proves his worthiness of the lady and she grants him her love. When she learns his name, as she now does, the two agree to marry. This is the point where Tennyson ends his tale, but in Malory a new test arises. Lyones and Gareth, unable to wait for marriage, plan a nocturnal assignation. They are prevented from satisfying their desires only by Lyonet—again in her role as guide and teacher. At the critical moment she sends a huge axe-wielding knight to attack Gareth. He beheads the intruder but Lyonet, using magic ointments, replaces the head, and the strange knight rises and departs. The same thing happens a second time, though this time Gareth is wounded by enchantment and can be cured only by Lyonet.

Before that problem is resolved (part of it never is—the strange knight simply disappears from the story) the scene shifts to Camelot. This is the first use in this tale of interlaced narrative—a new episode beginning while the other is left incomplete. The reason for its use at this point is obvious, since what happens next could well signal the end of the romance. All the knights whom Gareth has conquered come to Camelot to surrender to Arthur, and the Queen of Orkney reveals Gareth's identity to all. This is the logical end of the first half of the action, comparable to the *premerain vers* in two-part romances such as Chretien's *Erec et Enide*,[124] but the interrupted episode at Lyones' castle, with its slight suspense about the outcome of Gareth's wound, provides the occasion for the continuation of the tale. The theme demands this, since though he has won his lady, he must now prove his worthiness of her, just as, though he won his knighthood by fighting Kay and Lancelot at the beginning of the tale, he had to prove himself worthy of that state by the actions that culminate in the scene at Camelot. Moreover, he must now remove the stain of the attempted sin with Lyones, just as he had to remove the humiliation of his service as a kitchen knave. Finally, the rules by which he is operating require that he prove himself in the physical presence of those to whom his identity is revealed.

He therefore has Lyones arrange a tournament, with her hand as the prize. Gareth enters that tourney in disguise, and he triumphs over all. When he has thus defeated Arthur's best knights and proven he deserves Lyones, the heralds proclaim his identity to the assembled court.

But then he leaves the tournament. There is one other to whom his prowess must be proven. This is his brother Gawain. The last battle in a "Fair Unknown" romance is almost always a duel between the hero and a close relative, since the trace of the "Male Cinderella" motif in the "Fair Unknown" romances requires that the hero win not only knighthood and a lady but also the respect of his own family. And so Malory brings Gareth and Gawain together in battle, though he does not bother to motivate that battle by any chain of actions; the demands of the theme sufficiently account for the meeting. First Gareth encounters and slays an evil knight who has imprisoned thirty ladies. Then he meets and conquers the Duke de la Rouse, whose life he spares on the condition that he surrender himself to Arthur. Perhaps the feast that is an obligatory conclusion to this sort of tale accounts for these battles, since a celebration requires a parade of trophies such as the Duke and the thirty ladies provide. However, the order of battles, first without mercy and then with a life spared, is obviously intended to parallel the series of duels that precede the encounter with the Red Knight. Moreover, the battles are also required by the convention that every important duel must be preceded by one or more preliminary engagements. They show us the importance of the final battle, when Gareth meets and fights Gawain until the maiden Lyonet—in her final appearance as teacher—reveals their identities to one another. When Gareth has attained and proven himself worthy of knighthood, a lady, and membership in his own family, the theme of identity is complete, and the tale ends with his marriage to Lyones and his reception into the Round Table.

    Once we recognize that Malory is not simply writing a story about a "Fair Unknown," as Tennyson was, but is using that theme to provide the structure of his romance, its form becomes clear and what seemed a rather loose and digressive narrative is revealed as a well-proportioned, even elegantly structured work of art, constructed with some of the same regard for symmetry that we find in the better romances. The opening encounter with Lancelot is balanced with the final encounter with Gawain, and the tale falls into two nicely balanced halves, each with its sexual temptation, with its scene at Camelot, with its revelations of Gareth's identity—to Lancelot, to the general world of knighthood represented by Persaunte and Lyonet, and then, at the center of the tale, to Lyones, followed by a revelation of his name to the special world of knighthood represented by Arthur and his court, and then to Gawain. It is a carefully wrought pyramidal structure, with the center marked by the Queen of Orkney's arrival at Camelot and the two halves linked by the suspended episode with Lyonet that brackets that scene. Each of the halves ends with a union of Gareth and Lyones, first imperfect and then perfected as the tale returns to the point at which it began in Arthur's court.

This is not to say that the theme accounts for everything. I see no reason why Gareth fights four knights with color-names on his way to Lyones' castle instead of the three that we find in Tennyson, and obviously we could add or subtract an opponent without affecting the structure of the work. But there is a reason why there should be opponents, whether four, or three, or the two whom Gareth fights on his way to meet Gawain. Likewise, though from the standpoint of action we could shift around the episodes, from the standpoint of theme we could not; it is necessary that Gareth fight Lancelot at the beginning of the tale and his close relative, Gawain, at the end. Though the theme does not and probably should not account for all the parts in a work whose virtues include copiousness and variety as well as thematic integrity, it does account for the shape of the narrative and the "proportionateness" that unifies it.

V

I do not delude myself that this labored discussion of theme and symmetries will convince everyone that the Tale of Gareth (and, by implication, the *Morte Darthur*) is a great work, for there is nothing to prevent anyone from thinking that this sort of thematic unity is all very well but that unity of action is nevertheless a higher, better sort of unity. Likewise, though the tale and, I believe, the *Morte Darthur* as a whole have "proportionateness," neither the tale nor the book will pass our ordinary test for "organic unity"--the impossibility of adding or subtracting parts from the whole. That sort of unity, with each part growing naturally from another, the parts shaped and developed from within and "the fullness of its development one and the same with its outward form," [125] is doubtless a great source of pleasure. But a work like the *Pickwick Papers* is no less pleasant because it satisfies our taste for variety more easily than our demand for unity.[126]

In Malory's time variety was a virtue closer to the center of critical doctrine than it is today, and in the century after Malory lived, during the great Italian critical dispute in the course of which our ideas about unity were introduced into our critical tradition, variety was sometimes preferred to unity. This was, of course, an old idea. Medieval thinkers such as Hugo of St. Victor had argued that multiplicity was the basis of earthly beauty, since "perfect and infinite beauty can manifest itself only in an infinite number of forms." [127] It follows, as Edgar de Bruyne wrote, "that our vision of the beautiful, at least in this life, can only be a succession of beautiful perceptions—multiplicity, diversity, change, and succession combining themselves." [128] This sounds very like Coleridge's "mechanical unity"—"pictures on a motley screen."

Applied to literature, this theory of beauty in diversity yields Geraldi Cinthio's doctrine of romance. This sixteenth-century critic held that the writer of romance must tell the deeds of many men rather than the unified action of one man:

> For this diversity of action carries with it a variety which
> is delightful and furnishes ample opportunity for the in-
> troduction of episodes and pleasing digressions and

events which could never happen in that manner of poetry (i.e., fiction) which describes a single action.[129]

Cinthio, writing around a century after Malory and upholding
the old tradition against the newly revived classical assumptions, regards as virtues ("pleasing digressions") what critics
in our own time regard as faults ("lapses into digressive meanderings"). And he regards as indispensible the sort of *entrelacement* that Vinaver believed Malory rejected. "It has been
necessary for them," Cinthio says of the romancers, "after
speaking of one character to pass to another, breaking off the
narration of the first and entering into the deeds of the other."
This procedure is admirable because,

> There can be introduced into the composition loves, un-
> expected events, wrongs, vices, offenses, defenses, deceits,
> deeds of courtesy, justice, liberality, virtue, treach-
> ery, faith, loyalty, etc., and such other episodes, and there
> can be introduced such variety and delight that the poem
> will become most interesting.

There is a remarkable though general resemblance between
Cinthio's catalogue of delights and Caxton's description of the
Morte Darthur:

> For herein may be seen noble chivalrye, corteysye, hu-
> manyte, frendlynesse, hardynesse, love, frendship, cowar-
> dyse, murdre, hate, virtue, and synne.

Cinthio's list was intended to describe Ariosto's *Orlando Furioso;* Caxton's, the much earlier *Morte Darthur.* The two lists
coincide because they describe essentially similar works. And
the same kinds of objections have been made to the form of
both; Tennyson's opinion of Malory—"It has many fine things
in it but all strung together without art"—was anticipated by

centuries in the opinion of *Orlando Furioso* attributed to Galileo—"You may meet with a very good thing here and there in
it, but the whole is of but little value." [130]

To apply Galileo's Aristotelian or Tennyson's modern ideas
of unity to such works is to commit Saintsbury's first error of
criticism. Admirers of romance have recognized this from the
time of Bernardo Tasso in sixteenth-century Italy, to Jean
Chapelain in seventeenth-century France, to Richard Hurd in
eighteenth-century England, who advised, "Judge the Fairy
Queen by the classic models, and you are shocked by its
disorder; consider it with an eye to its Gothic originals and you
find it regular." [131]

It seems to me therefore that the next step in the criticism of
Le Morte Darthur will be to "consider it with an eye to its
Gothic originals." Here Vinaver will again supply an invaluable aid to criticism, for despite his opinion about the relation
of *Le Morte Darthur* to earlier romance, his perceptive essays
on the aesthetic of romance will supply the necessary starting
point for a new comparison.[132] When we better understand that
aesthetic and the modifications it underwent in the English
tradition, I believe that thematic analyses of the sort I have
applied to the Tale of Gareth will reveal in each of the tales a
quality of "proportionateness," a thematic coherence of the
sort that seems to underly the *Morte Darthur* as a whole.
Studies such as Charles Moorman's *The Book of King Arthur,*
though approaching the work from a much different point of
view, have already provided a good beginning for the definition of the thematic coherence of the whole book. Such an
approach will not solve all the problems in the criticism of the
Morte Darthur, but it will at least bring us closer to an understanding of Malory's form by providing us with answers to
Saintsbury's essential first questions—"What was Malory
trying to do?" and "Did he do it well?"

This will take time, for it involves a considerable readjust-
ment in our critical approach to the book. But the problem of

Malory's form has bothered critics since at least the time of Richard Stansby, and Saintsbury's questions have now gone unanswered for seventy years. A couple of years more will not matter.

In the meantime, I shall venture my own answers: Malory was trying to write a fifteenth-century English romance. And he did it very well.

Notes

[1] William Morris, *Works* (New York, 1966), XXII, ix.

[2] *Alfred, Lord Tennyson, A Memoir, by His Son* (New York and London, 1897), I, 193.

[3] Sir Walter Scott (ed.), *Sir Tristrem* (Edinburgh, 1804), p. lxxx.

[4] *A Connecticut Yankee in King Arthur's Court* (New York, 1901), ch. III. Direct quotations from Malory almost always put Twain's characters to sleep. During the recitation of "Sandy's Tale" (chs. XV, XIX), which Twain assures us in a footnote "is borrowed, language and all, from the *Morte d'Arthur*," the narrator, Hank, dozes off several times. R. H. Wilson, "Malory in *The Connecticut Yankee*," *Texas Studies in English*, XXVII (1948), 185–206, discusses Twain's use of Malory's work and his attitude toward it.

[5] Sir Edward Strachey (ed.), *Le Morte Darthur* (London and New York, 1891), pp. xiii–xiv.

[6] Andrew Lang, "Le Morte Darthur," in H. O. Sommer, *Le Morte Darthur*, II (London, 1891), p. xix. Lang adds that Malory's work is "of all jumbles the most pathetic and poetic."

[7] George Saintsbury, *A Short History of English Literature* (London and New York, 1898), p. 197.

[8] Tennyson, "To the Queen," a dedicatory poem subscribed to the *Idylls of the King*.

[9] Robert Southey, "Preface," *The Birth, Life, and Acts of King Arthur, etc.*, ed. Upcott (London, 1817), pp. xxxi–xxxii.

[10] Saintsbury, *A Short History*, p. 196.

[11] *The English Novel* (London, 1913), p. 25.

[12] H. S. Bennett, *Chaucer and the Fifteenth Century* (Oxford, rpt. with corrections 1961), p. 201.

[13] (Oxford, 1947) 3 Vols. I quote, however, from the one-volume

edition (Oxford, 1954). The Second Edition of the *Works* (Oxford, 1967) appeared too late to use.

[14] The best account is that of the modest discoverer, "The Finding of the Manuscript," in *Essays on Malory,* ed. J. A. W. Bennett (Oxford, 1963), pp. 1–6.

[15] C. S. Lewis, rev. of Vinaver's *Works* in *The Times Literary Supplement* (June 7, 1947), rept. in *Medieval and Renaissance Studies,* ed. W. Hoeper (Cambridge, 1966), p. 103.

[16] Vinaver, *Works,* p. xxxii.

[17] *Ibid.,* p. xxxiii.

[18] Whereas in 1947 Vinaver believed that the "arrangement in Winchester and in Caxton may be due to some intervening compiler" (*Works,* xxxv–xxxvi) he now holds that we "read Malory more or less as he thought one ought to read him and enjoy the arrangement and somewhat capricious sequence of romances as he intended it to be enjoyed" (*Essays on Malory,* p. 39). Vinaver's position has been further modified in the 'Introduction' to the Second Edition of the *Works,* which appeared after this essay was at the press.

[19] In his review Lewis objected to Vinaver's omission of these rubrics, which now, he asserted, have the charm of the marginal glosses in *The Ancient Mariner* (*Med. and Ren. Studies,* p. 107).

[20] *A Connecticut Yankee,* ch. XIX. Twain accentuates this and parodies what he thought was Malory's paragraphing when he quotes directly from the *Morte Darthur* (see note 4 above) and combines two of Caxton's chapters (I,xxv and xxvi) into one long paragraph.

[21] *Med. and Ren. Studies,* p. 110.

[22] "Caxton and Malory," *Essays on Malory,* p. 27.

[23] Lewis, "The English Prose *Morte,*" *Essays on Malory,* pp. 114–45.

[24] For a survey of the early editions, see Sommer, *Le Morte Darthur,* III (London, 1890), pp. 15ff.

[25] In the Harvard Library copy of this edition the woodcut frontispiece has been painted by a contemporary illuminator who may have added the word "Sauncete" that appears on the horse's trappings; the mounted knight bears a white shield with a red cross and is stabbing a green dragon. No other title page of this edition exists. However, Thomas East's edition bears on its title page the same figure without the word "Sauncete."

[26] Richard Stansby, "Preface," *The Most Famous and Ancient History of Prince Arthur, etc.,* ed. Thomas Wright (London, 1866), p. xxv.

[27] *Loc. cit.*

[28] Sommer, I, 44.

[29] Miss Shaw compares Caxton directly to the manuscript rather than to Vinaver's edition and concludes that Caxton "has made a coherent whole from his somewhat unsophisticated original, providing his reader with book and chapter divisions . . . rubrics . . . and reasonably consistent punctuation" (*op. cit.,* p. 143). Stansby's three-part division is more coherent than Caxton's twenty-one chapters, his punctuation better, and his language easier. On the errors in Caxton's edition, see Sommer, II, 21–25.

[30] See the remarks of Wright in his edition of Stansby: "No particular philological value is attached to the language of Caxton's edition, which would be repulsive to the modern reader, while all its value is retained in the reprint" [i.e., Stansby], p. xv.

[31] For a bibliography of nineteenth-century editions, see Vinaver, *Malory* (London, 1929), pp. 192–196.

[32] Wright, *ed. cit.* p. xiv.

[33] Strachey, *ed. cit.,* p. xxxii.

[34] *Alfred Lord Tennyson, A Memoir,* p. 194.

[35] Sommer, II, 14, quotes this from the preface to Strachey's first edition.

[36] Sommer, I, vii, note 1; Strachey objected to this; see the preface to his 1891 edition, p. xxxv.

[37] *Texas Studies in English,* XXVII (1948), 187, note 4.

[38] Though critics have often commented on this, *Morte* is common enough and the use of *le* for *la* is not all that unusual; see Karl Bartsch, *Chrètomathie de l'ancien français,* 12th ed. by Leo Weise (New York, 1951), pp. 319–20, with examples.

[39] *Malory* (Oxford, 1929), p. 10.

[40] W. J. B. Crotch (ed.), *The Prologues and Epilogues of William Caxton,* EETS, 176 (Oxford, 1928), p. 96.

[41] H. S. Bennett, *English Books and Readers,* 1475–1557 (Cambridge, 1952), pp. 211–14. The first English title page was printed in 1490, and the practice was established around 1530.

[42] R. H. Wilson, "How Many Books Did Malory Write?" *Texas Studies in English,* XXX (1951), 1–23.

[43] *Works,* p. xxxi.

[44] See Wilson, note 42 above; Brewer, "Form in the *Morte Darthur,*" *Medium Aevum,* XXI (1952), 14–24.

[45] *Essays on Malory,* p. 36.

[46] *Ibid.,* pp. 41–63.

[47] *Ibid.,* p. 36.

[48] *Works,* p. xxx.

[49] Thomas C. Rumble, "The First *Explicit* in Malory's *Morte Darthur," MLN,* LXXI (1956), 564–66.

[50] *Works,* pp. xxxvi–xxxvii; J. A. W. Bennett in a generally sympathetic review in *RES,* XXV, 161–67, raises some objections and C. S. Lewis in his review (see note 15 above) points out that part of Vinaver's argument is based on a mistranslation ("fir-tree" for "fyr," meaning "fire"). Vinaver rejects Bennett's criticism in *Arthurian Literature in the Middle Ages,* ed. R. S. Loomis (New York, 1959), p. 554.

[51] These are discussed by Wilson (note 42 above) and Brewer (notes 44 and 46) and Lumiansky, "The Question of Unity in Malory's *Morte Darthur," Tulane Studies in English,* V (1955), 29–39.

[52] *Works,* p. xxxix, note 1.

[53] See note 18 above.

[54] *Works,* p. 1398.

[55] *The Vulgate Romances,* ed. H. O. Sommer, II (Washington, 1908), 424–41.

[56] Cf. the passages cited by Mary Dichmann in *Malory's Originality,* ed. R. M. Lumiansky (Baltimore, 1964), p. 70, and compare *The Vulgate Romances,* II, 424.

[57] Brewer, *Medium Aevum,* XXI, 17.

[58] R. H. Wilson (note 42 above) has suggested that about half-way through the composition of a series of romances Malory decided to make a unified book.

[59] "Characterization in Malory's Tale of Arthur and Lucius," *PMLA,* LXV (1950), 877–95.

[60] (Baltimore, 1964). A number of unpublished theses have dealt with this problem, and they are listed, along with other relevant works, in the notes to the articles in this volume.

[61] Vinaver held that this "must be attributed not to *M* himself but to one of his early copyists"; *Works,* 1298, note on 56.4–5.

[62] That is the opinion, according to Lumiansky's "Introduction" to *Malory's Originality,* p. 4, at which all the contributors to that volume arrived. However, there is some truth in Vinaver's assertion (*Essays on Malory,* p. 37): "Remove from Malory's text all the occasional references to what is going to happen in a later work or to what has happened already in an earlier one, and nothing of importance will have been lost."

[63] Lewis, *Med. and Ren. Studies,* p. 110; quoted by Brewer, *Essays on Malory,* p. 42.

[64] There have been linguistic studies, such as Jan Šimko, *Word Order in the Winchester Manuscript and in William Caxton's Edition of Thomas Malory's Morte Darthur (1485)—A Comparison* (Halle, 1957); Vinaver discusses in some detail Malory's style in the "Introduction" to his *Works.* William Matthews, *The Ill-Framed Knight* (Berkeley and Los Angeles, 1966), makes a number of observations on Malory's style. Aside from these and scattered references in other works, there has been almost no discussion of this aspect of Malory's work.

[65] Vinaver's discussion of *entrelacement* in the *Works,* pp. xlviii–lii, is an excellent introduction to the subject.

[66] *Malory's Originality,* p. 17.

[67] Ferdinand Lot, *Études sur le Lancelot en prose* (Paris, 1918), pp. 17–26, is the *locus classicus.*

[68] *Essays on Malory,* pp. 13–14.

[69] See T. C. Rumble, "Malory's 'Works' and Vinaver's Comments; Some Inconsistencies Resolved," *JEGP,* LIX (1960), 59–69.

[70] *Medium Aevum,* XXI, 14.

[71] For the number of characters, see R. H. Wilson, "Malory's Naming of His Minor Characters," *JEGP* (1943), 364–85.

[72] R. H. Wilson, *Texas Studies in English,* XXX, 10–12.

[73] R. M. Lumiansky, *Tulane studies in English,* V, 29–39.

[74] See "Internal Chronology in Malory's *Morte Darthur,*" *JEGP,* LX (1961), 240–49, and *The Book of Kyng Arthur* (University of Kentucky Press, 1965), pp. 1–12.

[75] *Tulane Studies in English,* V, 39.

[76] See the chart printed in *The Book of Kyng Arthur,* p. 96.

[77] *Malory's Originality,* pp. 18–21.

[78] Though Vinaver believed "such irregularities are never found within any one of Malory's romances" (*Works,* xxxii), T. L. Wright notes inconsistencies within the Tale of King Arthur (*Malory's Originality,* p. 14); and in the Tale of Tristram there are contradictory accounts of the death of Marhalt (he dies of Tristram's blow in the first account and because of "false leeches" in the second). The outstanding contradiction in the book as a whole is the prediction at the end of the first tale that Pelleas will be one of the four to attain the Grail.

[79] See Jean Frappier, "The Vulgate Cycle," in *Arthurian Literature in the Middle Ages,* ed. R. S. Loomis (Oxford, 1959), pp. 295–318,

and Fanni Bogdanow, "The *Suite du Merlin* and the Post-Vulgate *Roman du Graal*," *ibid.*, pp. 325–335.

[80] *Tulane Studies in English*, V, 32; Vinaver also comments on this distinction in *Essays on Malory*, pp. 34–37.

[81] E. K. Chambers, *English Literature at the Close of the Middle Ages*, p. 19. Chambers had access to the Winchester Manuscript, evidently knew Vinaver's theory, and, in effect, refuted the separate-tales theory before it appeared.

[82] S. T. Coleridge, *Shakespearean Criticism* (London, 1960), I, 4.

[83] For example, Moorman, *The Book of Kyng Arthur*, p. 11.

[84] *Ibid.*, p. 76.

[85] *Sir Thomas Malory*, English Association Pamphlet, No. 51 (1922), p. 4.

[86] *Works*, p. xxv.

[87] *Tulane Studies in English*, V, 32.

[88] Vinaver, *King Arthur and His Knights: Selections from the Works of Sir Thomas Malory* (Boston, 1956); *The Tale of the Death of King Arthur* (Oxford, 1955).

[89] Tr. by R. C. Williams, *The Theory of Heroic Epic in Sixteenth Century Italy* (Baltimore, 1917), p. 13.

[90] *Texas Studies in English*, XXX, 10–11.

[91] *Essays on Malory*, p. 42.

[92] Ibid., p. 22.

[93] Quoted by Paul Dupont, *Antoine Houdart de la Motte* (Paris, 1898), p. 285.

[94] *Essays on Malory*, p. 22.

[95] *Shakespearean Criticism*, I, 4.

[96] E.g., P. E. Tucker, "The Place of the Quest of the Holy Grail in the *Morte Darthur, MLR*, XLVIII (1953), 391–97; R. T. Davies, "Malory's Lancelot and the Noble Way of the World," *RES*, N. S., VI (1955), 356–64; R. M. Lumiansky, "Malory's steadfast Bors," *Tulane Studies in English*, VIII (1958), 5–20; B. G. Bartholomew, "The Thematic Function of Malory's Gawain," *College English*, XXIV (1963), 262–67; F. Whitehead, "Lancelot's Penance," in *Essays on Malory*, pp. 104–13.

[97] Besides his discussion in the Introduction to the *Works*, see *Arthurian Literature in the Middle Ages*, p. 545: "There is undoubtedly in this collection a certain unity of manner and style; there is no unity of structure or design."

[98] Both passages are quoted, and the second translated by F. Bogda-

now, *Arthurian Literature in the Middle Ages,* pp. 330–31; see G. Paris and J. Ulrich, *Merlin,* SATF (Paris, 1886), I, 280, and II, 57.

[99] "Critical Approaches to Medieval Romance," in *Literary History and Literary Criticism,* ed. Leon Edel (New York, 1965), p. 26.

[100] *Arthurian Literature in the Middle Ages,* p. 545.

[101] George Saintsbury, *A First Book of English Literature* (London, 1914), p. 60.

[102] *The Book of Kyng Arthur,* pp. 2–3.

[103] *Don Quixote,* I, xlvii; quoted by Moorman, *The Book of Kyng Arthur,* p. 2, and Vinaver, *Works,* p. xlix; in the "Introduction" to *King Arthur and His Knights,* p. x, Vinaver notes the difference between Cervantes' opinion and Malory's probable views.

[104] The romantic tale of Guiscardo and Ghismonda was translated (from a French version) into English verse by Gilbert Banaster (d. 1487) and a new version of that translation was written in the late fifteenth century; *The Early English Versions of the Tales . . . From the Decameron,* ed. H. G. Wright, EETS, O.S. 205 (London, 1937). The English poem is far less "modern" than its source and omits most of the "realistic" elements in Boccaccio's story, such as the careful details of the assignation, delightfully specific in Boccaccio but completely ignored by the English writer.

[105] (Durham, North Carolina, 1960), esp. pp. 42–58.

[106] (Princeton, New Jersey, 1966), esp. pp. 335–446.

[107] *The Antecedents of the English Novel, 1400–1600* (Warsaw and London, 1963). Malory's work, she finds, is "the culmination and conclusion of an old style in tale-telling rather than the announcement of a new" (p. 78).

[108] *Literary History and Literary Criticism,* p. 25.

[109] Vinaver, *Études sur le "Tristan,"* pp. 37–58, surveys the manuscripts of the prose *Tristan.*

[110] J. B. Severs (ed.), *A Manual of the Writings in Middle English, 1050–1500,* Fascicle 1, I. Romances (New Haven, Conn., 1967), pp. 13–16, shows that the majority of surviving English romances were written in the late fourteenth and early fifteenth centuries. Between 1450 and 1500 thirty surviving English romances were written.

[111] H. S. Bennett, *English Books and Readers, 1475–1577,* esp. Ch. I; Bennett notes that Caxton "made little attempt to educate or lead public taste" (p. 17).

[112] *Works,* pp. xxxix, 1273, 1398.

[113] "Malory's Naming of Minor Characters," *JEGP.* XLII (1943),

364–85; "Addenda on Malory's Minor Characters," *JEGP,* LV (1956), 563–87; "Malory's Early Knowledge of Arthurian Romance," *Texas Studies in English,* XXX (1950), 33–50.

[114] (Berkeley and Los Angeles, 1966), esp. pp. 75–115.

[115] Matthews therefore identifies Malory as a Yorkshireman rather than the Malory first proposed by G. L. Kittredge, "Who Was Sir Thomas Malory?" *Harvard Notes and Studies in Philology and Literature,* V (1897); see Matthews, *The Ill-Framed Knight,* p. 243, note 2, for full bibliographical references.

[116] J. A. W. Bennett in his review of Vinaver's *Works* in *Res,* XXV, 161–67, notes that "Malory's realism and much of his sentiment are part of an English tradition" (p. 163).

[117] In the "Introduction to the edition of *Ywain and Gawain,* EETS, 254 (Oxford, 1964) A. B. Friedman and N. T. Harrington discuss these characteristics in the English translation and conclude that the "elegant and dilatory courtly romance of Chrétien" has become "a rapid-paced story of love and gallant adventure." I have in progress a brief study of *Arthur and Merlin* in relation to the French *Merlin* which shows that the English author works in much the same way as Malory.

[118] W. L. Guerin, in *Malory's Originality,* pp. 99–117.

[119] *Works,* p. lvi.

[120] C. S. Lewis, *The Allegory of Love* (Oxford, 1936), p. 300.

[121] For a full treatment of this theme see E. Brugger, "Der Schöne Feigling in der arthurischen Literatur," *Zeitschrift für romanische Philologie,* LXI (1941), 1–44; LXIII (1943), 123–173 and 275–328; LXV (1949), 121–192 and 289–433.

[122] See Edmund Reiss, *Sir Thomas Malory* (New York, 1966), pp. 100–110.

[123] Vinaver, *Works,* p. 1445, note to 305.5–308.13; "These pages offer a *prima facie* parallel to the central episode of *Sir Gawain and the Green Knight.*" There are other reminiscences of *Sir Gawain* and of other English romances; this tale seems to be Malory's most "English" romance.

[124] R. R. Bezzola, *Le Sens de l'aventure et de l'amour* (Paris, 1947), p. 88.

[125] Coleridge, *Shakespearean Criticism,* I, 198.

[126] Brewer, *Medium Aevum,* XXI, 16, notes the resemblance between Dicken's work and medieval romance (as does Lewis, *Allegory*

of Love, 299–300) and points out that the *Morte Darthur* is, in structure, superior to the *Pickwick Papers.*

[127] Quoted by Edgar de Bruyne, *L'Esthétique du moyen âge* (Louvain, 1947), p. 129.

[128] *Ibid.,* p. 130.

[129] Quoted by Williams, *Theory of Heroic Epic,* p. 9, as are the other quotations in the following paragraph.

[130] Joseph Spence, *Anecdotes of Books and Men,* ed. J. M. Osborne (Oxford, 1966), III, 52. Quoted from Cocchi, July 1732–April 1733. Osborne notes that he has been unable to find that passage in Galileo's works.

[131] See Williams, *Theory of Heroic Epic,* p. 22, for the opinions of Bernardo Tasso; Jean Chapelain, *Opuscules Critiques,* Societe des textes français modernes (Paris, 1936), p. 215 (where he offers a defense of the prose *Lancelot*); *Hurd's Letters on Romance and Chivalry,* ed. E. J. Morley (London, 1911), p. 118.

[132] In addition to the useful discussion in the "Introduction" to the *Works,* and to the essay already cited from *Literary History and Literary Criticism,* see his presidential address to the MHRA, *Form and Meaning in Medieval Romance* (Modern Humanities Research Association, 1966).

THE FAERIE
QUEENE

A. C. Hamilton

M odern criticism of *The Faerie Queene*—criticism,
that is, in the past half-dozen years—appears to be
taking two opposing approaches. One sets up elaborate interpretations that become increasingly learned, subtle, and
complicated; the other, in opposing explicit interpretation,
ends by being against interpretation itself. The best modern
criticism, based firmly upon the scholarship summarized in the
Variorum Spenser, seeks to apply that scholarship to a close,
critical reading of the text. The Variorum critics were concerned largely with the poem's background, with its sources
and its illustration of religious, moral, and historical matters in
the age, and with the poet's own life and beliefs. Reading the
poem was for them, apparently, a simple matter of selecting
certain words and translating them into moral and historical
equivalents in order to erect rigid levels of allegorical meaning. To modern critics, reading the poem is vastly complex:
more and more words are given their weight of allegorical
significance, and connections with the age are not only indirect
but complicated through the background provided by the
poem itself. The difference between the two approaches may

be illustrated, crudely but not unfairly, from the treatment of the first episode in the poem. Within these 28 stanzas, 252 lines or some 2,500 words, the Variorum critics weighted the words "Knight," "bloudie crosse," "Una," "Error," "bookes and papers," "faith," and "force," and regarded the rest as mere filler. Modern critics add many more words, such as those that describe the Wandering Wood and the Knight's response to it, and the monster in the cave and his response to her. Criticism is moving to the point where each word bears an equal weight of significance. In place of the older, single allegorical reading, "Holiness defeats Error with the aid of Truth," modern readers find that the poem's richly textured surface provides a number of other possible interpretations and provokes endless commentary. Now the problem is to decide which of the possible meanings are supported and maintained by the poem, and how any one of these may be singled out for statement, at the same time doing least harm to the others. Spenser's reference to his poem as "this rusticke Madrigale" describes the dilemma which confronts every critic: he needs half a dozen voices speaking at the same time and in harmony. Because of this simultaneity of meanings, the commentator may hope at best to violate the poem as little as possible. His further burden is that the poem, being an allegory, directs its own interpretation. Its continued metaphor continually invites the reader's response, yet its clear images resolutely resist all interpretation.

The poem first impresses any reader with its elaborate sophistication as a work of art, designed as though to delight and persuade the reader by its artistry without demanding to be understood. Its story is one of "Fierce warres and faithfull loves," of battles with monstrous foes or monsters of the earth, water, air, and fire, of endless quests and sudden flights, of long imprisonments and miraculous escapes. Its setting in fairyland is the desert wilderness, the mysterious forest, and the

perilous sea, higher paradises and the infernal regions, deep
caves, dark dungeons, and glittering castles. It is a mysterious
world of sudden brightness or confused enchantment: a world
of nearly forgotten memories, wonder and magic, a world of
dreams, visions, and nightmares, which engages the reader
upon the conscious and subconscious levels.[1] The poem begins
with "a tale which holdeth children from play, and old men
from the chimney corner," the story of a gentle knight and a
lovely lady, both unnamed, who enter a Wandering Wood to
escape a sudden storm. Through its enchantment they wander
in delight until they take the path to its center which leads to
the cave of a monster. Not until after the two-hundredth line,
when the lady cries "Add faith unto your force, and be not
faint," does there seem clear underlying significance pressing
upon a simple tale. Why "faith," and faith in what? The
irruption of meaning into what could have been enjoyed simply as a story lends weight to earlier details such as the knight's
battered armor, and to later details such as his proven worthiness to wear that armor. When this manner of reading is
extended, the poem may impress readers with its high seriousness as an English epic in which the knight is Saint George, his
lady the English Church, and their story a moral and historical
account of the English nation under Queen Elizabeth. The
poet may be regarded as the English Vergil, the spokesman for
the beliefs and ideals of his age.

The serious reading of the poem began in our century with
the study of the general background of the age as "reflected" in
the poem in an effort to supply the terms in which the poem
was read by a representative contemporary. Now, of course,
we are skeptical of knowing how any contemporary would
read the poem: we recognize that any number of world pictures may serve as possible background, that the backgrounds
are conflicting and contradictory, and that their application to

the poem is ambivalent and ambiguous. Yet this older historical approach did bring an informed reader to the poem, one who could expand his response beyond the record of his own sensitivity and sensibility, and who was equipped to relate the poem to the other arts and sciences. Further, in stressing the chivalric element in the poem, the historical critics saw the poem as a whole. They treated the heroic quests of the individual knights as these quests would lead to a religious, moral, and historical climax in the unwritten Book XII when, presumably, Gloriana as Elizabeth would appear with Prince Arthur (to be identified) by her side, flanked by the twelve knights who had returned in triumph from the quests to which she had assigned them. With this sense of the poem as a whole, the separate quests could be treated in a variety of ways, from simple tale of adventure to psychomachia, pursuit of a virtue, history, treatment of moral or religious doctrine, or spiritual pilgrimage.

Interest in the poem as epic thus became part of a broader interest in the poem as a "continued Allegory, or darke conceit," with set levels of significance hidden beneath the literal level. In his general introduction to the poem in 1948, Leicester Bradner found that the religious allegory of Book I was full and logical, while the national and personal allegories were incidental: hence "the killing of the dragon is the conquest of Satan, or sin, by the Christian man with the assistance of the two divine sacraments recognized by the Church of England. Still in the religious sphere, it may be interpreted as the victory of Christ over death and hell. There is no national or personal significance here." [2] Now Spenser is seen as the Renaissance saw Homer and Vergil, that is, in the tradition of those poets whose works were allegories of the life of the virtuous man and good governor. The concept of allegory was reconstructed from the grammarians, from mythological handbooks with their

analyses of classical myths into moral, historical, and cosmological meanings, from the fourfold exegesis of Holy Scripture
so far as it may be applied to profane literature, and from
other poems that were regarded as allegories.

Yet it became evident that efforts to discover from the
Renaissance a way to read Spenser's allegory were invariably
disappointing and usually a liability. His poem is a more
extended and flexible allegory than the grammarians allow.
Specific levels of interpretation are only intermittent. The influence of medieval scriptural exegesis must be countered with
the Protestant's renewed emphasis upon the literal level. Comparison with other poets helps little because only Spenser and
Dante wrote poems that were conceived and executed as continued allegories. Further, it is difficult to escape feeling that
interpretations are being imposed upon the allegorical poems
of other poets; with Spenser's poem alone, interpretation follows inevitably and continually from careful reading.

Modern criticism of *The Faerie Queene* begins with dissatisfaction over reading on rigid levels of allegorical significance.
Critics have been forced to admit many kinds of allegory in
the poem, from naïve allegory with its one-to-one correspondence between image and idea, to allegory with simultaneous
levels of significance, to kinds where allegorical levels cannot
be separated from the literal level. Some kinds suggest identification with traditional morality, theology, or contemporary
history; some suggest significant analogues or point to what
the poem and the analogues have in common; and some point
only to the work itself. Graham Hough notes that Spenser's
field of operation extends "from hieratic symbolism through
naïve allegory, allegory proper and the romance of types to the
free style allegory where thematic significance is picked up and
dropped at will." [3] Among more recent critics the concept of
allegory has become fully flexible. Thomas P. Roche, Jr.
writes:

> . . . the entire narrative of an allegorical poem is the vehicle of a continued metaphor and . . . the tenor may be any concept or object outside the poem that conforms to the pattern or patterns inherent in the narrative. . . . We cannot restrict ourselves to a sterile hunt for one-for-one relationships. There is no single meaning, at least no single meaning to be stated apart from the experience of the poem. . . . Allegory, as I read it, is not trying to present clear and distinct speculations about philosophical niceties. There is no single object to receive the entire energy of the vehicle; there are always complexes of large and simple ideas, which are illuminated and realigned.[4]

In *Spenser's Image of Nature,* Donald Cheney writes:

> In speaking of Spenser's "allegory" . . . I would point to a multiplicity of meaning, not to any supposed otherness of reference. I would suggest that allegory is far from being a lazy or intermittent exercise of the poetic faculty, but is instead a highly energetic collocation of awarenesses which demands an equally high degree of attentive response from the reader.[5]

Both concepts may be too liberal for other modern critics since they do not allow the poem to control and direct its own meanings, but most critics agree that wide-ranging meanings are preferable to any naïve, simple translation.

As meanings multiply under these more liberal concepts of allegory, however, they become more indefinite, suggestive rather than distinct, hints and allusions that stop short of identification, evocations or echoes of possible meaning rather than any clear meaning. One begins to read the poem not as strict allegory, in which one thing is said but another is meant, but rather as romance. To read epic or allegory proper involves finding what the poet is thought to have put there, a task safely relegated to the scholar, who alone may determine its meaning through a study of sources, influences, and general background. Since meaning is fixed, even predetermined, reading may be impersonal. By contrast, romance invites the reader's immediate response and demands his continued personal participation. Where meanings are multiple rather than single, fluid rather than fixed, and possible rather than given, the reader is actively engaged: responding and understanding become the same activity. Where no identifications but only a choice among suggestions may be made, the reader participates in the work by bringing meaning to what otherwise would remain a simple tale of adventure.

As epic, the poem is read against a general historical background to give relevance to its story. As allegory, it is read through translation into theology, moral doctrine, or history. As romance, it is read within an enveloping framework: first of myth, which provides relevant echoes and analogues, but then of the poem itself, which provides its own echoes and analogues. On the one hand, this sequence from epic to allegory to romance is an extension of meaning: it makes more words in the poem significant. On the other hand, it marks a shift from overt, external statements about the poem, to kinds of allegorical meaning attached to the poem, and then to suggestions of larger and internal meanings. Further, it marks a steady narrowing of focus from the general background, to the poem's relationship to the background, to the developing structure of the poem. In effect, this means a movement back to the first reading when the poem was enjoyed for its fiction, only now the pleasure of reading is attended by a more conscious awareness of the poem's artistry.

These stages of reading may be illustrated from the well-known stanzas that describe the Wandering Wood. These stanzas occur with dramatic suddenness at the outset of the knight's journey when he and the Lady flee from a storm to seek refuge in a "Faire harbour," the fair arbor in which they wander in delight. "Much can they prayse the trees so straight and hy," says the poet in order to enter himself upon the professional task of cataloguing the trees, each with its defining characteristic:

> Much can they prayse the trees so straight and hy,
> The sayling Pine, the Cedar proud and tall,
> The vine-prop Elme, the Poplar never dry,
> The builder Oake, sole king of forrests all,
> The Aspine good for staves, the Cypresse funerall.
>
> The Laurell, meed of mightie Conquerours
> And Poets sage, the Firre that weepeth still,
> The Willow worne of forlorne Paramours,
> The Eugh obedient to the benders will,
> The Birch for shaftes, the Sallow for the mill,
> The Mirrhe sweete bleeding in the bitter wound,
> The warlike Beech, the Ash for nothing ill,
> The fruitfull Olive, and the Platane round,
> The carver Holme, the Maple seeldom inward sound.
>
> (I.i. 8–9)

These stanzas are his signature, the first display of his craftsmanship as the poet of fairyland. The epic catalogue announces his "originals" in Chaucer, Vergil, Ovid, and back to Orpheus, the archetype of the poet's power to move trees and gather a forest around him as he plays upon his lyre. Spenser's device of linking the trees either to their uses by men or to their traditional associations has suggested to readers since Upton that the Wandering Wood, like Dante's *selva oscura,* is an emblem of man's life within society.

When the poem is read as an epic, these stanzas are ignored as a lull before the significant action, the defeat of Error, which shows how the English nation at the Reformation defeated the power of Rome. When the poem is read as an allegory, they are regarded on the moral level as preliminary to the encounter with Error: betrayed by pleasure, the knight almost falls prey to the monster. When the poem is read as romance, the Wandering Wood is related more directly to the action at its center. Then it will be noted, for example, that the labyrinth in which the knight wanders becomes the labyrinthine tail of Error which almost overpowers him; that the various trees of the Wood become the one tree of the knowledge of good and evil through which mankind falls into sin when Error vomits books and papers whose stink overpowers the knight's senses; or that the Wandering Wood is Eden within which the unproved knight meets Eve and the serpent is the dragon-tailed serpent with the woman's head, but—unlike Adam—does not fall.

In a further refinement of this approach, one that proceeds to focus more steadily inward, the setting of the Wandering Wood reflects, and even symbolizes, the inner state of the knight and his lady. Cheney argues that the catalogue of the trees reveals the psychological state of the knight (and apparently also of the lady): their praise of the trees "reflects man's confident moral dissection of his universe" (p. 24). Both are shown to be "content to identify the trees and append the appropriate moral or emblematic tags to each," while the final line of the second stanza "is turned against the presumption of the human compilers of such a catalogue" (p. 25). Cheney concludes that "this wandering wood is suggestive of a naïve and disjunctive reading of nature" (p. 27). Later he refers to "individuals like the early Redcross who are blind to those origins [in nature], choosing in their naïve idealism to translate every solid tree into an abstract value" (p. 65). He refers to the knight's "earlier, wholly naturalist faith" for "the catalogue of trees in I.i. had naïvely seen Nature as orderly and friendly" (p. 183). From this perspective, then, the book shows the knight's struggle to understand both his own nature and the nature that surrounds him. Through his adventures he advances from a youthful idealism to a mature sense of his own identity and the limits of the fallen world.

In her commentary upon the poem, Kathleen Williams interprets the stanzas in similar psychological terms: "The traditional tree-list, which separated from its context can seem a mere set piece, within its context has remarkable immediacy and narrative relevance. The formal descriptions are felt as the appreciative comments of the travellers . . . their pleasant excursion reveals itself as a potentially dangerous dabbling in interests which are not properly their concern." [6] From the perspective of the epic, on the other hand, though these stanzas would be ignored, the book as a whole would be seen to treat a larger drama than the psychological, one in which the knight's gaining of his identity is one sign of a larger revelation (ours rather than his) of a cosmic drama. In this drama his role is hardly more than that of a pawn in a contest between two Queens who carry many meanings—chiefly historical and ecclesiastical—in their roles as forces of good and evil, light and darkness.

The older and the modern readings of the episode need not be opposed, any more than a view of a painting in its particular details denies a view of its larger organization. They may agree if we recognize one of the basic laws of Spenser's fairyland: that Nature is always the same though always veiled. Her aspect varies according to the eye of the beholder. To the knight before he enters upon his quest, she appears as an enchanting wood or labyrinth in which he wanders; to the knight of temperance, she appears as Phaedria's Island or Acrasia's Bower of Bliss; to the state of "true feminitee," she appears as the flowering Garden of Adonis; and to the bold young lover, she appears as the happy garden that leads to the Temple of Venus with Love at its center. Only when the virtue of Holiness is realized, as far as it may be within the knight, does Nature become the restoring Eden with the Tree and Well of Life to sustain him in his final battle with the Dragon.

If modern criticism may accuse the old of simplifying interpretation, the old may proffer a lengthier list of charges. Modern criticism is over-serious and too relentless in pursuit of meaning; and in turning the poem inward upon itself, instead of expanding it outward, it becomes too confining. Why not press the fact that the knight and lady flee into the forest to escape the storm, and find psychological significance in their fear of getting wet? At one time the term "epic" was invoked to give weight to a simple tale of adventure; now, with chiefly psychological interpretation, there is danger that the poem will sink under its burden of meaning. The problem mentioned earlier is crucial here: what interpretations does an episode invite, sustain, and control? And how do they relate to the primary impact of the two stanzas as a traditional catalogue in praise of trees that displays the poet's craftsmanship and sets the scene of the poem in fairyland?

The shift from Variorum to modern criticism may be illustrated if we compare Maurice Evans' chapter on Spenser in his *English Poetry in the Sixteenth Century,* first published in 1955, with the revised chapter in the 1967 edition. What he says is revealing for our purposes because he seeks "to be generally informative rather than original."

In the first edition, the chapter opens with a historical introduction, followed by a section on Spenser's kind of allegory as it "demands a sustained intellectual effort and an unflagging sense of moral values" (p. 141). These moral values are illustrated in terms of the Aristotelian mean: Belphoebe is the personification of virginity, Amoret of physical love, Britomart of chastity, Florimell of female modesty; chaste lust is exemplified in Amoret, unchaste lust in Acrasia; the deficiency of chastity is pictured in Paridell and Hellenore, while excess of chastity is pictured in Malbecco. In the section devoted to Spenser's religion and his idealism, Evans notes that in Lust's seizure of Amoret "Spenser utters a stern and traditional warning against a sin which can exist within the confines of chaste matrimony" (p. 149). An analysis of Spenser's view of love ends with the claim that *"The Faerie Queene . . .* justifies human love by a blend of Platonic idealism and Christian marriage, which reconciles original sin with Platonism, and Courtly Love with religion" (p. 152). The blend of philosophical and religious abstractions in this sentence illustrates the older historical approach to the poem.

In the revised edition, the chapter on Spenser begins with general facts, such as the role of Arthur; and the section on Spenser's kind of allegory concludes that *"The Faerie Queene* forces us to read it with a strenuous and unflagging attention to detail, and to weigh, at the same time as we enjoy, the images" (p. 141). The change from "an unflagging sense of moral values" to "unflagging attention to detail" epitomizes the shift from Variorum to modern criticism.

This modern attention to detail is illustrated by the comment on Error's brood that swarms about the Knight's legs. Evans does not attempt to identify the brood upon some moral or religious level of significance, as did the Variorum critics, but draws our attention to the simile that describes how the knight brushes them away:

> As gentle Shepheard in sweete even-tide,
> When ruddy *Phœbus* gins to welke in west,
> High on an hill, his flocke to vewen wide,
> Markes which do byte their hasty supper best;
> A cloud of combrous gnattes do him molest,
> All striving to infixe their feeble stings,

That from their noyance he no where can rest,
But with his clownish hands their tender wings
He brusheth oft, and oft doth mar their murmurings.

(I.i. 23)

Evans comments:

> The horrible creatures attacking the lower members are
> suddenly metamorphosed into harmless gnats buzzing
> around the head, to be brushed away with the back of
> one's hand. The operative word effecting the change is, of
> course, 'shepheard'—Christ, the good shepherd, the rec-
> ollection of whom renders the most horrible heresies
> impotent in the light of faith. They may trouble his lower
> nature, but Red Cross has only to use his head to see
> them in their true perspective and fear them no more.
> Spenser has made a comment, therefore, on the relation-
> ship between faith and heresy, and on the unthinking
> ignorance which alone makes heresy to be feared (pp.
> 142–143).

Though this interpretation may be dismissed, being as flimsy
as the gnats themselves, at least Evans does not speculate upon
how Spenser must have suffered from flies in the fens of Allen.

In treating the allegory, Evans no longer translates the chief
characters into the moral terms suggested by Aristotle, but
translates everything—character, plot, setting, and rhetorical
devices—into the inner life of the hero. For example, the
characters who accompany the Red Cross Knight "personify
those aspects of his own nature which are relevant to his quest.
. . . The hero is surrounded by projections of himself which
act out in front of us an allegory of what is going on within the
mind" (p. 143). Identifications become much more complicated: Una is the knight's right reason; the Dwarf, the powers
of his soul; the Lion, his bodily instincts; Archimago, his

whole lower nature; the satyrs who befriend Una "symbolise the first yearnings in the fallen soul of Red Cross for a virtue" (p. 146), and so on. Reading the poem today seems a matter of painful intensity, to say the very least, more rigorous and relentless than it was little more than a decade earlier. Its direction is ever deeper into the forest.

One of the most recent critics, Donald Cheney, reads the poem "under the intensive scrutiny which has been applied in recent decades to metaphysical lyrics" (p. 7). He looks for "witty play on imagery" (p. 6), "ironic, discordant impulses" (p. 7), "rapidly shifting allusions" (p. 17), and the poet's "constant insistence upon the ambiguity of his images" (p. 20). "Irony" is his key term: "the reading of *The Faerie Queene* which I am proposing entails a close attention to continually shifting ironic perspectives" (p. 97). His work is studded with such phrases as "suggestive repetitions" (p. 49), "pattern of reverberating echoes" (p. 61), and "pattern of imagistic repetition" (p. 97). Such a critical approach allows him to respond to the poem freshly and with considerable sensitivity. Certainly the poem rewards his intensive scrutiny: it never falls dead in his hands.

Yet the dangers of his approach are all too obvious. How may a poem of some 36,000 lines be read with the intensity and concentration that may be accorded a lyric? After a while even a "rich patterning of bewilderingly complex echoes of imagery and plot detail" (p. 4) becomes simply noisy, and repetitions form a labyrinth from which the reader yearns to escape. Echoes and repetitions of what? Ambiguities may restrict, or even cancel out, larger, accumulated meanings; possible inferences may overwhelm plain meanings; and irony may become simply reductive. To interpret an episode by "the balance of emphases maintained through Spenser's dialectic" (p. 239) may inhibit fullness of response to what we are reading at the moment.

The range of comment on Belphoebe's encounters with
Braggadocchio (II.iii) and Timias (III.v) offers a good illustration of the modern approach. Since the first stands isolated
as a formal *digressio* within the firm rhetorical structure of
Book II,[7] it received little attention from the Variorum critics,
whose interest in plot and character allowed them little scope
beyond making some obvious comments upon Braggadocchio's intemperance in seeking to rape Belphoebe, or noting a
compliment to the Queen in Belphoebe's virginity. Yet any
reader of the poem is soon aware that Spenser lavishes his
powers of invention upon this episode, particularly in the
description of Belphoebe. Her entrance is as violent and star-
tling as the comparable entrance of the Angel in Canto viii:

> Her face so faire as flesh it seemed not,
> But heavenly pourtraict of bright Angels hew,
> Cleare as the skie, withouten blame or blot,
> Through goodly mixture of complexions dew;
> And in her cheekes the vermeill red did shew
> Like roses in a bed of lillies shed,
> The which ambrosiall odours from them threw,
> And gazers sense with double pleasure fed,
> Hable to heale the sicke, and to revive the ded.
>
> (II.iii.22)

Such extravagant language continues for another eight stanzas
to constitute the most elaborate description of any character in
the poem. Later she heals Timias, only to wound him again
through love, for she refuses to yield her virginity:

> That dainty Rose, the daughter of her Morne,
> More deare then life she tendered, whose flowre
> The girlond of her honour did adorne:
> Ne suffred she the Middayes scorching powre,
> Ne the sharp Northerne wind thereon to showre,

> But lapped up her silken leaves most chaire,
> When so the froward skye began to lowre:
> But soone as calmed was the Christall aire,
> She did it faire dispred, and let to florish faire.
> (III.v.51)

Though earlier scholars had noted that the encounter in Book II alluded to Aeneas' meeting with Venus in Book I of the *Aeneid,* nothing was inferred from this reference, and the image was read simply as an idealization of virginity.

Harry Berger, Jr., extended the mythological and literary traditions of the image by focusing upon the simile (II.iii.31) in which Spenser compares Belphoebe to Diana hunting and to Penthesilea when she shows herself before Troy. He argues that "she mysteriously combines in herself the two aspects presented by the simile in the guise of two different women: the skill, preoccupation, and abandon of Diana hunting; and the self-conscious poise of Penthesilea," and concludes that "there is a shade of the sinister about this ambiguity." [8] Roche sees in the description a parody of Vergil:

> The ambivalence of Virgil's presentation of Venus as Diana, that strange juxtaposition of normally conflicting tendencies, is repeated and elaborated in Spenser's later descriptions of Belphoebe. The combination of Venus-beauty and Diana-chastity, which confounded Braggadocchio, is present in Belphoebe's later appearances (pp. 100–101).

Similarly, Miss Williams argues that "Belphoebe is an ambiguous figure because she is an ideal creation of the ambiguous mind of man, whose loftiest aspiration is not free from his deepest self-indulgence"; consequently, although "Braggadocchio is base . . . he is only isolating and distorting an element that is really present in Belphoebe" (pp. 50–51). She finds the episode "endearingly absurd" and notes of Belphoebe's rejection of Timias:

> Her conquering radiance, her funny and rather touching lack of understanding of others, the degraded misery to which these qualities of hers reduce Timias, are all part of Spenser's comment on the worship of the lady as ideal. It is a sympathetic comment, but it is also ruefully amused and sceptical (p. 102).

Finally, Cheney notes of Belphoebe's care for her virginity: "a certain narcissistic obtuseness to the concerns of others is the price which she pays for her immunity to lust. She is even rather pathetic in her glorious isolation" (p. 102). To support his reading, he claims that the ambiguities of the imagery "constitute a means of tempering and informing our approval of the individual figures of the poem" (p. 103).

As applied to the images in the poem, but particularly to those in Books III and IV, this ambiguity stressed by modern criticism seems reductive and restrictive. There is never any need to respond to one image at the expense of another. Other images of the feminine free us, in fact, from such a need. If Belphoebe alone provided the anatomy of love that is displayed in Books III and IV, perhaps she would be exposed to our querulous response that she should maintain a more reasonable virginity. The presence of the others, from Britomart to Mirabella, most of whose states we naturally prefer, allows us to respond with sympathy and precision to Belphoebe's place in love's pageants. By relating the images, Spenser may treat each state as a model or pattern which flourishes in its absolute simplicity. (It is as such, surely, that she appears in Book II, in contrast to the great whore, Acrasia.) Such placing does not yield irony or ambiguity but clarifies and defines each image. The effect is to liberate our response.

Modern criticism seems to be moving in various ways to

expand interpretation of each episode of the poem while re-
stricting the fullness of response to particular images. Ever
since C. S. Lewis's *Allegory of Love* (1936) we have been
taught to restrain and qualify our response to the Bower of
Bliss by becoming aware of its deception, artifice, and sexless-
ness, thus learning to be much more on our guard than ever
Guyon was under the Palmer. The climactic moment is the
famous song heard by Guyon and the Palmer:

> Ah see, who so faire thing doest faine to see,
> In springing flowre the image of thy day;
> Ah see the Virgin Rose, how sweetly shee
> Doth first peepe forth with bashfull modestee,
> That fairer seemes, the lesse ye see her may;
> Lo see soone after, how more bold and free
> Her bared bosome she doth broad display;
> Loe see soone after, how she fades, and falles away.
>
> So passeth, in the passing of a day,
> Of mortall life the leafe, the bud, the flowre,
> Ne more doth flourish after first decay,
> That earst was sought to decke both bed and bowre,
> Of many a Ladie, and many a Paramowre:
> Gather therefore the Rose, whilest yet is prime,
> For soone comes age, that will her pride deflowre:
> Gather the Rose of love, whilest yet is time,
> Whilest loving thou mayst be with equall crime.
>
> (II.xii. 74–75)

The clear and powerful burden of "this lovely lay" (Spenser's
own description) is simply to counsel "Gather the Rose
whilest yet is time." Comparison of the song with its obvious
sources in Ariosto and Tasso shows that Spenser seeks to
overgo them by handling the *Carpe diem* theme more persuasively. The birds approve the singer's "pleasing words," and

the song becomes the greatest test of temperance in Guyon and the Palmer: "The constant paire heard all, that he did say,/ Yet swarved not, but kept their forward way."

Yet Cheney finds a "mood of stagnation" and "sense of futility" in the song, and he comments on "the essential joylessness" and the "tendentiousness" of the speaker's argument. "The singer's exhortation is a counsel of despair. . . . Spenser conveys a sense that the pursuit of love in such a context is in effect a pursuit of death" (pp. 100–101). Here as elsewhere, we are asked to entertain complexity and contradictions at the expense of simplicity and wholeness. Much of modern criticism counters the characteristic effect of Spenser's verse, which is one of fullness, immediacy, and expansiveness.

A close, critical reading of a poem of some 36,000 lines, which has the comprehensiveness of epic, the complexity of allegory, and the suggestiveness of romance, must yield increasingly elaborate interpretation. The immediate problem is not to add meaning, but to control it, so that our understanding of the poem becomes more inclusive and central. A major contribution to the solution of this problem is Rosemond Tuve's *Allegorical Imagery*.[9] Her earlier studies of Elizabethan and metaphysical imagery, and of images in Milton and Herbert, find an inevitable climax in a study of medieval allegorical imagery that points to Spenser, the greatest of all the image-makers. It is unfair to her book to concentrate solely, as I must do, on its importance to Spenser studies, for she presents extended interpretations of a number of medieval books, while she confines her treatment of Spenser chiefly to a hit-and-run attack on his modern critics. One of her interests in these early books, however, is the lessons they provide for reading Spenser.

The medieval books which have *The Faerie Queene* as their posterity—to adapt Miss Tuve's subtitle—are certainly remote from a Renaissance poem. For Spenser's treatment of the virtues she turns to the elaborate, abstract, and diagrammatic vices-and-virtues treatises seen in the *Somme le roi,* rather than to Aristotle, whom he cites as source. For his handling of romance she turns to medieval romance—and not to Malory but to the grail romances—rather than to Ariosto, whom he cites as precedent for his own poem. For the nature of his allegory she turns to sophisticated courtly allegory, such as the *Roman de la Rose,* to spiritual allegory such as the *Pélerinage,* and to Christological allegory such as the Old French *Queste,* rather than to Langland and Dante. Yet she does not treat these medieval books as Spenser's sources: "I do not much care whether the reader thinks Spenser read earlier Arthurian romances or not" (p. 435) she grants near the end of her study, though she is careful to choose only those which would have been available to a sixteenth-century reader. Her purpose is to uncover in them an art of reading allegorical imagery more satisfactory than what she finds in modern Spenser criticism.

The chief lesson that she derives from her study of medieval allegorical imagery is that the images should not be translated into other terms but should be preserved with their inherited meanings:

The unifying principle is not the *history* of a particular or an individual; the action is not a biography, a life, but an action. However varied the definitions of allegory, they are at one in raising to an extreme Sidney's remark about poetry, that it deals with things "in their universal consideration" so that we view abstractions themselves interacting. It was brilliant of Spenser to realize that a structure which weaves a tapestry before us is particularly well suited to allegory, where pattern must steal upon us. He was also supremely successful at this secret conveying of unparaphrasable meaning, and we should not obscure the success by re-writing his stories into their allegories, but resolutely claim whole images with all their depicted feelings as the sole true statements of his allegorical meanings (p. 370).

Accordingly, she argues against overreading, imposed allegories, and rigid interpretation. Her motto for reading Spenser would seem to be "Damn braces, bless relaxes." A primary lesson learned from the early romances, the presentation of sympathetic quick insights into all manner of feelings, may be gained only if we read with "free and leisurely interest and pleasure"; instead she finds modern criticism "bent rather upon detecting an unflagging awareness of significances and upon seeking equivalents in signification for each separate movement in the narrative" (p. 377).

The lesson that she applies specifically to reading Spenser's allegory is the need to retain his images:

A great imaginative allegorist like Spenser will combine these various ways of trying to read truth in ancient images—seeming to evoke rather than impose, making full use of significances which had come to inhabit an image by virtue of its post-classical history of use. His primary method is to deepen meaning by reading moral images symbolically (not symbols in origin), so that they bring into play large conceptions of the moral order of the universe, and the actions debate or portray before us man's profound spiritual dilemmas (p. 226).

Her argument throughout is that the continued metaphor of allegory should be preserved as a metaphor. Such a lesson may be derived also from Sidney when he urges the reader to possess the poet's image in his imagination and to use that image "but as an imaginative ground-plot of a profitable invention." [10]

This stress upon the image limits psychological, biographical, and historical readings. Miss Tuve notes of the *Roman de la Rose* that if we take the story out of the metaphorical sphere "we may see some very neat and amusing disguises for portraying historical events, or we may see some subtle mind-movements within a consciousness under the stress of emotion, but we have not seen the broad sweep of ideas in action, exploring problems of any time and any place, which allegory provides for us when metaphorically read" (p. 249). Similarly for Spenser, she argues that he is "interested less in dramatic struggle than in investigating through actions and images the nature and definition of a virtue" (p. 124). Her extended chapter on "Allegory of Vices and Virtues" shows what precise knowledge of the virtues and their relationship lay at hand in the medieval tradition, ready for use by a Renaissance poet who conceived of his craft in Sidney's terms as "that feigning notable images of virtues [and] vices" (p. 103).

If Miss Tuve's subject had been Spenser, perhaps her general argument would have been qualified or stated more precisely. The sheer variety of Spenser's allegory almost forbids any general statement about his images. Sidney's remark that in the work of the right poets "all virtues, vices, and passions [are] so in their own natural seats laid to the view, that we seem not to hear of them, but clearly to see through them" (p. 108) has special relevance to *The Faerie Queene*. In Spenser the virtues are expressed only through the characters: they are not seen apart from virtuous action. According to the medieval scheme of virtues cited by Miss Tuve, the first of the Seven Gifts was Timor Domini (fear of the Lord), which nourishes the virtue of Humility. "This radical virtue . . . is what we watch slowly taking shape as we read Book I—a virtue built of clear-sighted realization of man's dependence on and grateful faith in his divine Lord" (p. 125). Such realization and faith is the reader's, however, and not the knight's. He remains silent at those points where he may be expected to express humility. Though he defeats Error only by adding faith to his force, the praise of victory belongs to him:

> Well worthy be you of that Armorie,
> Wherein ye have great glory wonne this day,
> And proov'd your strength on a strong enimie,
> Your first adventure.

(I.i. 27)

When he is rescued from Orgoglio's dungeon, the lesson taught him is "That blisse may not abide in state of mortall men" (I.viii. 44). He is saved from taking his own life when he is reminded that he is chosen by God. After he slays the Dragon, Una praises God and thanks her knight "That had atchiev'd so great a conquest by his might" (I.xi. 55), a line that gains special emphasis as the final line of the canto.

In Book I Spenser is more interested in the nature and definition of Holiness than in the knight's inner struggle, in arms rather than the man, although one needs to distinguish between the outer foes, such as Error, in the first half of the book, and the inner foes, such as Despair, in the second half. In contrast, Book II shows the tension between Guyon and the virtue of Temperance which he strives to embody. In contrast to both books, Britomart cannot be seen apart from her virtue of chastity. Further, any discussion of Spenser's use of earlier traditions of the virtues must take into account his claim that in the discipline of virtue he does not form men as they are now but according to the antique use:

> For that which all men then did vertue call,
> Is now cald vice; and that which vice was hight,
> Is now hight vertue, and so us'd of all.

(V.Pr. 4)

He may have intended to upset these earlier traditions. The knight of Holiness falls easily into sin; the knight of Temperance yields to the irascible and concupiscent passions; the knight of chastity pursues a stranger in order to yield herself to him; the knight of Justice submits himself willingly to an Amazon; and the knight of Courtesy abandons his quest, although to do so shames him forever.

In limiting the moral and psychological readings of Spenser's poem, Miss Tuve emphasizes the spiritual allegory. By applying the medieval concept of the two chivalries, the moral struggle that is also a spiritual pilgrimage, she hopes to deliver him "from the slicing machine which reading on different 'levels' has turned into of late. It will sometimes at least restore the depth of a reading that does not reduce human life to a psychomachia, spiritual life to morals and images to axes and hammers" (p. 55). If I understand her argument correctly, she interprets even Book II as a spiritual allegory. Temperance is Augustine's "rightly directed love" rather than the Aristotelian mean: "Guyon does not have to learn how to have just enough love of the world, a reasonable amount of lust. He is to love good *instead*" (p. 131). Though Mammon's cave shows the evils of *concupiscentia,* the imagery of the episode and the Angel "prove us right in our feeling that we have been in hell" (p. 51). Verdant in the Bower shows "the final death of the soul" (p. 31).

Again, however, the variety in the poem complicates general readings. In the Mammon episode, spiritual allegory would be at odds with the moral allegory. It is not sufficient for Guyon to love good, and he cannot reply to Mammon simply, "Get thee behind me, Satan." Mammon presents an argument that he must answer and a temptation that he must undergo and resist. To take account of the variety even within an episode, I cite the word "hore" in the Argument to the Canto:

> Guyon findes Mammon in a delve,
> Sunning his threasure hore.

Part of this second line is repeated in the next canto: the Palmer arrives "Where *Mammon* earst did sunne his threasury." If we agree with C. S. Lewis that Mammon's hoard is grey because it is not gold—he suns it that it may become gold —[11] the line reinforces the otherworldly suggestions of the episode. Yet "hore" may signify only "grey with age." Mammon's treasure is covered with dust, as rust hides the gold of his coat and "dust and old decay" cover his golden cave, and needs only to be "turned upsidowne, to feede his eye" with the sight of gold. Such use may remind us of the Book of Job, "the treasures of the deep that are hoary," or of the gnomes in folklore who sun their treasures in order to enjoy their beauty, until they are interrupted by strangers. Yet Spenser's source may be Horace's ode on temperance (2.2), in which he urges that man should govern his appetites and praises one who can pass by great heaps of treasure and not be tempted. The ode opens with the observation that metal loses its luster when hidden in the earth but shines through right use:

> Nullus argento color est avaris
> abdito terris, inimice lamnae
> Crispe Sallusti, nisi temperato
>   splendeat usu.

Guyon's opening argument against Mammon is that he hides his wealth "apart/ From the worldes eye, and from her right usaunce" (II.vii. 7). If he is called upon to love good instead of the world, as Miss Tuve urges, he is also called upon to claim the world from Mammon's rule. To risk here a general comment: all of Spenser's virtues, but especially Temperance, show man how to live in this world, not how to forsake it.

Spenser chose to write a profoundly secular poem. Miss Tuve's comment on Guillaume's *Pélerinage,* that "the Pilgrim is a spirit, and his pilgrimage the return to his heavenly inheritance and parent" (p. 173), shows how radically that work and its medieval tradition differ from *The Faerie Queene.* Spenser chose not to write a spiritual pilgrimage even in Book

I. He does not treat the Red Cross Knight's final pilgrimage to the Heavenly City, not even the climactic earthly battle that starts him upon that pilgrimage, but only a preliminary action, a qualifying round, in which he seeks to gain worship and honor from the Faery Queen. His subject is an earthly battle for earthly love which Contemplation judges in spiritual terms to be vain:

> But deeds of armes must I at last be faine,
> And Ladies love to leave so dearely bought?
> What need of armes, where peace doth ay remaine,
> (Said he) and battailes none are to be fought?
> As for loose loves are vaine, and vanish into nought.
>
> (I.x. 62)

Yet Miss Tuve identifies allegory with spiritual allegory: "strict allegorical figures are always urging the one great basic significance—the mystery of the soul's victory" (p. 308). Such a concept makes a spiritual allegory of the Old French *Queste* with its narrowness of focus, its reduction of life to the pursuit of a single goal and achievement of that goal solely through sexual purity, and the simple religiosity of the inevitable hermits with their pat explanations. It cannot accommodate the fullness of *The Faerie Queene*.

Miss Tuve's book is a major contribution to modern Spenser criticism because her emphasis upon spiritual allegory opens the poem to more comprehensive interpretations and resists the inevitable movement of modern Spenser criticism to narrow and rigid readings. Miss Tuve's most salutary warnings are made against "too precise or doctrinaire" readings (p. 409).

> The notion of levels, unfortunately now a critical cliché, has served us very ill, for the connection is always open between the literal and the shadowed deeper meaning. The apprehension of both is simultaneous, and the move-

ment should be vertically free—if we must make do with
a spatial image (p. 413).

In this matter, the art of reading medieval allegorical imagery
is fully supported by Renaissance poetics. Only by reading the
literal level in its depth may we preserve the image from being
translated into crude and misleading "equivalents."

As meanings multiply in modern criticism, there arises the
problem of overreading. It is discussed by Miss Tuve through
the standard crux in Book II: "Why does Guyon faint?" [12] If
we ask that question, all too surely we shall get an answer or
many answers. He faints because he breathes fresh air at last,
because he has been three days without food and water, because he has crossed a threshold from another world, because
the Angel, the Palmer, and Prince Arthur are hovering in the
wings, or because genre requires him to. Miss Tuve dismisses
the question on the ground that Spenser did not mean the faint
to be puzzling. "For faints are standard behavior for heroes of
romances. . . . we expect someone to faint who has been in
actual and continued contact with the supernatural world; if
evil is intimated, exhaustion and shock are the usual reactions
displayed to crossing that threshold" (p. 416). Or we may say
that Guyon faints because Spenser wants a moment of supreme irony and reversal: the knight whose motto is watch
and wait, see and endure, now in his greatest triumph falls
helpless before those enemies whom earlier he had reduced to
the position in which they discover him. Or we may say that
his victory over Mammon, being achieved by greater and
greater restraint upon his senses, causes his fall. For in this
most rational of the books, the state of astonishment or the
benumbing of the senses is a convention to project the action
to a level beyond the rational. Whatever answers are proposed,
none will be found satisfactory. Still, the overreading required
to dismiss previous answers should lead to a larger understand-

ing of the book and the poem so that the question itself no longer matters. The worst charge against any interpretation is not that it involves overreading, or that it is wrong, ingenious, or incomplete, but that it restricts our deepening pleasure in reading the poem.

The major problem of modern Spenser criticism is not over-reading, imposed allegories, or strained identifications, but failure to be aware of the nature and limitations of interpretation. Modern criticism focuses ever more sharply but more narrowly as it subjects the poem to its intensive scrutiny. If we assume with Sister Pauline Parker that the poem is "primarily and fundamentally a Christian poem," [13] it is sufficiently capacious and central to confirm our assumptions. If we seek for themes, all too surely we shall find them. Since allegory is a continued metaphor, we must supply meanings by establishing connections with morality, philosophy, or religious doctrine. Since the poem is a romance in which meanings are only suggested and allusive, we must give them shape. Often interpretation gives more insight into the reader or his critical assumptions than into the poem.

Though Spenser's poem may seem exposed to endless subjective interpretation, as an allegory it strongly directs its own interpretation. Miss Tuve argues that his images contain inherited meanings and that their earlier use shows the art of reading them on the spiritual level. I would argue that Spenser controls his meanings through the structure of images within each book, the relationships between the books and groups of them, and the unity of the whole poem. For example, the poem provides various frameworks to guide our reading. Book I reveals man's spiritual life in its vertical perspective from hell to heaven, and so clarifies the nature of the knightly quest; in Book II a moral order gives a horizontal norm against which Guyon's experiences are judged; in Books III and IV (and part of V), a framework of love, courtship, and marriage surrounds the various pageants of love; in the rest of Book V, historical England is juxtaposed against certain events in the poem; and in Book VI the framework is the poem itself. Again, the poem's characteristic movement is always inward, rather than outward or forward to a resolution. The focus of each book is not upon an achieved state but upon some central vision of ordered movement that points before and after; and its climactic vision is revealed in the harmony of the dance,

> An hundred naked maidens lilly white,
> All raunged in a ring, and dauncing in delight

which disappears as soon as it is seen. Invariably, this central vision expands beyond any level of interpretation. In his book on *Allegory,* Angus Fletcher develops the interesting suggestion by Northrop Frye that continuous allegory prescribes the direction of commentary and thus restricts the reader's freedom.[14] Further study of *The Faerie Queene* may show how subtly Spenser manipulates the response of his readers.

In the future, criticism may recognize the limitations of interpretation. For a poem which is such an elaborate dance of meanings, it becomes clear very quickly that interpretation is a matter of saying what the poem chooses not to say, and certainly not in the critic's words, or making explicit what the poem prefers to keep implicit. It forces a reading which the work obstinately resists or withholds for the moment of its own choosing. Even on the simplest level we fault the poem by prose statement. We cannot say that the Red Cross Knight and Una enter the Wandering Wood, because Spenser carefully refrains from naming them. The knight is not named until he proves himself worthy of his armor, and until his parody appears in the disguised Archimago. Una is not named until Duessa usurps her role. All interpretation violates the poem's subtlety, complexity, and wholeness by rationalizing its imaginative statements. It seems designed to protect us from the fearful exposure to the work itself. "We have our philosophical persons to make modern and familiar, things supernatural and causeless. Hence it is that we make trifles of terrors, ensconcing ourselves into seeming knowledge when we should submit ourselves to an unknown fear."

At the present moment the poem needs less commentary and less interference with the reader's response by telling him the story or providing him with a guide. It needs more scholarship to equip the reader and more criticism to allow him to approach the poem as a whole. Once criticism has brought an informed reader to the poem, it should leave him alone. As much may be said for any imaginative work, but it needs to be said with special emphasis for allegory, whose images depend upon the response that they awaken in readers, and above all for Spenser's allegory, whose end is not understanding but virtuous action. *The Faerie Queene* is not meant to be understood but to be possessed. We look for moral meaning when we should be attending to released moral energy.

If the limitations of interpretation are recognized, we may return to the scholarly matters that exercised the Variorum critics.[15] Now that Miss Tuve has related medieval romances to the poem without being distracted by "source-hunting," there is need for a similar study of Renaissance romance, chiefly Ariosto. The tradition of medieval allegory behind the poem should be extended to Langland and Dante, and then to Renaissance allegory. In his study of allegory, Fletcher notes: "It has been felt with increasing surety in recent years that Spenser's aim was not simply to write allegory; he is too concerned with mystery and with the rationally inexplicable aspect of an eternal destiny" (pp. 321–322). The concept of allegory implied here is split-level allegory. Spenser's poem is always peripheral to generic treatments of allegory because it breaks all definitions of the mode; yet for this reason it could be taken as central in a study of the genre. The considerable influence on Spenser criticism of Edgar Wind's *Pagan Mysteries in the Renaissance,* illustrates the need for extended studies of Spenser's use of iconography and emblems, alchemy and astrology. We have never taken seriously the Renaissance cult of the poet as the curious universal scholar, though A. D. S. Fowler's book has demonstrated Spenser's use of number symbolism [16] and Frank Kermode shows Spenser's use of initiation rituals in the Cave of Mammon episode.[17]

Besides extending essential scholarship, particularly into the arcane, Spenser critics could well attend to the most difficult of all levels, the literal. To cite one small matter: in the course of producing an annotated edition of *The Faerie Queene,* I have been surprised continually by Spenser's precise use of language and his play on alternate meanings of words, where I had thought words used vaguely for their suggestiveness. Spenser may be a greater craftsman in words, and in more interesting ways, than we have allowed. His etymologizing, for example, needs a separate study. For other levels, it is possible that even historical allegory could be allowed, provided that proper safeguards were set up.

One direction of modern Spenser criticism in the future is clear from the recent studies by Roche, Cheney, and Williams. While Books I and II have dominated all earlier criticism and dictated approaches to the whole poem, the later books will serve that role. This emphasis is fully justified: pastoral scenes dominate increasingly until the pastoral episodes in Book VI strike most readers as an inevitable and natural climax to the poem that we have.

In Book I the pastoral motifs are muted, though the stages of the knight's fall and final triumph are given antithetical pastoral settings. Book II is strongly anti-pastoral: the pastoral setting in Phaedria's Island, the Garden of Proserpina (an infernal pastoral), and the Bower of Bliss are opposed to the heroic activities of the knight, all of which take place upon the plain or in the Castle. (Belphoebe in the wilderness stands apart from this pattern, as she stands apart from the action.) The pastoral dominates Books III and IV: most of the action takes place in the Garden, the forest, the seashore and the sea, and the scenes of evil are the house of Malbecco and the house of Busyrane. The garden and the castle merge for the first time in the poem in the climactic Temple of Venus. It becomes clear that Book V deliberately excludes the pastoral, and that difficulties over its interpretation should begin with this fact. (Artegall in woman's clothes in Radigund's prison engages in the pastoral activity of spinning.) Book VI counters the previous book by being entirely pastoral, not only in the central scenes that treat Calepine and Serena, but in Calidore's pastoral retreat and in his vision of the dancing maidens. Upon one level, that vision is the climax of two opposing lines of imagery: on the one hand, the binding of Acrasia which (on the level of allegory) occasions the flight of Florimell is followed by various images of women in flight, being abused, tortured, and slandered until their sufferings gather into the image of the naked Serena bound upon an altar, about to be eaten by cannibals. On the other hand, the visions of Belphoebe, Amoret in the Temple of Venus, Britomart as Isis, and Mercilla in her court are fulfilled in Calidore's vision of the hundred naked maidens dancing in delight as they surround the three graces who both dance and sing as they encircle Colin's heavenly maid. Modern readers will grant the rightness of this pastoral vision as a resolution to the poem that we have, as they may grant also that in a coda to this poem the Goddess Nature herself should appear to answer the claims of Mutability. For Spenser is the poet of "faithfull loves" rather than "fierce warres." Venus is the tutelary deity of his poem: in the Proem she is invoked in her own person while Mars must appear "In loves and gentle jollities arrayed." Spenser's statement in the Proem that he is "now enforst a far unfitter taske,/

For trumpets sterne to chaunge mine Oaten reeds," sounds like a complaint. Throughout the poem the thin strains of the oaten reed may be heard above the stern trumpet. Even for the apocalyptic slaying of the Dragon, he seeks out the "second tenor." He is much happier when he may harness the Muses in the pastoral vein.

An emphasis on pastoral may counter the prevailing seriousness of modern Spenser criticism and restore awareness of the poem as a play of the imagination. Berger's term, "conspicuous irrelevance," which he applies to Spenser's similes, may be extended to the whole poem, provided we recognize such irrelevance as the flowering and end of human activity. At the present time it is invariably more rewarding to talk to a reader who finds Spenser to be "camp" than one who reads the poem as though he were going to school or attending church. As Book VI comes to dominate our approach to the whole poem, we may regain the sense that the poem is enjoyable to read and understand. The one key to its reading is that understanding follows only from a deepened and extended appreciation, and not the other way around.

At this point we should recognize that the poem is more than pastoral or romance, and that it includes all literary kinds. In his chapter on Spenser in *The Poet and his Faith,* A. S. P. Woodhouse writes:

> There is scarcely a genre that it does not involve or draw upon—epic narrative, chivalric quest, the whole range of allegorical poetry as the Middle Ages had developed it, not to mention pastoral idyll, emblem, interlude, and masque. And within its ample confines it gathers up all the principal elements of the Elizabethan cultural inheritance: the wealth of Greek and Roman philosophy, poetry, and myth, mediated through the classical Renaissance; the treasure of the Christian tradition, mediated

through the Reformation; the inheritance of medieval
chivalry and romance. . . . All these things *The Faerie
Queene* assembles and in measure co-ordinates. . . .[18]

Because of its scope, the poem should appeal increasingly to
modern readers as a work that is central to life and art, and to
their relation. It is a work upon which a literary education may
begin and to which it may constantly return.

Notes

[1] Here, and in the discussion of allegory and the Wandering Wood, I
have borrowed some sentences from my introduction to *The Selected
Poetry of Spenser,* Signet Classic, 1966. Further, I have incorporated
into this essay a review-article, "Spenser's Pastoral" which originally
appeared in *ELH,* 33(1966), 518–531.

[2] Leicester Bradner, *Edmund Spenser and "The Faerie Queene"*
(Chicago, 1948), p. 125.

[3] Graham Hough, *A Preface to "The Faerie Queene"* (London,
1962), p. 111.

[4] Thomas P. Roche, Jr., *The Kindly Flame: A Study of The third
and fourth books of Spenser's "Faerie Queene"* (Princeton, 1964), p.
31.

[5] Donald Cheney, *Spenser's Image of Nature: Wild Man and Shepherd in "The Faerie Queene,"* Yale Studies in English, Vol. 161 (New
Haven, 1966), p. 7.

[6] Kathleen Williams, *Spenser's "Faerie Queene": The World of Glass*
(London, 1966), p. 2.

[7] I have argued this point in "The Visions of *Piers Plowman* and *The
Faerie Queene,"* in *Form and Convention in the Poetry of Edmund
Spenser,* ed. William Nelson (New York, 1961), pp. 20–27.

[8] Harry Berger, Jr., *The Allegorical Temper: Vision and Reality in
Book II of Spenser's "Faerie Queene,"* Yale Studies in English, Vol.
137 (New Haven, 1957), p. 140.

[9] Rosemond Tuve, *Allegorical Imagery: Some Mediaeval Books and
their Posterity* (Princeton, 1966).

[10] Sir Philip Sidney, *An Apology for Poetry,* ed. Geoffrey Shepherd
(London, 1965), p. 124.

[11] C. S. Lewis, *The Discarded Image* (London, 1964), p. 106.

[12] This crux is discussed at some length by Berger, pp. 3–38.

[13] M. Pauline Parker, *The Allegory of the "Faerie Queene"* (Oxford, 1960), p. 3.

[14] Angus Fletcher, *Allegory: The Theory of a Symbolic Mode* (Ithaca, 1964), pp. 304–305. Frye makes his suggestion in *Anatomy of Criticism* (Princeton, 1957), p. 90.

[15] As I suggested earlier, there has been no sharp break in the scholarship; cf. particularly William Nelson, *The Poetry of Edmund Spenser* (New York, 1963), pp. 158–60, on the Wandering Wood, and pp. 210ff. on Spenser's use of Plotinus.
The strength of future Spenser studies is evident in recent doctoral dissertations, such as those by A. R. Cirillo, Martha Craig, Carol Kaske, T. K. Dunseath, and Alice Blytch which extend considerably our understanding of the poem. I regret that the submission date for this manuscript—August 1, 1967—prevents me from including the criticism of Paul J. Alpers in his *The Poetry of "The Faerie Queene,"* Princeton, 1967. See my forthcoming review article of his book in the *Journal of English Literary History*.

[16] Alastair Fowler, *Spenser and the Numbers of Time* (London, 1964).

[17] Frank Kermode, "The Cave of Mammon," in *Elizabethan Poetry* (Stratford-upon-Avon Studies, 2, 1960), pp. 151–173.

[18] A. S. P. Woodhouse, *The Poet and His Faith* (Chicago, 1965), p. 21.

KING LEAR

Ernest William Talbert

K *ing Lear* is a problem." With those words a perceptive
critic began his study of Shakespeare's drama.[1] The
tragedy is indeed a problem. It is concerned with man and the
universe in which he lives, and since man and his universe will
remain inscrutable for some time to come, the problems that
King Lear poses, by the very nature of the mystery and tragedy
of life, cannot be resolved easily. In other words, *King Lear* is
a problem—as it should be.

Nor is it surprising that during the past twenty years well
over six hundred critics, at least, have attempted to analyze
King Lear. Directions taken by R. B. Heilman and others have
been continued and scarcely any group of words has been
ignored in attempts to formulate the themes and problems
apparent in the tragedy.[2] Even a study concerned with "the
ways in which the *forms* of experience and of mental outlook"
have been altered by different means of communication begins
with an analysis of *King Lear*.[3] This, too, is as it should be;
and the great disagreement among critics—although it may
not be as it should be in the best of all possible worlds—is
certainly inevitable and nearly always enlightening.

One question has remained constant, however. Does Shakespeare affirm certain values and certain judgments related to man and his universe, or does he question and even deny them? To list the answers, with their qualifications of other answers, or even to illustrate their range fully is quite impossible within the limits of this essay. But as the phrasing of the preceding question implies, two emphases that in general contradict one another are apparent. I shall illustrate that contradiction very briefly, and then I shall discuss a somewhat similar disagreement involving different approaches to the drama. The two topics are not mutually exclusive, but a separate consideration of them provides a basis for evaluating current approaches to this tragedy and current analyses of it.

One dominant emphasis in the criticism of *Lear* can be described as a continuation or a merging of earlier interpretations by A. C. Bradley and R. W. Chambers. Although Bradley would not allow a theological interpretation of the world to be present in any Shakespearean tragedy, he believed that Lear was redeemed. According to R. W. Chambers, during the course of the drama a purgatory gives way to a paradise of true love.[4] In this very general vein of criticism, emphases vary and critics differ greatly in their interpretation of speeches and scenes. They nevertheless see a basic optimism in the play's logic, and they may conclude that the pagan world of *King Lear* is permeated, or even transformed, by the values of the Christian Renaissance.[5] This general point of view can be illustrated by a few quotations:

> *King Lear* is a triumph of dramatic construction which in its total effect, like *Hamlet* and *Othello,* affirms justice in the world, which it sees as a harmonious system ruled by a benevolent God.[6]

In this tragedy, suffering humanity is given an "almost mystical dignity," and in the last scene,

. . . we recognize a supreme value that the ancients never knew, a value which surpasses—for us, at least—even the Sophoclean value of justice: the value of love.[7]

All this titanic expenditure of effort and suffering to teach two stupid old men how to love? Yes; and rightly; for the colossal extravagance of means, the cosmic excess of upheaval and waste, celebrates the range and importance of the nature of man. At such times, even the supreme powers of the universe (whatever and wherever they may be) humble themselves before man. . . .[8]

In the play itself there is nothing wanton. There is justice, mercy, sacrifice, and redemption.[9]

Shakespeare traces the soul's journey from the pit of chaos, to a point where it seems about to unfold celestial wings.[10]

As Lear dies, there is

. . . the moving certainty that here we are watching Lear slip round the corner of this known world of time and space into a kind of fourth dimentional world, with a glimpse before he disappears of what he sees already around that corner of eternity, his beloved Cordelia awaiting him there, her lips smiling again for Lear.[11]

This play dramatizes the "tragic suffering of those who find regeneration" and the "tragic waste of those who sink from sin to sin." It holds "the mirror up to nature (and grace)," and in the paradox that it is a profoundly Christian drama about a pre-Christian world, *King Lear* is "undeniable proof that it is possible to write Christian tragedy." [12]

In this very general vein of criticism, action and characters in *King Lear* sometimes have been said to be analogous to Christ in his passion and Christ in his saving grace. More than twenty years ago J. Dover Wilson considered it "impossible to contemplate the death of Lear without thinking of Calvary," and G. Wilson Knight saw "a miniature Christ" in Lear, as in Shakespeare's other tragic protagonists. As Russell A. Fraser points out in his study of Shakespeare's poetics, Lear *"fantastically dressed"* is likened to Christ, "the king of fantastics": "O thou side-piercing sight!" [13] At times, an analogy between Cordelia and Christ has been emphasized. Some of Paul N. Siegel's conclusions illustrate this tendency. In the reunion of Lear and Cordelia, the protagonist "as if from purgatory" hears "the celestial music" and sees "the angelic radiance" that he is to attain. The miracle of Lear's redemption is thus "analogous to the redemption of mankind," and the "unmistakable" analogy between Cordelia and Christ is completed by her "ignominious death." A "brand of heaven" releases the souls of Lear and Cordelia and enables them "to become reunited in eternal bliss." [14]

As might be expected, this last tendency has met vigorous opposition. The method used has been called an unwarranted extension of "the medieval method of Biblical exegesis," and the point has been made that although Shakespeare undoubtedly believed in Christ's redemption of mankind and in a Christian eschatology, he did not dramatize either. Whatever redemption the hero attains is "not through Divine Grace but, like the Greek hero, through his own efforts." What is Christian in the drama is psychological and ethical only. [15]

It will be remembered that L. L. Schücking denied Lear's purification, and E. K. Chambers argued that there was no final victory of good. Similarly, numerous writers during the past twenty years have maintained that *King Lear* cannot be interpreted in the light of Christian morality. [16] D. G. James points out that in this tragedy the wholly good is "altogether proof against all that is brought against it." He nevertheless insists that we "must raise our minds to the height" of Shakespeare's "bleak and merely exploratory vision." "The play's action is terrible in all conscience; but there is no crumb of Christian comfort in it." [17] Although John Lawlor considers *King Lear* a tragedy of positive family relationships, much as R. G. Collingwood did, Lawlor otherwise sees only a negative endurance and a tragic illusion in the drama.[18] Others have insisted that pessimism permeates *King Lear* and is "in Shakespeare himself," since it is not in the inherited story. The "toughness of despair in and behind the writing" is constantly "jolted into the foreground." [19] In this second very general vein of criticism, any "epilogic vision" that reunites Lear and Cordelia in eternity is denied, and it has been argued that as Lear dies he does not believe Cordelia to be alive. If he does, this "hope where none is possible" is "the last joke played by the universe against Lear." From an entirely different point of view, Northrop Frye contrasts the inner tragedy of Gloucester with the outer tragedy of Lear. The one is "morally explicable," the other ends in a "vision of absurd anguish." [20]

This forceful opposition to the first vein of criticism mentioned here can be illustrated further by the analyses of Nicholas Brooke and of J. Stampfer. Brooke believes that in *King Lear* Shakespeare has created a universe in which "Nature has no moral order" and "has no need" of either an all-embracing destructive evil or its "unequal opposite." The ending "is the most painful thing in our, perhaps, in any, literature." We must face it "without any support from systems of moral . . . belief at all." The "greatness of *King Lear* is in the perfect completeness of its negation, and in the superb energy with which it is enforced." [21] In a somewhat similar manner, Stampfer writes that in this tragedy "even those who have fully repented, done penance, and risen to the tender regard of sainthood can be hunted down, driven insane, and killed by

the most agonizing extremes of passion." As a consequence, in
King Lear "we inhabit an imbecile universe." [22] Even an emphasis on the paradox or paradoxes said to be embedded in
this drama also has led to different, and even contradictory,
conclusions.[23] And so it goes.

If we do "inhabit an imbecile universe" in *King Lear,* then
we are close to the view of Jan Kott, who sees in the tragedy an
anticipation of the theater of the absurd, and specifically an
anticipation of Samuel Beckett's *Endgame.* Shakespeare is
"our contemporary," and *King Lear* emerges in all of its purposeful and cruel grotesqueness as it dramatizes a nihilistic,
meaningless "decay and fall of the world." [24] But Kott's analysis ignores a great deal that is explicit in Shakespeare's drama.
Maynard Mack, Alfred Harbage, and others have made it
quite clear that the Beckett-like bleakness in the production of
Peter Brook, who was influenced greatly by Kott's discussion,
distorts and obscures—and, one might add, oversimplifies—
the text of Shakespeare's *Lear* just as much as did Nahum
Tate's redaction.[25]

A distortion of Shakespeare's text was also apparent in
Herbert Blau's production of Lear. It was based on a "subtext"
that was in turn based on "nothing"—the "nothing" that in
Lear's words comes of "nothing." Yet Blau's "nothing" could
develop three series of electronic sounds that competed with
Shakespeare's words for thirty-five minutes during the heath
scenes. Maynard Mack remarks that "We may safely guess
which factor won." [26]

One might ignore these productions were they not illustra-
tive of two points that should be made. In the first place, there
is a "nothing" that runs through Shakespeare's drama and is
enlarged by cognate allusions and, indeed, by entire enactments involving Mad Tom. Even if they do not focus on this
particular development, those who write in the second general
vein of criticism make us aware of this. "Nothing" and noth-

ingness, however, is only one allusive development in a complex and expanding pattern of meaning. By itself it does not constitute either text or subtext. No one should forget those who write in the first general vein of criticism.

In addition, the use of the word "nothing" may have meant more to Shakespeare's contemporaries than it does to a modern reader. William R. Elton points out that Lear's repeated exclamation about nothing coming of nothing could carry a meaning "centrally relevant to the religious crisis of Shakespeare's age" and, by extension, a meaning that was also "crucial" to scientific development. "Creation *ex nihilo* . . . implies providence," and God's creation of the world from nothing was being defended vigorously by theologians. Especially after the appearance of the *nova* of 1572, belief in an eternally changeless heaven and in a world made for men was being shaken. As a result, "nothing" and its cognate allusions may have had "a pointed religious irony in the play" and produced an impact upon a Jacobean audience more complex than any impact it might have upon our contemporaries. This argument is one detail in *"King Lear" and the Gods.* From his analysis of the drama, Elton argues that Shakespeare's tragedy was meant to be "syncretically pagan."

> By depicting a superstitious pagan progressing toward doubt of *his* gods, Shakespeare secured for the play the approbation of the less speculative devout, who saw in its direction the victory of the True Faith. . . . Moreover, he obtained for it the interest of those more troubled and sophisticated auditors who were not to be stilled by pious assurances in the unsteady new world of the later Renaissance.

For those more sophisticated auditors, the drama would intensify their doubts of a conventional providence and their horror of an "all-dissolving chaos." [27]

The point just made leads to some familiar questions. All would agree that as one excludes from consideration what a work of art does not present, one must become immersed in everything that is presented. But does not each person and each generation see something different in any enduring work of art? Need one consider what historical scholarship points out as being important in the past, even though that is not as important, if important at all, in the present? Perhaps these and similar questions explain the interest shown during the past twenty years in the approach of myth-critics and ritualists. They at least seem to be concerned with something that may explain the impact of *King Lear* in a much more primitive or universal way than anything pointed out by others. Such an approach may also avoid or cut through any bothersome disagreement about the meaning of a drama.

In his defense of his method and in his criticism of those who are concerned with Shakespeare's themes, John Holloway argues that Shakespeare's tragedies are "an extension or elaboration" of rites of human sacrifice. He sees demonstrable similarities between the victim of the ritual hunt and the tragic protagonist, whose suffering is "almost a chosen end" of life as he has lived it and as he is separated from society. Ordeal, human scapegoat, and sacrificial victim energize the drama's action. The total enactment is of overriding importance. It produces "a momentous and energizing experience" that "sensitizes the recipient" so completely that he may not be "necessarily or clearly aware" of the extent of that sensitization. The experience is comparable to the way in which primitive societies attempt to establish a relationship between the participants in rituals and the "world of unseen and holy powers." By that experience "quotidian life" is revitalized, and since the experience is "extra-calendrical," the "sacrificial rhythm of the tragedy itself" ritualizes reality.[28] Here, in other

words, is an approach applicable to past, present, and future
—something that may explain, in part, why Shakespeare's
tragedies endure.

As I have argued elsewhere, any approach that whittles
away the entire enactment of a drama until *King Lear, Macbeth*, and *Antony and Cleopatra* can be spoken of in one way,
and in the same breath, obviously leaves a good deal else to be
examined. Not to see the forest for the trees may be short-
sighted perhaps, but not to see the trees for the forest probably
will be disastrous. The nature of society in Shakespeare's tragedies varies greatly. As Arthur Sewell indicates, the conflict in
Lear is not so much between the individual and society as it is
within society itself.[29] Lear chooses to go into the storm because he will not submit to an association in which power
alone determines one's relationship to others: "I pray you,
father, being weak seem so." In view of the banishment of
Cordelia and Kent, there is irony here, but at the same time
the recipient's sympathies are being shifted. Kent has returned
and now supports Lear. An audience has heard the Fool's lines
at Albany's castle. Albany has questioned Goneril's conduct.
Lear has admitted his folly, injustice, and "jealous curiosity";
and he has restrained his "more headier will." The viciousness
of this group to whom Lear refuses to submit is then intensified. One example will suffice:

> Though well we may not pass upon his [Gloucester's] life
> Without the form of justice, yet our power
> Shall do a court'sy to our wrath, which men
> May blame but not control.

When one is concerned with the impact of *King Lear* upon an
audience, not to realize Shakespeare's changing emphasis and
his development of a conflict *within* society is to court critical
disaster. Holloway's approach may be pertinent for those concerned with the nature of tragedy, but it is inadequate for an

analysis of an individual work of art as a whole. Myth-critics
and ritualists themselves have made this very point, although it
is sometimes obscured by their terminology.

Several years ago, Robert Hapgood published a useful article entitled "Shakespeare and the Ritualists." [30] Especially no-
ticeable in his survey is the "wide variety of contexts" in which
the words "myth" and "ritual" are used: Elizabethan ceremo-
nies, folk motifs, festal celebrations, the conventions of the
Elizabethan drama, literary tradition in general, and the
"myths" of literature which enact a variety of human emotions. Quite understandably, Hapgood also quoted Wimsatt
and Brooks to the effect that during the preceding ten or
fifteen years criticism by myth and ritual origins had become
our "hugest cloudy symbol." The "symbol" is also a very
inclusive one. By exercising a bit of ingenuity, one might
extend the previous list to include nearly every form of historical scholarship and literary criticism. The cloudiness and in-
clusiveness of the "symbol" tempt one to repeat what is said to
have been Lord Melbourne's favorite question: "Can't we
leave it alone?"

I am afraid that we cannot leave it alone, but at the moment
it might be well to consider only one definition of "tragic
myth." If *King Lear* enacts the regeneration of its protagonist
and creates a paradise of love after a purgatory, then inasmuch
as Lear is a king, the enactment created from the beginning
until his reunion with Cordelia promises to approximate what
has been described as the basic myth of tragedy. It promises to
do this by its universal nature and not, as Herbert Weisinger
phrases it, because the myth has been "baptized Christian."
The protagonist, "in whom is subsumed the well-being of the
people and the welfare of the state, engages in conflict with a
representative of darkness and evil." A "temporary defeat is
inflicted" on him, but "after shame and suffering he emerges
triumphant as the symbol of the victory of light and good over

darkness and evil, a victory sanctified by the covenant of the settling of destinies which reaffirms the well-being of the people and the welfare of the state."

> In the course of the conflict there comes a point where the protagonist and the antagonist appear to merge into a single challenge against the order of God; the evil which the protagonist would not do, he does, and the good which he would, he does not; and in this moment we are made aware that the real protagonist of tragedy is the order of God against which the tragic hero has rebelled.

In this manner, *hybris,* potential in all of us, is purged by the suffering of the hero, who is given a "vision of victory" but who does not attain it.[31]

As T. R. Henn, Weisinger, and Hapgood discuss *King Lear,* they point out that the "moment of illumination" at the end of the fourth act becomes "the double tide" of sorrow and rejoicing, or "the shambles," or the "maimed rites" of the fifth act. The settling of destinies is said to be "mishandled and misplaced," and one reads that "Here is Golgotha indeed." [32]

Aside from the basic tragic myth, ritualistic and mythic components of *King Lear* have been named. The drama enacts, for example, Ordeal of the Riddle, Debasement of the King, Mock King–Fool King–Holy Fool, Duel with the Unknown Champion, Slaying of the Old King.[33] We might ask, nevertheless, "What has been achieved?" Hathorn points out the obvious fact that "the greatness of the literature . . . does not depend merely on the mythical nature of its subject-matter," [34] and Hapgood insists that to stop at the discovery of the myth is a grave error. The discovery should be "the starting point for discriminating the unique qualities which give each work its identity." He believes that the sympathy created for Lear should not be minimized, and that one should not speak of Lear's death as being welcome because it releases the audience from its identification with the hero. In this tragedy, our hopes for a "sacrificial ritual" that will transform the life of the community are encouraged, but they are also confronted "with the unregenerate way things are." By this maiming of the ritual, "a unique balance" is achieved between "fulfilling our hopes for a successful sacrifice and disappointing them." A conclusion that is both "numenous and true" results. We take satisfaction in the purging of the royal scapegoat" and yet "mourn the death of the royal hero." [35]

The fact remains, however, that if the destinies of society are "mishandled and misplaced" in *King Lear,* or if the rites are "maimed," then the emotional and imaginative impetus of this work of art ultimately exists outside the area of those destinies and those rites. It seems logical to assume that this impetus of the drama was Shakespeare's essential concern and, consequently, should be our essential concern. The point can be illustrated further by choosing two variations upon this general approach and commenting briefly upon each. One is concerned with the "rituals" created by Shakespeare in *King Lear*. The other interprets the Lear myth psychologically.

In the first study, the meaning of "ritual" is extended to include "any speech or situation which will be felt by participants or spectators to be predictable in important respects." With this definition, ritual in *King Lear* becomes allegory and accords with the "mythic, the folkloristic nature of the story." The tragedy then becomes "one enormous parody after another of the ritualistic opening of the play." Finally, ritual loses "all relevance to the King" and both Cordelia and Lear are no longer of importance. They have passed beyond ritual and "cannot be expressed or comprehended by any of its forms —this fact is their greatness and their tragedy." [36] One may object to the circular reasoning and the subjective, unstable definition of "ritual," but it seems more pertinent to me that this approach again ignores any emotional or imaginative development that becomes important to Shakespeare's characters and thereby animates their existence outside or "beyond" even as inclusive a definition of "ritual" as this one.

Consider also an analysis of *King Lear* based upon the "myth dream" or the "basic fantasy" of parental punishment. We are told that we hear the voice of a hurt child armed with a punitive impulse when Lear refuses to submit to those who would turn bonds into bondage and who value power only. Such an analysis of Lear's choice seems to me to be the result of looking at a work of art through the wrong end of binoculars. The parental punishment fantasy and the dream that the bad siblings also will be punished may explain the appearance of the Lear myth in its many primitive forms. But let us pause when we hear that the spectator has it both ways as Shakespeare's tragedy closes and as the full force of this "archetypal fantasy" results in the death of both parents: Edgar actually kills his father, and the conclusion dramatizes the crowning punishment of "I'll die and he'll be sorry." [37] Again, this interpretation diminishes and ignores Shakespeare's enactments, including his representation of the effect of those deaths upon his other characters.

Even if we are "sensitized" by echoes from a racial unconscious, a repetitive ritual, or an archetypal fantasy, those echoes certainly should not be magnified and, like Herbert Blau's electronic sounds, overpower Shakespeare's text. By the nature of their approach, myth-critics and ritualists abstract structure from its context. Thus they tend to ignore the conceptual apprehensions that arise from the complexity of this tragedy and that produce what D. A. Traversi has called its "expanding pattern of meaning." [38] This pattern of meaning quite obviously involves language, character, and action. As L. C. Knights indicates, in *King Lear,* as in all great drama, "Poetry and situation release and bring into relation the differ-

ent meanings" of ambiguous key-words until they "vibrate" in
the recipient's mind "beyond the limits of the specific in-
stances." The result is the opposite of that achieved by what
Martin Foss has called "symbolic reduction." "Just as there is
interplay and tension between the different senses of the key-
words, so there is interplay and tension between the different
key-words themselves and all other elements of the drama." In
"the upward surge of the metaphoric process" new directions
for imaginative thought appear. The energy in this "drive of
interest" is "an energy of understanding" brought about by
"the reader's imagination responding to the imagination of the
poet," and the imagination "thus conceived is an instrument of
knowledge." As Northrop Frye indicates, "it is not what the
characters have learned from their tragic experience, but what
we have learned from participating in it, that directly confronts us." In contrast with comedy, tragedy individualizes the
audience, "nowhere more intensely" than in a drama like
Lear. Our "awareness survives the play, and gives it a death-
and-resurrection pattern. . . ." [39] At the very least, the "metaphoric process" with which Knights is concerned arises from
what is explicit, constant, and pervasive in the increasing impact of the drama.

"*King Lear* as Metaphor" represents one of Knights'
skirmishes with historically minded scholars. His point is not
that scholarship is irrelevant but that it may exclude considerations of the greatest relevance. Knights is pleading for the
liberty of interpretation, not for license. He argues that one
must be concerned with the way in which Shakespeare's ideas
permeate the dramatic action and demand our imaginative
response and with the way in which those ideas are not simply
expressed philosophically but are relived. Just as it is hard to
conceive of anyone's resisting his admonitory skirmish, so
Knights appreciates the way in which historical scholarship

can aid one in "grasping more firmly what is essential" to a Shakespearean drama "as an ever-present work of imagination." [40] This approach, I submit, is especially helpful in analyzing *King Lear* as a whole.

Consider the stark outlines that Shakespeare gives his characterization. Bradley, of course, had called attention to this aspect of the drama, as Maynard Mack reminds us. "The persons surrounding" Lear

> . . . are in some sense (. . . as in the Morality plays) extensions of himself, who will struggle to assist or defeat him, and most show a monolithic simplicity and singleness of being which makes them representatives, as Bradley saw, of the Morality tendency "to decompose human nature into its constituent factors." [41]

Perhaps the constant tendency to comment upon this feature of the drama has resulted from the popularity of the word "archetype" and from an increasing interest in the way in which the Morality play seems to be reflected in later drama.

Much depends upon the definition of the term, but if "archetype" means "an element in one's literary experience as a whole," [42] then a dominant feature of *King Lear* probably can be called archetypal and can be related both to Shakespeare's literary experience and to his audience's. In his chapter "Archetype, Parable, and Vision," Maynard Mack briefly reviews what has been pointed out in this respect and enlarges the parabolic background of *King Lear* by referring to additional motifs that give an "exemplary and emblematic" meaning to both the pattern of the entire tragedy and the tissue of its enactments. One reads of the Abasement of the Proud King, of Virtue Locked Out, of the Messenger of the King (or of the God) Turned Away. Parallels in Morality plays and in earlier Shakespearean dramas are pointed out as they are applicable both to the characters surrounding Lear and to incidents that create a sense of journey to "some form of commitment"—a journey that had also been taken by "a far more ancient dramatic hero, variously called Mankind, Everyman, Genus Humanus, Rex Vivus, Rex Humanitas, Magnificence, etc." [43]

Shakespeare, no less than Ben Jonson, knew the Morality play, and in his earlier dramas the spectacles that Shakespeare created could bind different enactments together. More than twenty years ago, W. B. C. Watkins argued that one of the two major techniques in *King Lear* was that of "symbolic stylization." [44] A great deal of what one finds in Russell A. Fraser's *Shakespeare's Poetics in Relation to "King Lear"* substantiates this point of view. With an almost profuse richness, archetypal patterns are developed by emblematic situations. [45] One example will suffice. Those who finally are asked to sustain the "gor'd state" had been "locked out" together. Kent was in the stocks when Edgar became "Poor Turlygod! poor Tom!" and between those enactments an audience would hear, "Fortune, good night; smile once more; turn thy wheel!"

The intensified simplicity that gives to character and action a symbolic quality produces such a compression that one's apprehension of an enactment may be extended in a variety of ways. Details from the studies of L. C. Knights, Maynard Mack, and Kenneth Muir illustrate this. In "one act of apprehension" we have "fire and whirlpool, bog and quagmire, whirlwinds and star-blasting, the web and the pin (cataract), squint eyes, hare-lips, and mildewed wheat"—and then "our sense of natural calamity stretches on and on." [46] That one proud king had to feed with the palace dogs may be reflected in "The little dogs and all" that bark at Lear—"Tray, Blanch, and Sweetheart." [47] Yet the specific names also provide a backward glance at different circumstances never dramatized. The entire mock trial of Goneril and Regan is the *"reductio ad absurdum* of Lear's view of his own role as dispenser of justice." At the same time this trial by "a mad beggar, a dying Fool, and a serving man" evokes the Biblical words, "He hath put down the mighty from their seat, and hath exalted the humble and the meek." [48] Pathos and absurdity permeate our apprehensions of justice, and our notions of wisdom and folly are turned upside down, as tears mar the "counterfeiting" of Edgar.

Any apprehension, however, exists only to be transmuted into another. Constantly one is carried forward to other apprehensions that enlarge or qualify what has just been perceived. As a result, one cannot ignore or underestimate the approach of those who are concerned with ideas that permeate the action or with unfolding concepts that run beneath a number of enactments. Through this approach, I believe, one can evaluate the conflicting opinions about the nature and the effect of *King Lear* as a whole. Consider some enactments permeated by the ideas of justice, patience, endurance, and briefly note how those ideas are related to other concepts, as meanings expand and then are resolved. The enactments are characteristic of *King Lear,* and the concepts are involved in its tragic resolution.

As C. J. Sisson and others have indicated, the first scene dramatizes the great injustice done Cordelia.[49] Primarily, Lear fails to recognize and reward true love and service. Among other considerations, Shakespeare's development of the characters of France and Kent makes this clear.[50] Lear is also one who has "ever but slenderly known himself." As Paul A. Jorgensen points out, the Renaissance meaning of "to know oneself" carried with it overtones suitable to modern psychology and involved, for Lear, a number of insights, including an understanding of what love really means and a knowledge of what it is to be a man.[51] An understanding of one aspect of love and a knowledge of what it is to be a man might also be subsumed in justice, and from Lear's initial violation of that cardinal virtue, there will be developed other apprehensions and emotions related to this complex of ideas and to Shakespeare's portrayal of his central figure.[52]

As it has been indicated, Shakespeare begins to modify his portrayal of a proud king and angry father as he dramatizes Lear at Albany's castle and Lear entering Gloucester's castle and seeing Kent in the stocks. As John E. Hankins has pointed out, the Psalmist, no less than Lear, considered the ingratitude of children "an unnatural aberration from universal laws," and as Miss E. Catherine Dunn has indicated, in both a pagan and a Renaissance world, ingratitude was considered the greatest of injustices.[53] After the division of the kingdom, those who are aligned against Lear and Gloucester violate the natural bonds of justice, and in spite of a public contract entered into at the center of a kingdom, Lear is stripped of his ceremonious necessities by an abhorrent ingratitude.[54]

In such a context, when Lear pours forth the torrents of his wrath, he is acting as King James counselled his son to act whenever he found "a notable iniurie." Lear wishes to be touched with "noble anger" and not to be overcome by grief. With the tears that stain his cheek, his grief would then become "the whetstone of his sword." [55] But he does not know that he has a sword. He is unaware of the forces of Cordelia and France, and he does not know of the thirty-five or thirty-six knights whose actions will deny the Fool's adage about the great wheel. As a result, Lear's anger has become anguish, and this archetypal figure is becoming the prodigal father. The Fool's verses about "fathers who wear rags" reminds one of this, as do Cordelia's later lines:

> And wast thou fain, poor father,
> To hovel thee with swine and rogues forlorn,
> In short and musty straw? [56]

Yet to Cornwall, as Lear is "locked out," he is simply "the old man." From more than one point of view, Shakespeare indicates that we are meant to follow Gloucester, Kent, and the nameless Gentleman and to protest what is happening.[57] At the same time, as Lear refuses to submit to a monstrous ingratitude that respects power only, he calls upon the gods for patience. It is an absolute, not a ceremonious, necessity for him; and the concept of patience will unfold into different patterns of thought during scenes that dramatize Lear and Gloucester in their agony.

Again I find historical scholarship helpful. Patience might be one of the four attributes of fortitude. The two active attributes of this cardinal virtue were manifested usually in prosperity and may be designated roughly as magnificence and, then, confidence or trust or magnanimity. Fortitude's passive attributes, manifested especially in adversity, were patience and perseverance. Thus, in spite of a slight disagreement by recent critics, the patience spoken of in *King Lear* does not need to be either Stoic or Christian. It can be both. In explanations of the cardinal virtues, discussions of patience were buttressed by classical, Biblical, medieval, and contemporary citations. It was an ethical commonplace and an eternal verity, and it is treated in this manner by such writers as Elyot, La Primaudaye, and William Leighton. In their discussions of fortitude, as in Shakespeare's dramas, it might be pointed out that men cannot be Stoical stocks, and into those elucidations of the four parts of fortitude, admonitions against suicide found their way, as they had into earlier Morality plays.[58]

In adversity, Lear strives to achieve patience and insists that he will endure, even as he perseveres in balancing offense with retribution as regards both his daughters and himself. But when he sends the Fool into the hovel, Lear also shows a magnanimity comparable to that shown by Julius Caesar. On a plain during a great storm Caesar sent one of his captains who was ill at ease into a peasant's hut, the only shelter available. According to La Primaudaye, Caesar thereby surmounted the weakness of his body by the magnanimity of his heart.[59] Quite fittingly, then, Lear never gives way to despair. In the scenes that follow, intensify, and anticipate Lear's enactments, Gloucester does attempt to commit suicide. He is saved from despair by Edgar, and although Gloucester falls into "ill thoughts again," he admits that one must endure. Patience and endurance are concepts permeating these enactments. If men cannot achieve the "free and patient thoughts" whereby they can bear affliction and, in Sidney's words, all else that "the foolish world may lay upon" them, yet they must endure "Their going hence, even as their coming hither:/ Ripeness is all." As J. V. Cunningham demonstrates, the metaphor ending the line "shifts our point of view from a man's attitude toward death, from the 'readiness' of Hamlet and 'Men must endure' of the first part of Edgar's speech, to the absoluteness of the external process of Providence, on which the attitude depends." [60]

According to Alvin B. Kernan, the attempted suicide of Gloucester and the awakening of Lear when he is reunited with Cordelia represent, respectively, the allegorical and the symbolic modes of reconfirming "traditional views of the values and meaning of life." [61] From a different point of view, I shall return to Lear's free and patient thoughts in adversity. Before then, vistas of mankind's delirious guilt and suffering have been revealed, but so have affirmations of man's struggle for justice and for fortitude and man's realization of a humanity common to both wretches and kings. Anyone who had read the *Governor,* as Shakespeare probably had, would know that a realization of man's common humanity was subsumed in justice and led to *caritas.* A ruler must know himself, that is, he must know that he is "verely a manne, compacte of soule and body, and in that all other men be equall vnto" him. The governor "shal also by the same rule know all other men, and shall nedes loue them . . . ." The man of fortitude, as Leighton and others indicated, also showed benevolence by giving alms and relieving the poor.[62] These concepts permeate Lear's prayer after the Fool's entrance into the hovel, just as they permeate Gloucester's giving his purses to Tom.

As a consequence, enactments involving justice, attributes of fortitude, and their relationship to man's common humanity qualify Lear's bidding the winds blow the earth into the sea and his calling upon the thunder to "Strike flat the thick rotundity o' th' world!/ Crack Nature's moulds, all germans spill at once/ That makes ingrateful man!" Because of his own manifest guilt, the "close pent-up guilts" of others, and especially because of the great injustice of ingratitude, Lear would have things "change or cease." This varies from Macbeth's willingness to have "nature's germans tumble all together,/ Even till destruction sicken." But even if the speeches were not different, Lear's magnanimous gesture and his prayer should keep any apprehension of his desire from being described as "nihilistic." This king now knows that he is but a man, exposed to feel what wretches feel, and the prayer itself is a great deal more than "nothing"—even though man physically is a "poor, bare, forked animal."

Similarly, I believe, a few critics—most noticeably some concerned with rites or maimed rites—misinterpret the desire of both Lear and Gloucester to shake their superflux to others. What is expressed is not so much a vision of a society never achieved, as it is a representation of the actions of magnificent and magnanimous men, who live, as all men must, in a harsh world filled with inevitable inequities. *Caritas* permeates these particular revelations. To say this is not to deny that the drama extends to its recipient vast reaches of agony, of natural calamity, and especially of human viciousness. In the complex development of Shakespeare's enactments, the one is the corollary of the other.[63] Constantly the apprehensions of a recipient are stretched in opposite directions, as if he, too, were on the rack of Lear's world.

As L. C. Knights, for example, has indicated, the idea of justice continues to unfold until it reaches the ambiguity of "None does offend, none, I say none; I'll able 'em." He has referred to the *reductio ad absurdum* of justice in the mock trial and to Lear's "weighing of retribution against offense." Knights then writes,

> "None does offend" because we are all as bad as each other. That is one sense. But because at more than one point Lear has now admitted his own guilt and involvement, there is a bridge to the second sense; "none does offend" because at the most fundamental level of all no one has a right to condemn. And what is held in tension is not only two senses but two basic attitudes—utter revulsion ("Give me an ounce of civet, good apothecary, To sweeten my imagination"), on the one hand: on the other an unconditional and unquestioning charity. . . .

Underlying the two extremes, we might add, is the idea of man's common humanity. From this enactment one is then carried forward "alert and engaged" to the immediately succeeding scene when "all forms of proportionate justice" are brushed aside by the four words that answer an awakened Lear: [64]

>   . . . for your sisters
> Have, as I do remember, done me wrong:
> You have some cause, they have not.
> *Cordelia.*   No cause, no cause.

In the imaginative and emotional drive of the tragedy, the concepts with which we have been concerned reach climactic moments and then are resolved into other apprehensions. With the defeat of Cordelia's forces, Gloucester's "free and patient thoughts" become "ill thoughts again"; but in the immediately succeeding scene Lear's struggle for fortitude reaches a climax. For the second time in the drama an audience sees Cordelia weep, and it is then that Lear describes how they "will sing like birds i' th' cage." The struggle for patience, which ten lines earlier became endurance and ripeness only, now becomes a tranquility that transcends adversity. It is comparable to the tranquility spoken of by Boethius' Mistress Philosophy and comparable also to that achieved by Cicero's best souls.[65]

At the same time, the ground is laid for the resolution of this climax into another one. To D. A. Traversi, the "shadow of the way of the world" falls across this scene.[66] In the enactment, I submit, there is more than a shadow of the world. The joyous and enduring contentment of a love of blessing and forgiveness is pitted against the "packs and sects of great ones/ That ebb and flow by th' moon." Edmund, in command of the guard surrounding these prisoners, is certainly one of those great ones, and it is his command that interrupts Lear's consolation just as those transitory packs are mentioned. As a consequence, by the enactment there is created once more a mutual and an uncompromising opposition, not simply between Lear's fortitude in adversity and the factions of worldlings, but also between his fortitude and an almost perdurable viciousness. From this, the events that take place in prison develop. As Lear speaks, an enduring union that can be shattered only by "a brand from heaven" also exists with the "good years" that will devour Goneril and Regan "flesh and fell." There will be no rejoicing, however, when the two sisters have been destroyed by their own evil prosperity. Only then will there be weeping. An uncompromising opposition but yet a natural affection had been expressed briefly when, at Gloucester's castle, Lear promised to trouble Goneril no further (2. 4. 221–23). Now the climax of Lear's fortitude in adversity repeats but intensifies the earlier situation.

What has just been pointed out contributes greatly to the restless nature of *King Lear,* and it seems to me that any critic who would analyze the work as a whole must consider its ceaseless movement. The swift current of events is reported or dramatized in relatively short scenes. Minor and nameless characters thrust themselves upon one's attention. Two love triangles emerge suddenly. Throughout the drama action swiftly follows resolution. This restlessness is much more apparent in *Lear* than in *Richard II,* where Shakespeare also dramatized the Abasement of the Proud King. Only Albany hesitates in *Lear.* The rapidity with which will leads to action, the shifting and unexpected results of action,[67] the sudden appearances of unexpected characters and of new relationships, the mingling of wisdom and folly, and the shifting patterns of thought never allow an audience to remain on settled ground for any length of time. Nothing illustrates this more clearly than Shakespeare's conclusion.

One other consideration probably should be kept in mind when one turns to that conclusion. As it has been indicated, in *King Lear,* more than in Shakespeare's other tragedies, the conflict is within society and arises from what human relatedness means to individuals. Miss Gardner writes that "What we honour and what moves us in Lear is his vulnerability," [68] and in a world of human relatedness vulnerability is inescapable. Edgar's feigned madness increases when his father is involved in the action, but Edgar came to Gloucester's mind though his mind was "then scarce friends with him":

> . . . I lov'd him, friend,
> No father his son dearer. . . .

Because of Edmund, Goneril poisons her sister and kills herself, and Regan is tormented by the thought that Edmund may have been "conjunct/ And bosom'd" in her sister's "forfended place." "Down from the waist they are Centaurs," but their consuming lust is for another human and that "dark and secret place" to which "strange œilliads" lead.[69] Human relatedness animates the "monolithic simplicity" of the characters. It also complements and qualifies their abstract nature. The villainous "whoreson," who had been kept in foreign parts, finally rejoices that yet he was beloved. An audience sees Cordelia weep when she and Lear are prisoners. She is "a queen/ Over her passion," but as a loving daughter she is neither outside nor above Fortune. As far as Lear is concerned, the benevolence which "is proprely called charite" and which subsumes or is subsumed in justice gives way to the intense and fervent love between him and Cordelia.[70] This is the positive aspect of human love and service that Shakespeare emphasizes as he approaches man's ultimate vulnerability.

Nearly all critics agree that by the end of the fourth act something like a redemption, or metamorphosis, of Lear has occurred,[71] but a Christian interpretation of the drama based upon an extended analogy between Cordelia and Christ seems to me to neglect what has just been pointed out. From viciousness, natural calamities, and human agony, values and concepts emerge that are inseparable from man's involvement with man. Any general pattern of Christian redemption, be it unbaptized and mythic or reduced to a ritualistic repetition, represents most inadequately the apprehensions that arise from ideas permeating the action. The world of King Lear is a pagan one.[72] Although its values are magnified and are those of the Christian Renaissance, they are thoroughly human. They are also inseparable from a Christian pessimism about the nature of man.[73] It seems to me, then, that an analysis of the work as a whole leads to a conclusion which recognizes the conflicting apprehensions arising from the drama but relates those apprehensions to the human condition and to the basic emotions and traditional values of life.

For reasons that are much the same, I believe other critics extend their apprehensions too far in the opposite direction, especially when they see in the conclusion an "ultimate negation" or a vision of a burial place, a shambles, and an imbecile universe. The final scene cannot be locked within any one concept. Even a critic who insists that no moral belief can support Shakespeare's conclusion writes that values, nevertheless, remain.[74] In its conclusion the drama is as restless as ever. The final lines, however, express emotions into which the tragedy is resolved, for Shakespeare has provided us with a speaking audience on the stage. By considering their apprehensions and emotions, we again may be able to grasp what is essential with some degree of firmness.

Before Lear's final entrance, as many have pointed out, justice permeates the action once more, but its context has been widened. Justice in man's relationship to man is supplanted by a judicial combat. Edmund's wheel comes full circle, and Edgar comments upon the course of celestial justice as it also has affected his father. For Gloucester, darkness has led to darkness.[75] Then, with an intensified shock—provided by the Gentleman crying for help as he enters with a bloody knife—Lear's lines about evil destroying itself come true, and the deaths of Goneril and Regan also are spoken of as a judgment of the heavens. As will be true of Edmund, those sisters have died offstage, and one remembers Giraldi Cinthio's statement that deaths "come about behind the scenes, because they are not introduced for commiseration but for the sake of justice."[76] In Shakespeare's words, "This judgment of the heavens, that makes us tremble,/ Touches us not with pity." Like Edgar after the mock trial, Albany now speaks as if he were both critic and audience. Pretty clearly, Shakespeare is thinking of the tradition in which tragedy was said to stir "the affects of admiration and commiseration." At the sudden justice apparent in the death of the vicious sisters, there is a fearful wonder, but not the wonder, the startled admiration, the "shocked limit of feeling," which is aroused in conjunction with woe or commiseration.[77] These last emotions are stirred by the final, central spectacle.

Shakespeare, nevertheless, works justice into his conclusion again, and it is once more a justice that involves man's relationship to man. The justice that Albany at first would effect is the restoration of Lear. Friends will then be rewarded and foes punished. But when the central spectacle has run its course, there is a resurgence of *caritas*. Albany resigns any claim to the kingdom in favor of the "friends" of his "soul" who have endured from the beginning in love and service. Concern for the "general woe" of a "gor'd state" supplants retribution. As our myth critics remind us, a transformation of the life of the community hovers about Albany's resignation, but these "rites" are not so much "maimed" as they are harmonious with an earlier metaphoric process. More important, Albany's act of charitable justice in a world of human relatedness results from the final emotional and imaginative thrust in Shakespeare's re-creation of the old Lear story.

Upon Lear's entrance with Cordelia in his arms, the apprehensions of an audience that had just seen and heard about acts of celestial justice are stretched suddenly in the opposite direction. No judgment of the heavens has intervened for Cordelia, and those on stage are overwhelmed by what they see:

> Howl, howl, howl! O! you are men of stones:
> Had I your tongues and eyes, I'd use them so
> That heaven's vault should crack. She's gone for ever.

What unfolds in its entirety is paramount—not simply as it is expressed by words but as it is expressed by the mass, the proportion, and the action of a spectacle thrust upon both audiences. As his lines tell us, Lear encounters a helpless amazement. The spectators on stage are "Stone-still, astonish'd with this deadly deed." [78] Shakespeare preserves this basic situation, and the attention of all is constantly and ultimately focused upon what Miss Gardner has called a secular *Pietà*. Not to recognize this, I submit, is to stand "aloof from the entire point." The inscrutable relationship between the gods and men is overpowered by this "spectacle of love and grief and innocence dead." [79]

As the central spectacle runs its course, Shakespeare's variation from the old tale is emphasized for anyone who might remember Holinshed's cut illustrating Cordelia's suicide with a dagger. Cordelia did not despair. Nor did Lear. With an astonishing vigor he killed the slave hanging his daughter. Although the rack of this tough world has now caused Lear to lose his "free and patient thoughts," he nevertheless endures; and as his request for a mirror, his joy at a stirring feather, and his thinking he hears a faint voice show, he endures with hope.

Lear's age and his troubles have spoiled a vigor in combat that might have saved Cordelia. But that Lear is "old now,/ And these same crosses spoil" him is also applicable to the fact of his "ripeness." [80] The simple knowledgeable statement anticipates another climactic moment, since death is common to all men. As with Gloucester, and to a lesser degree with Kent, this king is but a man whose heart is finally unable to withstand being stretched between two extremes. All knew that a contraction of the heart caused by great grief could be fatal, and its expansion by joy or hope was a similar commonplace.[81]

As they have watched the central spectacle, the audience on stage has felt a grief so "cheerless, dark, and deadly" that the sight has seemed an image of a doom when all shall die. Kent has attempted to intrude into the spectacle, but because of Lear's preoccupation with Cordelia, those on stage vainly present themselves to the king. The drama, however, is not resolved until Lear's death, and then Kent, Albany, and Edgar again express their emotions. If Lear dies believing that Cordelia lives, they do not begrudge him that illusion nor do they draw any inference from it.[82] Lear should not be tortured further, and when Kent expresses that belief, he also uses language suitable to the enactment and to Renaissance criticism. What he has felt about Lear "upon the rack of this tough world" is compressed into the statement that "The *wonder* is he hath endur'd so long." Albany's reaction is that resurgence of *caritas* whereby the final lines are left to Edgar; and when Edgar speaks, even as regal authority is transferred, woe and wonder demand expression.

Bacon wrote that in contrast with reason, poetry submits the "shows of things to the desires of the mind." This tragedy denies the precept. Its conclusion, like Bacon's reason, "doth buckle and bow the mind into the nature of things." *King Lear,* nevertheless, achieves "a more ample greatness" than nature ordinarily provides.[83] Lear's words about his spoiled age stir one's memory of Lear praying in the storm or consoling Cordelia, and among other considerations the final lines spoken by the ruler of a reunited kingdom express commiseration and repeat the "wonder" of Lear's endurance:

> The weight of this sad time we must obey;
> Speak what we feel, not what we ought to say.
> The oldest hath borne most: we that are young
> Shall never see so much, nor live so long.[84]

In *King Lear,* "great winds of suffering" "howl through the world," as Miss Nowottny phrases it,[85] but a wondrous endurance has sustained Lear's victory and defeat. Edgar's lines conclude one of Shakespeare's themes and accord with Philip W. London's conclusion that Lear is perhaps "the most monumental personage in all literature." [86] The present interpretation of those lines also harmonizes with the conclusions of

Maynard Mack, the critic whose words began this essay:

> Tragedy never tells us what to think; it shows us what we
> are and may be. And what we are and may be was never,
> I submit, more memorably fixed upon a stage than in
> this kneeling old man whose heartbreak is precisely the
> measure of what, in our world of relatedness, it is possi-
> ble to lose and possible to win. The victory and the defeat
> are simultaneous and inseparable.

> When we come crying hither, we bring with us the badge
> of all our misery; but it is also the badge of the vulnera-
> bilities that give us access to whatever grandeur we
> achieve.[87]

Notes

[1] Maynard Mack, *"King Lear" in Our Time* (Berkeley, 1965), p. 3.

[2] Twenty-one years ago Robert Bechtold Heilman signed the Fore-
word to *This Great Stage: Image and Structure in "King Lear,"* (Baton
Rouge, La., 1948). What was then an example of the "new criticism"
has become a landmark in the appreciation of the artistic integrity of
this drama. Also in 1947, Moody E. Prior's discussion of *Lear* was
published: *The Language of Tragedy* (New York), pp. 74–93. W. H.
Clemen's study of Shakespeare's imagery had appeared earlier: *Shake-
speares Bilder* (Bonn, 1936). It was revised and augmented later: *The
Development of Shakespeare's Imagery* (Cambridge, Mass., 1951).
One might also mention George R. Kernodle, "The Symphonic Form
of *King Lear*," *Elizabethan Studies and Other Essays in Honor of
George F. Reynolds* (Boulder, Colo., 1945), pp. 185–91. Other studies
of Shakespeare's language and themes will be cited. As a result of these
many discussions, Bradley's strictures are seldom mentioned. See the
Introduction to *King Lear*, ed. Kenneth Muir (Cambridge, Mass.,
1959), pp. xlviii–li. This is the text used here. A survey of trends in the
criticism of *Lear* during the preceding twenty-five years is provided by
R. W. Zandvoort: *"King Lear": The Scholars and the Critics,* Medede-
lingen der Koninklijke Nederlandse Akademie van Wetenschappen,
Afd. Letterkunde, Nieuwe Reeks, XIX. 7 (Amsterdam, 1956).

[3] The tragedy presents a "new strategy of culture and power," resulting from the way in which the age was "poised between medieval corporate experience and modern individualism" (Marshall McLuhan, *The Gutenberg Galaxy* [Toronto, 1962], pp. 1–17). From such a point of view *King Lear* is a social document rather than a complex work of art. Although such an approach is fairly constant, it does not constitute a major emphasis in the criticism of the tragedy during the past twenty years. For recent comparable studies—with a Marxist emphasis, however—see Mohit Sen, "Betwixt Damnation and Impassioned Clay: The Dialectics of *King Lear*," *Osmania Journal of English Studies*, IV (1964), 77–88, or Hildegard Schuman, *"König Lear,"* *Shakespeare-Jahrbuch*, C/CI (1964/1965), 192–207.

[4] Bradley, *Shakespearean Tragedy* (New York, 1937), p. 285; Chambers, *King Lear, The First W. P. Ker Memorial Lecture* (Glasgow, 1940).

[5] See, for example, John F. Danby, *Shakespeare's Doctrine of Nature: A Study of "King Lear"* (London, 1949) and " 'King Lear' and Christian Patience," *Cambridge Journal,* I (1948), 305–20, reprinted in *Poets on Fortune's Hill* (London, 1952); J. C. Maxwell, "The Technique of Invocation in 'King Lear,' " *MLR,* XLV (1950), 142–47; L. C. Knights, *"King Lear* and the Great Tragedies," *The Age of Shakespeare,* ed. Boris Ford (London, 1955), p. 232; Roy W. Battenhouse, "Shakespearean Tragedy: A Christian Interpretation," *The Tragic Vision and the Christian Faith,* ed. Nathan A. Scott, Jr. (New York, 1957), pp. 61–62. To James L. Rosier, for example, the drama is implicitly Christian through its logic that substantiates living in accordance with reason, custom, law, restraint: "The Lex Aeterna and *King Lear*," *JEGP,* LIII (1954), 574–80. Emphasizing the universality and power of evil and hence of deep human pain, H. B. Charlton nevertheless believes that there is an "underlying assumption" that "goodness somehow triumphs," though it pays a heavy mortal cost: *Shakespearean Tragedy* (Cambridge, Eng., 1961), pp. 215–16 (printed first in 1948).

[6] Irving Ribner, *Patterns in Shakespearian Tragedy* (London, 1960), pp. 116–17.

[7] Harold S. Wilson, *On the Design of Shakespearian Tragedy* (Toronto, 1957), pp. 208–9.

[8] John Wain, *The Living World of Shakespeare* (New York, 1964), p. 173.

[9] M. D. H. Parker, *The Slave of Life: A Study of Shakespeare and the Idea of Justice* (London, 1955), p. 135.

[10] John Vyvyan, *The Shakespearian Ethic* (London, 1959), pp. 204–5.

[11] Charles Jasper Sisson, *Shakespeare's Tragic Justice* (Scarborough, Ont., 1961), pp. 75–6.

[12] Virgil K. Whitaker, *The Mirror Up To Nature: The Technique of Shakespeare's Tragedies* (San Marino, Cal., 1965), p. 240. See also John M. Lothian, *"King Lear": A Tragic Reading of Life* (Toronto, 1949), p. 27; George Ian Duthie's Introduction to his edition of *King Lear* (Cambridge, Eng., 1960), pp. l–li; or R. W. S. Mendl, *Revelation in Shakespeare* (London, 1964), pp. 152–59. Although Thomas McFarland argues that the play is "not reducible to Christian coordinates," his discussion of reduction "to the brink of nothingness" and of renewal in *King Lear* falls, in general, into this category: *Tragic Meanings in Shakespeare* (New York, 1966), pp. 127–71. As far as the logic of the drama is concerned, even an existential and a Jungian interpretation can be included here: David Horowitz, *Shakespeare: An Existential View* (New York, 1965), pp. 82–6; James Kirsch, *Shakespeare's Royal Self* (New York, 1966), pp. 269–70, 293, 318–19. James V. Baker's article, "An Existential Examination of *King Lear*," *College English*, XXIII (1962), 546–50, falls less easily into this category than does the discussion by Horowitz.

[13] Wilson, *Six Tragedies of Shakespeare* (New York, 1929), p. 46; Knight, *Principles of Shakespearean Production* (New York, 1936), p. 231; Fraser, *Shakespeare's Poetics in Relation to "King Lear"* (London, 1962), p. 127.

[14] *Shakespearean Tragedy and the Elizabethan Compromise* (New York, 1957), pp. 173–86. For similar emphases before and after 1957, see Geoffrey L. Bickersteth, *The Golden World of "King Lear,"* Annual Shakespeare Lecture of the British Academy (London, 1947); Robert Speaight, *Nature in Shakespearean Tragedy* (London, 1955), pp. 103, 120, 129–30; Terence Hawks, *Shakespeare and the Reason* (London, 1964), pp. 192–93; Martin Lings, *Shakespeare in the Light of Sacred Art* (New York, 1966). Lear also has been called "a self-image" and a symbol of God, as well as a Lucifer figure at the play's beginning: Danby, *Nature,* pp. 177–78, 180; Abraham Schechter, *"King Lear": Warning or Prophecy* (Brooklyn, N.Y., 1956); Honor M. V. Matthews, *Character and Symbol in Shakespeare's Plays* (London, 1962), p. 144.

[15] Zandvoort, p. 241. Roland Mushat Frye argues that Christian doctrine in the dramas is consistently anthropocentric: *Shakespeare and Christian Doctrine* (Princeton, 1963). He also suggests (p. 51)

that one of Christianity's "greatest contributions . . . to Shakespearean drama" may have been its recognition that life denies a prudential morality. Reference to Lear and the Greek hero constitutes part of the argument in Richard B. Sewall's *The Vision of Tragedy* (New Haven, 1959), p. 73. See also Sylvan Barnet, "Some Limitations to a Christian Approach to Shakespeare," *ELH*, XXII (1955), 81–92; G. R. Elliott, "Shakespeare's Christian, Dramatic Charity," *Theology*, LVI (1953), 459–63; Philip Gray, "Christian Tragedy and Shakespeare," *Claremont Quarterly*, IX. iv (1962), 29–39.

[16] Schücking, *Character Problems in Shakespeare's Plays* (New York, 1922), pp. 185–90; Chambers, *Shakespeare: A Survey* (London, 1925), pp. 246–47. Although their conclusions are not cited in the paragraphs that follow immediately, in this general category one might place such diverse works as Clifford Leech, *Shakespeare's Tragedies and Other Studies in Seventeenth Century Drama* (New York, 1950), pp. 7–11, 13–14; George Orwell, *Shooting an Elephant and Other Essays* (London, 1950), pp. 49–50; and John Peter, *Complaint and Satire in Early English Literature* (Oxford, 1956), pp. 211–12.

[17] *The Dream of Learning* (Oxford, 1951), pp. 80, 92–3. For an emphasis upon Shakespeare's exploration "in terms of a paradox," see Geoffrey Bush, *Shakespeare and the Natural Condition* (Cambridge, Mass., 1956), pp. 127–28, also 118–21.

[18] *The Tragic Sense in Shakespeare* (New York, 1960), e.g., pp. 181–82.

[19] G. B. Harrison, *Shakespeare's Tragedies* (London, 1951), pp. 159, 183; T. B. Tomlinson, *A Study of Elizabethan and Jacobean Tragedy* (Cambridge, Eng., 1964), p. 38. This emphasis is repeated, for example, by Minas Savvas, "*King Lear* as a Play of Divine Justice," *College English*, XXVII (1965/1966), 560–62.

[20] Harrison, p. 183; J. K. Walton, "Lear's Last Speech," *Shakespeare Survey*, XIII (1960), 11–9; Tomlinson, p. 38; Northrup Frye, *Fools of Time, The Alexander Lectures, 1966* (Toronto, 1967), pp. 114–15. See also John D. Rosenberg, "King Lear and his Comforters," *Essays in Criticism*, XVI (1966), 135–46.

[21] *Shakespeare: "King Lear,"* Studies in English Literature, No. 15, ed. David Daiches (London, 1963), p. 60, and Brooke's "The Ending of *King Lear*," *Shakespeare, 1564–1964,* ed. Edward A. Bloom (Providence, R.I., 1964), p. 87.

[22] "The Catharsis of King Lear," *Shakespeare Survey*, XIII (1960), 4, 10.

[23] For example, out of "nothing" "comes nothing less than all"

(Richmond Y. Hathorn, *Tragedy, Myth, and Mystery* [Bloomington, Ind., 1962], p. 194). Looking "on Cordelia's lips for something," Lear "finds again 'nothing' " (Norman N. Holland, *The Shakespearean Imagination* [New York, 1964], pp. 257, 259–60). See also Andrew Riemer, "King Lear and the Egocentric Universe," *Balcony: The Sidney Review,* No. 5 (1966), 33–42; Philip W. London, "The Stature of Lear," *University of Windsor Review,* I (1965), 173–86; Rosalie Colie, *Paradoxia Epidemica: The Renaissance Tradition of Paradox* (Princeton, 1966), pp. 461–81; etc.

[24] *Shakespeare Our Contemporary,* trans. Boleslaw Taborski (New York, 1964), p. 91.

[25] Mack, pp. 28–32, 38–40; Alfred Harbage, *Conceptions of Shakespeare* (Cambridge, Mass., 1966), pp. 72–75. Among other considerations that make Kott's criticism unsatisfactory is the fact that the societies in *Lear* and in the theater of the absurd differ greatly; see below and James L. Roberts, "The Role of Society in the Theater of the Absurd," *Literature and Society,* ed. Bernice Slote (Lincoln, Neb., 1964), pp. 229–40.

[26] Herbert Blau, "A Subtext Based on Nothing," *Tulane Drama Review,* VIII.ii (1963), 122–32; Mack, p. 36. For a different treatment of "nothing" and a conclusion similar to that which will be expressed here, see Sigurd Burckhardt, *"King Lear:* The Quality of Nothing," *Minnesota Review,* II (1961), 33–50. A useful survey of productions of *Lear* is provided by Esther Merle Jackson, *"King Lear:* The Grammar of Tragedy," *SQ,* XVII (1966), 25–39; see also Charles Landstone, "Four Lears," *Shakespeare Survey,* I (1948), 98–102; Mack, pp. 26–7; Lorraine Sherley, *"King Lear:* The Stage, Not the Closet," *Shakespeare 1964,* ed. Jim W. Corder (Fort Worth, 1965), pp. 71–9, especially.

[27] *"King Lear" and the Gods* (San Marino, Cal., 1966), pp. 179–82, 338.

[28] *The Story of Night* (London, 1961), pp. 8–9, 19, 135–47, 151, 153–54.

[29] *Character and Society in Shakespeare* (Oxford, 1951), pp. 108–20. In connection with the sentence that follows immediately, see Edwin Muir, *The Politics of "King Lear,"* *The Seventh W. P. Ker Memorial Lecture* (Glasgow, 1947) and R. C. Bald, " 'Thou, Nature, Art My Goddess': Edmund and Renaissance Free Thought," *Joseph Quincy Adams: Memorial Studies,* ed. James G. McManaway *et al.* (Washington, D.C., 1948), pp. 337–49.

[30] *Shakespeare Survey*, XV (1962), 111–24. See also O. B. Hardison, Jr., "Symbol and Myth: More Questions than Answers," *Bucknell Review*, XII. i (1964), 17–28.

[31] "Myth and Ritual Approach to Shakespearean Tragedy," *Centennial Review*, I, (1957), 153–54, reprinted in *The Agony and the Triumph* (East Lansing, 1964). See also Weisinger's "Myth, Method, and Shakespeare," *Jour. of General Education*, XVI (1964), 39–40.

[32] T. R. Henn, *The Harvest of Tragedy* (London, 1956), p. 86, and see pp. 154–55; Weisinger, *Cent. Rev.*, I, 160; Hapgood, "Shakespeare's Maimed Rites," *Centennial Review*, IX (1965), 494, 508.

[33] Hathorn, p. 178; Henn, pp. 83–8; Herbert Weisinger, "Myth and Ritual Approaches," *Shakespeare Newsletter*, XIV (1964), 28–9.

[34] Hathorn, p. 28.

[35] *Cent. Rev.*, IX, 494, 508.

[36] William Frost, "Shakespeare's Rituals and the Opening of *King Lear*," *Hudson Review*, X (1957–58), 577–85.

[37] Marvin Rosenberg, "The Lear Myth," read to English 5, MLA, New York Dec. 28, 1966; or see R. Hector Currie, "The Energies of Tragedy: Cosmic and Psychic," *Centennial Review*, XI (1967), 229–32. In his essay Currie ignores much that is explicit in Shakespeare's text in order to emphasize the concept that *Lear* is a tragedy of "psychic stress" in the context of an "archetypal myth of creation"; thus Lear's "final cry" is "one of horror."

[38] "King Lear," *Scrutiny*, XIX (1952), 130. The essay, printed in three parts, was reprinted but slightly condensed in *An Approach to Shakespeare* (Garden City, N.Y., 1956), pp. 181–213.

[39] Knights, *"King Lear* as Metaphor," *Further Explorations* (Stanford, 1965), pp. 169–85; Frye, pp. 116–20.

[40] See also "Historical Scholarship and the Interpretation of Shakespeare," *Further Explorations*, pp. 138–54. That one should be concerned with ideas that permeate the action has been expressed by others. Donald Stauffer, for example, writes of "judgments implicit or stated" in the outcome of the plots and of Shakespeare's "choric or touchstone figures": *Shakespeare's World of Images* (Bloomington, Ind., 1966), p. 369 (first printed in 1949). Reuben A. Brower suggests that "plot" is "the dramatic sequence perceived in the progress of meanings": "The Heresy of Plot," *English Institute Essays, 1951*, ed. Alan S. Downer (New York, 1952), p. 69.

[41] P. 58. See also one aspect of Heilman's conclusion. The "kinds of moral capacity" in Lear and Gloucester "are externalized in their

children" and "the saving perspective, which brings evil into focus, is possible to man even after he has made serious mistakes"—this is the play's "ultimate assertion" (p. 290). Thus Heilman's conclusion falls into our first general category, although it is not extended as far as is O. J. Campbell's emphasis on the Morality pattern in *Lear:* "The Salvation of Lear," *ELH,* XV (1948), 93–109. See also K. W. Salter, " 'Lear' and the Morality Tradition," *N&Q,* CXCIX (1954), 109–10.

[42] Northrop Frye, *Anatomy of Criticism* (Princeton, 1957), *e.g.,* pp. 99–102.

[43] Pp. 43–80. For similarities in Shakespeare's earlier plays, see also, Matthews, pp. 139–43.

[44] "The Two Techniques in *King Lear,*" *RES,* XVIII (1942), 1–26, reprinted in *Shakespeare and Spenser* (Princeton, 1950).

[45] For a general discussion of emblematic situations, see Fraser, pp. 1–16. The situation of Kent and Edgar is mentioned briefly (p. 14).

[46] *Further Explorations,* p. 179.

[47] Mack, p. 50.

[48] Muir, Introduction to *King Lear,* p. xlviii. See also Helen Gardner, *King Lear,* The John Coffin Memorial Lecture, 1966 (London, 1967), pp. 8–10.

[49] For example, Sisson, p. 91; Knights, *Further Explorations,* pp. 179–80. Dorothy C. Hockey, "The Trial Pattern in *King Lear,*" *SQ,* X (1959), 388–95.

[50] In addition, for a dramatic pun on *love,* with one meaning determined by the word derived from O. E. *lofian* ("praise," "estimate the value of"), see Terry Hawks, " 'Love' in *King Lear,*" *RES,* X (1959), 178–81, and, for example, Harold Skulsky's discussion, especially of the first scene, *"King Lear* and the Meaning of Chaos," *SQ,* XVII (1966), 3–17. See also Jonas A. Barish and Marshall Waingrow, " 'Service' in *King Lear,*" *SQ,* IX (1958), 347–55.

[51] *Lear's Self-Discovery* (Berkeley, 1967), p. 94 and throughout. One learned to know oneself through the tutorship of nature, of the harsh world, and of affliction, as well as by understanding one's passions and one's body. Others have only touched upon Jorgensen's central point: e.g., Sewell, pp. 83–5; Matthews, pp. 145–57. Edmund H. Creeth also points out that "a saving realization of one's error" differentiates Shakespeare's tragic heroes from typical Elizabethan ones: "Moral and Tragic Recognition," *Papers Michigan Acad. Science, Arts and Letters,* XLV (1960), 381–94.

[52] The relationship between justice and knowing oneself to be a man

is pointed out below. The law of nature might also be subsumed in justice: e.g. *Wilson's Arte of Rhetorique, 1560,* ed. G. H. Mair (Oxford, 1909), p. 32. Because of James's proposal to unite England and Scotland, one should mention also Lear's division of his kingdom and the chaos that results: John W. Draper, "The Occasion of *King Lear,*" *SP,* XXXIV (1937), 176–85; Ribner, pp. 118–19; Barbara Heliodora Carneiro de Mendonça, "The Influence of *Gorboduc* on *King Lear,*" *Shakespeare Survey,* XIII (1960), 41–8. For the wisdom and justice of Lear's original plan, however, see Harry V. Jaffa, "The Limits of Politics: An Interpretation of *King Lear,* Act I, Scene I," *American Political Science Review,* LI (1957), 405–27. See also G. R. Elliott, "The Initial Contrast in Lear," *JEGP,* LVIII (1959), 251–63; John W. Velz, "Division, Confinement, and the Moral Structure of *King Lear,*" *Rice University Studies,* LI. i (1965), 97–108. The articles by Jaffa and Elliott would qualify any view of Lear as a completely foolish old man and of the first scene as "a tissue of nonsense" or sheer myth—a view expressed, for example, by Frank O'Connor, *Shakespeare's Progress* (New York, 1960), p. 133.

[53] Hankins, "Lear and the Psalmist," *MLN,* LXI (1946), 88–90; Dunn, *The Concept of Ingratitude in Renaissance English Moral Philosophy* (Washington, D.C., 1946), pp. 13, 21–3, and throughout. See also Roland Frye, pp. 187–88.

[54] Lear's ceremonious necessities can be glossed by a passage in William Perkin's *The Whole Treatise of the Cases of Conscience.* The Puritan divine writes that goods and riches are necessary to nature and necessary to a "man's state, condition, and dignitte [*sic*]": *Works* (Cambridge, 1609), II, 144, col 2, C. See also Richard Hooker, *Works,* ed. John Keble *et al.* (Oxford, 1888), I, 239, 240; 217, 250–51.

[55] For Lear's anger, see *The Political Works of James I,* ed. Charles Howard McIlwain (Cambridge, Mass., 1918), p. 41; *Macbeth,* 4. 3. 228–29; Robert P. Adams, "King Lear's Revenges," *MLQ,* XXI (1960), 223–27. On the relationship between Lear's speech, ingratitude, and the storm, see E. Catherine Dunn, "The Storm in *King Lear,*" *SQ,* III (1952), 329–33, and Hankins, *MLN,* LXI, 88 (Psalms 144:4–8). On the relationship between Lear's speech and, in particular, the appearance of Mad Tom, see E. M. M. Taylor, "Lear's Philosopher," *SQ,* VI (1955), 364–65, and Dean Frye, "The Context of Lear's Unbottoning," *ELH,* XXXII (1965), 17–31.

[56] Note also Battenhouse, pp. 85–6; Robert E. Fitch, "Shakespeare:

The Uses of Religion," read to English 5, MLA, New York, Dec. 28, 1964; Susan Snyder, *"King Lear* and the Prodigal Son," *SQ,* XVII (1966), 361–39.

[57] See also E. A. Block, *"King Lear:* A Study in Balanced and Shifting Sympathies," *SQ,* X (1959), 499–512. I believe Block might have given more emphasis to the reaction of Albany when he learns the cause of Lear's anger and sees his grief (1. 4. 303–4, 307, 310–13, 321–22). Shakespeare's changing emphasis in the portrayal of Lear might evoke actualities, and not simply because of our modern social conscience. There were the generous but grievously mistreated Elizabethan and Jacobean fathers Ralph Hansby, Sir William Allen, and Brian Annesley of Lee with his Youngest-Best named Cordell. Sisson, pp. 80–3; Sir Gyles Isham, "The Prototypes of King Lear and His Daughters," *N&Q,* CXCIX (1954), 150–51.

[58] A Christian patience in *Lear* is advocated by Danby, *Cambg. Jour.,* I, 305–20. Stoicism and a harsh Stoic world is advocated by Hiram Haydn, *The Counter-Renaissance* (New York, 1950), pp. 636–51. In addition to Stoicism, McFarland refers to Gnosticism, Epicureanism, and a concept comparable to Spinoza's "good"; pp. 133–68. A grafting of Renaissance Stoicism upon traditional Christian piety and upon the Morality play is advocated by O. J. Campbell, *ELH,* XV, 93–109. See also Norman T. Pratt, "From Oedipus to Lear," *Classical Journal,* LXI (1965), 49–57. For further details related to the present emphasis upon English discussions of the cardinal virtues, see my "Lear, the King: A Preface to a Study of Shakespeare's Tragedy," *Medieval and Renaissance Studies,* ed. O. B. Hardison, Jr. (Chapel Hill, N.C., 1966), pp. 83–114. I cite that study here because I did not differentiate patience and endurance sufficiently. For despair and the temptation to suicide in five Morality plays, see William O. Harris, *Skeleton's Magnyfycence and the Cardinal Virtue Tradition* (Chapel Hill, 1965), pp. 121–26. Some of Mad Tom's lines anticipate the focal point of Gloucester's despair.

[59] *The French Academie* (London, 1618), pp. 111–12. This portion of the compilation had been published at various times since 1586.

[60] *Tradition and Poetic Structure* (Denver, Colo., 1960), p. 140. H. Rossiter-Smith points out a parallel in Cicero's *De Senectute.* "Ripeness is All," *N&Q,* CCX (1965), 97. For Sidney's words, see *Complete Works,* ed. Albert Feuillerat (Cambridge, Eng., 1922), II, 110.

[61] "Formalism and Realism in Elizabethan Drama: The Miracles in *King Lear,*" *Renaissance Drama,* IX (1966), 59–66.

[62] *The Boke Named the Gouernour* (London, 1537), pp. 164v–166r (III. 3). The pertinence of Elyot's first sentence to Lear's unbuttoning apparently is ignored by D. Frye, *ELH*, XXXII, 17–31. See also, Sir William Leighton, *Vertve Trivmphant* (London, 1603), stanzas 143 through 145, including one on prayer.

[63] See, for example, Barbara Everett, William Empson, Kenneth Muir, John F. Danby, Emrys Jones, John Holloway, "The New *King Lear*," *Critical Quarterly*, II (1960), 325–39; III (1961), 67–75, 167–68.

[64] *Further Explorations*, pp. 182–83. At the same time, as Traversi remarks, "insanity and fresh vision" are in juxtaposition. *Approach*, pp. 187–88. It seems to me that what Knights points out adequately answers those who would read Lear's lines of sexual horror back into his characterization and see Lear's interest as "ridiculous and sordid"; e.g., William Empson, *The Structure of Complex Words* (London, 1951), p. 138. The reference to Centaurs will be implicit in the later complex of meaning involving a wheel of fire, Ixion as the father of the Centaurs, and Lear with bestial daughters. As most critics realize the expanding meaning of the entire play is paramount.

[65] Interpretations comparable to the present one seem to be accepted generally. What is expressed is contentment, not resignation; and hence overtones of the pastoral appear in this anti-pastoral. See Mack, pp. 65–6. The present interpretation, I believe, answers adequately Hathorn, p. 193, or, for example, John M. Munro, "The Problem of Choice in *King Lear*," *South Atlantic Quarterly*, LXIII (1964), 243–44. Munro's "choice" also seems to be too far removed from the words of Shakespeare's text. See Robert K. Presson, "Boethius, King Lear, and 'Maystresse Philosophie,' " *JEGP*, LXIV (1965), 420; and Cicero, *Tusculan Disputations*, I. xvi–xxviii, xxx. Cicero's discussion also gives a non-Christian, and hence a universal, validity to Cordelia as a "soul in bliss" when Lear speaks of being bound upon a wheel of fire. That the tragedy was designed for universality is the argument of Winifred Nowottny, "Shakespeare's Tragedies," *Shakespeare's World*, ed. James Sutherland and Joel Hurstfield (London, 1964), pp. 48–78.

[66] *Approach*, p. 212.

[67] From a different point of view, Maynard Mack writes that the "inscrutability of the energies that the human will has power to release" is "assigned the whole canvas," pp. 96–7.

[68] P. 22.

[69] Also in contradiction of Empson's comment about Lear's "ridicu-

lous and sordid interest," note that the "sex horror of the play comes chiefly by way of the strongly expressed revulsion of the sympathetic characters from a self-evident foulness": Robert H. West, "Sex and Pessimism in *King Lear*," *SQ*, XI (1960), 57. See the comment below on Edgar's statement about celestial justice and Gloucester.

[70] The quotation is from Elyot's *Gouernour*, p. 121v: "Beneuolence, if it doo extende to a hole countreye or citie, is proprely called charite . . ." (II. 8).

[71] See, for example, as recent a critic as Marion Bodwell Smith, *Dualities in Shakespeare* (Toronto, 1966), pp. 40–1: "All the play is in these lines," i.e., 4. 7. 60–70.

[72] For those who can see no reason for the spelling "gods' " rather than "God's," see T. M. Parrott, " 'God's' or 'gods' in *King Lear*, V, iii, 17," *SQ*, IV (1953), 427–28.

[73] Although my emphasis varies from Kenneth Myrick's, see his "Christian Pessimism in *King Lear*," *Shakespeare, 1564–1964*, pp. 56–70.

[74] N. Brooke, *Shakespeare: "King Lear*," p. 60.

[75] "The punishment is exemplary like the act. The blindness is not what will follow from adultery, but what is implied in it. Darkness speaks to darkness": Mack, p. 70.

[76] Allan H. Gilbert, *Literary Criticism: Plato to Dryden* (Detroit, 1962), p. 257.

[77] The "affects" are so defined by Sidney: Gilbert, pp. 432, 459–61. See also Cunningham, pp. 142–63; Jasper Heywood's translation of *Troades*, 11. 1143, 1136–37, in *The Tenne Tragedies of Seneca* (Spenser Society, 1887), II, 118; and, for example, as regards *admiratio*, Bernard Weinberg, *A History of Literary Criticism in the Italian Renaissance* (Chicago, 1961), pp. 188, 239, 401, 489, 565, 752.

[78] *Rape of Lucrece*, 1. 1730.

[79] Pp. 27–8. If we are to follow Shakespeare's emphasis, even as we read his drama, it seems to me that we should not forget that *Lear* was written to be performed. It may be blasphemous from a detached point of view to protest any manifestation of the all-powerful gods, or of an omnipotent Deity, and to speak of one like Cordelia as being gone forever (Elton, p. 254). But this is a tragic drama, not an essay. Both Kent and Edgar had been "big in clamour" and Kent had "bellow'd out/ As he'd burst heaven." In the elevated language of Elizabethan and Jacobean tragedy, Lear's lines are a heightened cry of agony, introducing the woe and wonder of the final enactment. If any repre-

sentation of grief is convincingly human, surely this one is. Note how Shakespeare's prosody transforms "terms of common grief" into an "uncommon language"—including the thoroughly human pronunciation of Cordelia's name differently when Lear calls her a second time.

Corde/lia/ Corde/lia! Stay/ a lit/le. Ha!
What is't/ thou say'st?

Winifred M. T. Nowottny, "Some Aspects of the Style of *King Lear*," *Shakespeare Survey*, XIII (1960), 56–7. Although one may object to some of her interpretations (for example, that of Lear's prison speech), see also Betty Kantor Stuart, "Truth and Tragedy in *King Lear*," *SQ*, XVIII (1967), 167–80: ". . . there is relief in knowing the worst and hearing it expressed in the best possible manner" (p. 180). The importance of spectacle and prosody is illustrated constantly by John Russell Brown, *Shakespeare's Plays in Performance* (London, 1966), e.g., pp. 11–12, 15, 134–36. For Shakespeare's characteristic emphasis on the grieving character, see Horst Oppel, "Shakespeare und das Leid," *Shakespeare-Jahrbuch,* XCIII (1957), 38–81.

[80] The meaning is related to "Ripeness is all," and the statement is necessarily apprehended along with Lear's reference to a former vigor. These considerations are ignored, I believe, by those who speak of Lear's lines as expressing "the commission of a confirmed murder . . . and a final heroic vaunt," or who interpret the speech as showing vainglory: Elton, p. 259; Sears Jayne, "Charity in *King Lear*," *SQ*, XV (1964), 283–84. Among other considerations one cannot forget the completely sympathetic portrayal of Cordelia.

[81] La Primaudaye, pp. 466–67, 468; G. Smith, "A Note on the Death of Lear," *MLN,* LXX (1955), 403–4.

[82] See also Mack, p. 116. We cannot be sure that Lear dies believing Cordelia alive, but Shakespeare's technique, I believe, points in that direction. There is his characteristic triple preparation for what will be dramatized (the glass, the feather, the faint voice). The two extremes of grief and joy accord with the figure of the rack. From Lear's point of view, the final brief enactment repeats but intensifies his longer endurance unto joy (from 2. 4 through 5. 3. 26). Gloucester's death and Kent's trance anticipate Lear's death but vary from it in that Lear's belief is an illusion and his death is dramatized. Some critics argue that Lear never achieves wisdom or achieves too little too late. Others maintain that in the conclusion Shakespeare indicates how human experience destroys anyone who has tried to comprehend it all or who has seen through the world. Both points of view, I believe, move too

far from the words of the text: Keith Rinehart, "The Moral Background of *King Lear,*" *University of Kansas City Review,* XX (1953), 228; Warren Taylor, "Lear and the Lost Self," *College English,* XXV (1964), 509–13; James Land Jones, *"King Lear* and the Metaphysics of Thunder," *Xavier University Studies,* III (1964), 51–80; in contrast with Paul J. Alpers, *"King Lear* and the Theory of the 'Sight Pattern,' " *In Defense of Reading,* ed. Reuben A. Brower and Richard Poirier (New York, 1962) pp. 133–52; Isadore Traschen, "The Elements of Tragedy," *Centennial Review,* VI (1962), 215–29; Herbert Weisinger, "A Shakespeare All Too Modern?" *Arizona Quarterly,* XX (1964), 293–316.

[83] *Of the Advancement of Learning,* ed. G. W. Kitchin, Everyman's Library, No. 719 (London, New York, 1915), pp. 82–3. James, *Dream of Learning,* is concerned with Bacon as well as with *Hamlet* and *Lear.*

[84] For a defense of the reading in the Folio, which gives the lines to Edgar, see Muir's edition, p. 219, and Theodore C. Hoepfner, " 'We That Are Young,' " *N&Q,* CXCIX (1954), 110. Interpretations of the final lines as a "sort of hushed envy" or a "hope which is a benediction" contradict interpretations that refer to the lines as a "frail and hopeless flourish" or an expression of exhaustion: Empson, *Complex Words,* p. 157; Josephine Waters Bennett, "The Storm Within: The Madness of Lear," *SQ,* XIII (1962), 155; in contrast, for example, with Bush, p. 15; Holland, pp. 259–60; John Shaw, *"King Lear:* The Final Lines," *Essays in Criticism,* XVI (1966), 261–67. Once more, I believe we should stay as close to Shakespeare's words as possible.

[85] *Shakespeare's World,* p. 72.

[86] *Univ. Windsor Rev.,* I, 185.

[87] Mack, p. 117. See also Winifred M. T. Nowottny, "Lear's Questions," *Shakespeare Survey,* X (1957), 97; R. B. Sewall, p. 79; or, in part, William Rosen, *Shakespeare and the Craft of Tragedy* (Cambridge, Mass., 1960), p. 51.

PARADISE LOST

Irene Samuel

If the attacks mounted by Pound, Eliot, and Leavis against Milton's verse, and by A. J. A. Waldock and William Empson against his views, together with the answers they have elicited, did in fact preempt the field of comment on *Paradise Lost* as literary journalists assume they do, it would be simplicity itself to summarize the past quarter-century as a battle in which the issues were posed by Milton's antagonists and then met head on by Milton's defenders. The chief materials for such a survey are available in *Milton: a Collection of Critical Essays*, edited by Louis L. Martz (1966); they were most recently rehearsed by Patrick Murray in *Milton: the Modern Phase* (1967)—although Christopher Ricks had fairly ended the controversy over Milton's style (*Milton's Grand Style*, 1963) and Helen Gardner had pronounced it dead in the opening pages of *A Reading of Paradise Lost* (1965). Miss Gardner ought to have been right—and was, alas, wrong. Any number of writers will probably go on making capital of Milton's twentieth-century opponents.

Even omitting all such spurious controversies, we can hardly take into account all the pertinent work of the last twenty-five years. Bibliographies and such collections of essays as those by Frank Kermode (*The Living Milton*, 1960) and Arthur Barker (*Milton: Modern Essays in Criticism*, 1965) may tell more about trends than a survey can, and even they cannot suggest what is said in the lecture-halls and classrooms of several countries. Like other reports on trends, mine may falsely imply that what is printed constitutes the whole body of opinion. Moreover, this is not the place to deal with a great many valuable studies: the editions by Helen Darbishire (1952–5), Merritt Y. Hughes (1957, revising his 1935 edition), and Douglas Bush (1965), or the special work *On the Composition of Paradise Lost* by Allan H. Gilbert (1947), on *Milton's Imagery* by Theodore Banks (1950), on his diction by Edward S. LeComte (*Yet Once More*, 1953; *A Milton Dictionary*, 1961), and on *Milton's Grammar* by Ronald D. Emma (1964). From my survey I also exclude all work, including my own, that falls outside or does not illustrate main trends.

As the diatribes against *Paradise Lost* have fallen off, more critics evidently start from the assumption that Milton, a great conscious artist, achieved his intended effects. They agree less than ever on the intention, on the critical issues the poem raises. Six years ago Arthur Barker ("Recent Studies in the English Renaissance," *SEL* 1, 1961) could confidently say " 'heroism' . . . is still the central problem (as it is the central theme) of *Paradise Lost*." Milton studies have since shifted direction or revealed latent tendencies. Then it seemed that everyone must decide whether Satan was hero or fool, whether Adam, Christ, God, Milton himself, or the reader could be proved the hero of *Paradise Lost*. If an epic poem demands a hero, A. S. P. Woodhouse's solution ("Pattern in *Paradise Lost*," *UTQ* 22, 1953) was doubtless right: a joint Christ-Adam supplies the hero. Satan, though allowed some heroic qualities, is too patently neither central nor designed to hold our sympathies, and at best illustrates "the pagan heroic in its more primitive and amoral form." The Messiah, while clearly furnishing the standard of Christian heroism, has only a superhuman role within the action. Adam, the "man" of the opening phrase, though obviously the chief human agent, does little that can be called specifically heroic. Milton as his own hero was merely a weak joke; and making the reader the hero seemed just as unlikely to be a serious suggestion, until Stanley Fish worked the "harassed reader" through the poem in *Surprised by Sin* (1967). A poet as punitive as Fish makes Milton out to be was indeed demanding either heroism or masochism from his reader.

Perhaps the issue all along was rather the relation of *Paradise Lost* to the tradition of heroic poetry. That the question "Who is the hero?" was for a time discussed at such length suggests that commentators are determined to match the poem to their preconceptions. As the poem gets matched to an ever greater variety of preconceptions, only the question *"How shall we read it?"* could now summarize the central problem. Our era multiplies uncertainties, distrusts firm clear outlines. Under the impact of its preferred critical postulates, the subject and genre of *Paradise Lost* hardly remain fixed: commentary no longer unanimously grants that Paradise was lost, that Adam and Eve fell, or that Milton's is a heroic poem.

Is *Paradise Lost* the most epic of them all, the last possible epic, a nearly impossible fusion of epic conventions with a wholly unheroic theme, or a contradiction of the very terms it uses? And disagreements concern not only placing *Paradise Lost* in the epic genre. Readers differ also on whether the poem is the ultimate tragedy, or has rather—its tragic element localized more or less narrowly—the force of a *commedia*. With new estimates of the genre have gone new structural readings; and as genre, structure, and theme bear on one another, the central themes of *Paradise Lost* multiply. The relevance of the Christian tradition, in whole or in part, has been explored, as well as the relevance of Milton's own *Christian Doctrine,* sometimes to suggest that Milton organized

Paradise Lost as a declaration of Christian teaching, to set forth the whole celestial cycle, demonstrate divine Providence, or instruct the fallen reader in the way to the inner Paradise. For many such interpreters, the fall is unequivocally fortunate and the final books no tragic aftermath but the *telos* at which the whole aims. Those who take the *felix culpa,* the inner Eden, or victorious Providence as the central theme find in the last books, and especially in the exalted lines spoken by Adam on learning of his Redeemer, the crux of the whole. But such interpreters are not alone in giving new emphasis to the end. Along with Books X–XII, the middle third of the poem (Books V–VIII) has won fresh scrutiny, again with no unanimous conclusions on purpose and meaning.

Faced with the centrifugal positions maintained in the last twenty-five years, we are fortunate to have a sure starting point: in 1942 C. S. Lewis's *A Preface to Paradise Lost* set many of the questions that would occupy scholars for the next quarter-century. Taking issue with Milton's most eminent denigrators, as well as with such eminent defenders as Denis Saurat and E. M. W. Tillyard, Lewis asserted the propriety of the ritualistic style in *Paradise Lost* to its genre, secondary epic, rescued its theology from charges—and praises—of heresy, argued the agreement of its positions with central, traditional Christianity, and explained the whole action as turning on the Elizabethan doctrine of hierarchy or degree. If Lewis did not provide an entirely satisfactory reading, he cleared away some highly unsatisfactory misreadings. For a time, a flurry of answers continued to assert that Satan was the hero, however little Milton—and C. S. Lewis—admitted it; now only the rare eccentric argues for that view. Perhaps a naive reader here and there went on talking about the famous "organ voice"; the phrase has happily disappeared from currency in discussions of Milton's style. Even when Lewis could not entirely approve a part of the poem—the treatment of God in

Book III, say, or the presentation of future history in Books
XI–XII—and even when he exaggerated or misconstrued a
point, his comments were fructifying.

In large agreement with C. S. Lewis, Douglas Bush in
Paradise Lost in Our Time (1945) and John S. Diekhoff in
Milton's Paradise Lost (1946) explored the convictions Milton wrote into his poem. Diekhoff, accepting Milton's own
poetic and rhetorical theory as guidelines, established the logical coherence of the poem in chapters on Satan's evil, man's
guilt, God's justice, providence, and mercy, and the way of
virtue, as Milton conceived of them. Douglas Bush, out of his
comprehensive humane vision of the moods and predicaments
of the post-war years, read *Paradise Lost* as a poem very much
needed by our era, speaking pertinently on lasting issues of
ethics and politics. To Bush's later succinct treatment of the
poem in *English Literature in the Earlier Seventeenth Century,* especially in the revised edition of 1962, every student,
from freshman to advanced scholar, must constantly return to
regain perspective. In much the same way every student must
return to James Holly Hanford's *Milton Handbook* (4th ed.
1946) and to the preface and notes by Merritt Y. Hughes in
John Milton: Complete Poems and Major Prose (1957).

The Style

On the style of *Paradise Lost* C. S. Lewis satisfied few
readers long. Accepting the very qualities "new" critics objected to, Lewis argued that secondary epic properly seeks
large effects and therefore does not reward scrutiny of verbal
texture, that Milton rightly aimed to evoke stock responses
rather than to shape a language minutely and precisely revealing subtleties of thought. The "solemn" ritual style of *Paradise
Lost* does the poet's "thinking and poetizing" for him. Some

readers evidently agreed: C. M. Bowra (*From Virgil to Milton,* 1945) found the style all "on the same sublime level," and defended it as "cold, even inhuman"; and B. Rajan (*Paradise Lost and the Seventeenth Century Reader,* 1947), arguing that an epic style cannot be dramatic, that its proper virtues are clarity, force, assertion, simplicity, found *Paradise Lost* working its stately effects through sweep and accumulation in a style "stiff, homogeneous and architectural." But those who studied the detail of individual passages found a far greater variety and subtlety than such descriptions allowed for. Their persuasiveness is evident from Rajan's modification of his comments on "The Language of *Paradise Lost*" in his edition of Books I and II (1964).

In *Answerable Style* (1953) Arnold Stein, applying to *Paradise Lost* the criteria of the "new" critics, remarked that its style has at least three determinants: its relation to the grand style demanded of Renaissance epic, its relation through the specifically Christian epic to Scripture, and also its relation to the poet's declared aim of creating something as yet "unattempted." Milton's problem is to secure variety within a unified style; and Stein explored his success—through the use of ironies arising from the vast difference between Satan's perspective and God's providence, through the use of style to characterize speakers, through the constant play on "the reader's expectation . . . to secure . . . very precise effects." Stein might grant something like Lewis's position in saying that Milton does not have to think *about* his language, but can think *through* it, or in attributing to Milton's style "the conscious impersonality of a great artist"; his comments on the correspondence between sound and sense, the play of motion and arrested motion, "the mastery of perspective" throughout the poem in fact showed something different. So too Don Cameron Allen (*The Harmonious Vision,* 1954) might echo Lewis in explaining that Milton's visual images are to be grasped in the large with the reader supplying "the unexpanded terms of his description"; he had in fact shown something different in his explication of how Milton gets effects with imagery of light and motion. Indeed Stein and Allen between them have elicited a spate of studies, Stein on the subtle correspondence of style and meaning in *Paradise Lost,* Allen on the effects of light and dark, falling and rising motions, as these interweave to form significant patterns in the poetic texture.

In 1954, F. T. Prince's *The Italian Element in Milton's Verse* established the similarity between Milton's blank verse and the patterns evolved by Tasso and Della Casa, to show that their theory and practice determined much that had been thought peculiar to the diction, constructions, and prosody of *Paradise Lost.* Milton achieved what he intended: an artificial language that would combine with the magnificence Tasso demanded for heroic verse, the "vigorous freedom of Elizabethan English," a wide "range of verbal harmonies and contrasts" that could include "effects of bareness and simplicity" as well as "an incessant . . . verbal wit." The felicity with which the intricate word order creates emphasis and excitement, the sheer intellectual energy in the handling of language led Prince to conclude that "Miltonic diction is . . . but one aspect of a form of poetry in which everything is unified: matter, meaning, emotion, method."

Prince's conviction that the style of *Paradise Lost* is subtle, supple, and precise within its range of grandeur is supported by the work of Isabel Gamble MacCaffrey (*Paradise Lost as "Myth,"* 1959) and Roy Daniells (*Milton, Mannerism and Baroque,* 1963). Mrs. MacCaffrey demonstrates Milton's "centripetal method" of accumulating examples, expressive of recurrence and permanence in a universe composed of correspondences, to enrich the few dominant images of the archetypal world he is creating. As Mrs. MacCaffrey clarifies the methods by which Milton thickens the texture of his poem, Daniells clarifies the methods by which he preserves a Baroque unity through devices of "subordination, superimposition, merging, interaction, and dynamic flow."

For Christopher Ricks (*Milton's Grand Style,* 1963), the criteria of effectiveness proposed by Milton's chief denigrators are fully applicable to the style of *Paradise Lost.* Explicitly countering Lewis's defense of its ritual character, Ricks uses the work of Milton's eighteenth-century editors to elaborate the precision, variety, and flexibility with which Milton handles words, syntax, inversions, verse patterns, pauses, stresses —grammar and metrics in the widest sense—to achieve a style that meets the severest "standards of relevance and consistency." *Paradise Lost,* with only occasional lapses, shows an extraordinary command of "nervous energy, subtle involution, . . . and linguistic daring." The grand style proves superbly exact as well.

But what larger intentions these local precisions correspond to Ricks does not attempt to discuss. Miltonists, however, though they otherwise scarcely agree, generally insist that *Paradise Lost is* its meanings. The devices of style can only be estimated in relation to the large purposes of the poem, and indeed the large recognized purposes apparently determine what stylistic devices various scholars perceive. Thus Anne Davidson Ferry (*Milton's Epic Voice,* 1963), concerned with the narrative voice through whose inspired and compelling accents alone the reader hears all that he hears in *Paradise Lost,* finds the distinctive tone of that unique voice combining judgment and sympathy, heroism and lyricism in a "cool luminosity." For Stanley Fish, concerned with what befalls the "guilty" reader in his progress through the poem, the distinctive stylistic device is the "intangling" assured by traps of syntax, diction, metrical stress, and postponed explanations. Evidently until we agree on what *Paradise Lost* as a whole is and does, on where to locate its center, its core, we risk praising Milton for stylistic virtues he might have scorned and attributing to him subtle effects that contravene his deepest convictions.

The Center: Plot or Patterns

In 1942 C. S. Lewis could assume that the core of *Paradise Lost* is the fall of Adam and Eve, and argue that its central doctrine is the violation of degree on which their fatal disobedience turns. But Rajan, though he partly agreed, subordinated all the doctrine that the seventeenth-century reader would have expected—and found—to the balanced construction Milton invented. Rajan saw the action as dividing into two halves, each beginning with a destruction that is then contrasted with a creation. Many parallels link the destructive phases of the heavenly and earthly halves, somewhat fewer the constructive phases; the antitheses in each half between the creative and the destructive are most numerous. Thus *Paradise Lost*—while as an epic for its own time it uses convictions then universally accepted on hierarchy, order, Christian liberty, Christ as second Adam, and the struggle of Everyman against Satan—more important, creates "a symbolic pattern of repetition and recurrence" whose symmetry is "a token of ultimate order." If its theme is the violation of degree, its core is the Elizabethan habit of seeing analogies throughout the cosmos.

The shift of focus from central action to central patterns has characterized much commentary on *Paradise Lost* since Rajan. For M. M. Mahood too (*Poetry and Humanism,* 1950), although the fall turns on the disruption of hierarchy, the greatly important element becomes the parallels and subtle parodies through which the poem works. Eden is a dream stage for the "enactment of a collective . . . myth embodying

a psychological experience of the race," and the chief movements of the poem are less the events through which Paradise
is lost than the shifts from one stage to another of the cosmic
setting. The beginning fixes human life as the center; the poem
then opens out, with Books I–III an "agitated outward circle,"
from which Book IV shifts to the still center of this "vortex-
like cosmos." We follow movements from the center to the
outermost circumference of a multisphered cosmos, noting
how its symmetry is marred in Book IX, with disorder spread-
ing its rift in Book X and the new dimension of history introduced in Books XI–XII. In the ultimate restoration, to come
outside time, what is to be restored is the symmetrical balance
of the universe.

Arnold Stein, while giving more weight to the drama of the
fall, also saw *Paradise Lost* as going beyond the dramatic to a
"great and central mythic vision" where all perspectives lead
to God's idea, and the smaller circle of man's creation, fall,
and redemption is contained within the great circle that starts
from and ends in God. Stein has much more than that to say;
he provides illuminating readings of the War in Heaven as a
complex metaphor, of Hell as the place where defiance and
separation prove their nature, of the Garden as a "compressed
myth of natural sympathy and order." But his chief effect has
been, along with Rajan and Miss Mahood, to shift the focus of
many commentators from the sequential action to patterns of
myth, metaphor, and structure.

Thus for William Madsen ("The Idea of Nature in Milton's
Poetry," *Three Studies in the Renaissance,* 1958), stressing
the related cosmological, moral, and artistic designs, Milton
uses a series of contrasts—creation vs. destruction, order vs.
disorder, light vs. darkness—to establish "analogical relationships between the various levels on which the great Christian
epic moves." A main concern of *Paradise Lost* is still to assign
man his place in those hierarchic levels and see what results

when he fails to keep it. And the essential conflict in Milton's poem, as in Christian thought generally, is still between love of self and love of God.

But for Rosalie Colie ("Time and Eternity: Paradox and Structure in *Paradise Lost," JWCI* 23, 1960), what is of chief moment is the structure through which Milton resolves two central paradoxes of Christianity: the relation between time and eternity, and again between man's free will and God's foreknowledge. The whole narrative, from Christ's elevation to Doomsday, is itself a mere "parenthesis" in eternity, though it includes all human history, whether as compressed in God mind in Book III or as spread out in time in Books XI–XI To establish such relations, structure is all important: *Paradi Lost* both begins and ends in the midst of things; its two halv emphasize thematic structure, Books I–VI beginning and en ing with the same event, the fall of Satan and his rebels, Boo VII–XII proceeding from the creation of the cosmos to recreation at Doomsday; the central Books V–VIII unite p and future; the last speech of Adam concerns time and et nity. Through its very structure *Paradise Lost* illustrates two central paradoxes to give its reader the Christian exp ence of their force.

With Mrs. MacCaffrey's *Paradise Lost as "Myth"* (19 the shift of emphasis to pattern is complete. The poem comes "an arena for movements" corresponding to Milt central myth of the dark voyage of the soul from separa through initiation, to return—a circular mythic journey requires pattern in both the narrative and the verse textu express its "primordial reality." Thus "the major action r duces the plan of the whole universe," with time rath "series of horizons" than "a process lived through," and most crucial change in history" treated not as an argumen in terms of the "causes of moral events." Milton pref chronology a folded structure returning on itself spiral

ion, with recurrence, retrospect, and anticipation the chief keys to his pattern, as his three-tiered stage—Heaven, Hell, and the Garden—offers a geography suited to the quasi-time-less motions in his "severely structured universe." The poem presents "all history in a huge triptych." The "poison of time" which Satan brings into Paradise, the difference between be-fore and after, can only temporarily mar the cyclic pattern of the unfallen world, whose essential structure is a pyramid, its roots in Hell, its crown in Heaven, its hierarchical geometry the "visible image of God's eternal plan." *Paradise Lost* is therefore not tragic, but a *commedia* ending with a *Paradiso*.

Starting from a view similar to Mrs. MacCaffrey's, Jackson Cope (*The Metaphoric Structure of Paradise Lost,* 1962) finds in Milton's Ramism the ground for his having preferred an "atemporal and nonsequential" form like that of *Finnegan's Wake* to a sequential form like that of the *Odyssey*. The Ramist "place" logic, together with the Ramist insistence that words correspond to things, influenced Milton's poetic so that metaphors of "light and darkness, blindness and vision, falling and rising" become the *topoi* out of which *Paradise Lost* is created. But in the same year, agreeing rather with Mrs. Mac-Caffrey's cycle of separation, initiation, and return, Charles Monroe Coffin ("Creation and the Self in *Paradise Lost*," ed. C. A. Patrides, *ELH* 29, 1962) interpreted *Paradise Lost* as the *sequence* in human and divine relations of "association, dissociation, reassociation." A year later Roy Daniells, prefer-ring to study the poem in relation to the sculpture and archi-tecture of its time, favored the Baroque concepts of unity, power, and will as determining the patterns of *Paradise Lost*. Daniells sees the poem as an "artifice, full of power and pur-pose and predetermination," in which everything is "totally subdued to one idea, the indisputable pre-eminence of the will of God."

Tragedy or *Commedia?*

No doubt patterns have largely displaced action as center of *Paradise Lost* because the poem has been read as such different actions. C. S. Lewis, Diekhoff, and Bush substantially agreed that the central action is the fall of man. Presumably the only alternative was the fall of Satan, or a poem on two falls. Elio Chinol (*IL Dramma Divino e il Dramma Umano nel Paradiso Perduto,* 1958), asserted with Rajan that the action of *Paradise Lost* falls into two distinct parallel halves, a divine and a human drama, linked by the theme of rebellion against God and through the character of Satan, but of separate and equal importance. Like A. J. A. Waldock (*Paradise Lost and Its Critics,* 1947) and E. M. W. Tillyard earlier (*Milton,* 1930), Chinol found a tension in Milton between the poet who creates the magnificent Satan and the theologian who condemns him. To be sure, the poem progressively reveals the reality of evil and liberates Milton—and thus the reader—from the myth of Satan; still it reflects the large gap between the poet's human experience and his doctrine, and is itself split into two dramas.

For A. S. P. Woodhouse too ("Pattern in *Paradise Lost,*" *UTQ* 22, 1953; *Milton the Poet,* 1955) there are both a divine and a human action in *Paradise Lost,* but the human tragedy is subsumed under a divine comedy. While the movement of the poem from the superhuman to the human is essential to its pattern, Christ, the protagonist of the supernatural action, provides the standard of heroism, and Adam is the protagonist only of the human action. Woodhouse, although noting correspondences in the fourfold setting (a Heaven of order and liberty, an earth that reflects Heaven until after the fall, a Chaos of disorder, a Hell that perverts both order and heroism) and exploiting such a repeated pattern as the hand-in-hand motif, still assumed that sequence matters and reveals central meaning. His reading harks back to something like C. M. Bowra's comment that Milton's scheme, while in the fall itself recalling Greek tragedy, goes beyond the recognition of error with which Greek tragedy stops, to show the meaning of recovery and the good to come.

But the new trend goes far beyond Bowra and Woodhouse in removing tragedy from Milton's poem. Frank Kermode may insist that *Paradise Lost* is tragic since what we chiefly feel is the change from joy to woe ("Adam Unparadised," *The Living Milton,* 1960); and an outsider to Milton studies, Harry Levin, may even call *Paradise Lost* "the tragedy of tragedies" ("Paradises Heavenly and Earthly," *HLQ* 29, 1966). For an increasing number of writers *Paradise Lost* is a *commedia.* The new view derives partly from the discontinuity introduced by stressing patterns in place of plot, partly from a new reading of a comic vein in the poem. While C. S. Lewis regarded Satan as a comic figure because a fool, most earlier critics assumed with Bowra that literary epic of its very nature excludes the comic vein. *Paradise Lost,* they thought, contains only traces of sardonic humor, as in the Limbo of Vanities. With Arnold Stein's reading of the war in Heaven as a huge burlesque, new possibilities opened. Thus Joseph Summers finds "burlesque, parody, and comedy" as essential in Milton's poem as "the heroic, the divine, and the tragic," and argues that only preconceptions about epic poetry and about the man John Milton have prevented general recognition of the many passages where *Paradise Lost* "approaches or achieves comedy" (*The Muse's Method,* 1962).

More important to the new reading of *Paradise Lost* as a *commedia*—since tragedy too may involve comic scenes, especially English tragedy—the fall has grown progressively more fortunate since A. O. Lovejoy (following the precedent of

Cecil A. Moore and Allan H. Gilbert, as Diekhoff—in agreement with the thesis—noted) announced the paradox ("Milton and the Paradox of the Fortunate Fall," *ELH* 4, 1937).
When E. M. W. Tillyard displaced the crisis from the fall in
Book IX to the reconciliation in Book X ("The Crisis of
Paradise Lost," Studies in Milton, 1951), he gave further
impetus to the *felix culpa* as Milton's central theme: even
before the redemption Adam and Eve were proving from what
small and humble things God—and they—could achieve
greater good for man. M. M. Mahood stressed Milton's
"earned" faith that the fall, while not commendable, proved
fortunate thanks to the Mercy that draws good out of evil. For
Millicent Bell ("The Fallacy of the Fall in *Paradise Lost,"
PMLA* 68, 1953) there is no real fall since Adam and Eve
were fallen from the start, and their growth in human understanding to the "triumphant victory" of the end constitutes the
climactic central theme.

Wayne Shumaker ("The Fallacy of the Fall in *Paradise
Lost," PMLA* 70, 1955) and H. V. S. Ogden ("The Crisis of
Paradise Lost Reconsidered," *PQ* 36, 1957) gave detailed
answers to Mrs. Bell's thesis that an "imperfect" Adam and
Eve were as good as fallen right along and to E. M. W.
Tillyard's thesis that Book X contains the turning point of the
poem. But the fall continues fortunate. Jacques Blondel (*Milton, poète de la Bible dans le Paradis Perdu,* 1959) finds the
Augustinian *felix culpa* throughout the poem, especially as it
points less backward to the lost Eden than forward to the
"Paradise within." Roland Frye (*God, Man and Satan,* 1960)
argues that because of the fall "earlier human mutability is
now replaced by an unbreakable promise" and thus by "an
existential assurance of God's grace" far happier than the lost
Eden. Mrs. Ferry returns to the paradox involved in the *felix
culpa,* but concludes that the world gained is an improvement
because it contains a "growth in self-knowledge and experi-

ence" that offsets the doomed simplicity and innocence, and even more because it makes possible a conclusion in which the cycles of "descent and ascent, loss and restoration, departure and return" are finally harmonized.

So thoroughly does G. A. Wilkes (*The Thesis of Paradise Lost,* 1961) believe the evil of the fall "finally absorbed into [God's] providential scheme" that he argues the significant issue in *Paradise Lost* is not how or why man falls but how Providence responds to produce greater good for man. And William Marshall (*"Paradise Lost: Felix Culpa* and the Problem of Structure," *MLN* 76, 1961) even complains that Milton fails of his didactic purpose in *Paradise Lost* because he does not adequately dramatize the greater good of man's redemption. So too J. B. Broadbent argues (*Some Graver Subject,* 1960) that Milton does not treat the *felix culpa* theme with enough lyrical joyfulness because he goes about his "attempt to celebrate Christian culture" too mechanically. For Marshall and Broadbent *Paradise Lost* is a *commedia* not quite achieved inasmuch as the good fortune of the fall is inadequately driven home.

As the action, the sequence of occurrences, and the emotional response these invite recede in importance, the affirmations that *Paradise Lost* is a *commedia* like Dante's mount. For Northrop Frye (*Five Essays on Milton's Epics,* 1966) the end of *Paradise Lost* absorbs both hope and disillusion into serenity, and the return of Eden is more than achieved as God again is all in all. J. R. Watson ("Divine Providence and the Structure of *Paradise Lost,*" *Essays in Criticism* 14, 1964) and John Shawcross ("The Son in His Ascendance," *MLQ* 27, 1966) find the triumph of divine Providence through the Savior determining the whole structure of the poem. In a dwindling minority, Thomas Greene (*The Descent from Heaven,* 1963) holds that the hope glimpsed at the end remains distant so that the curve of the action is a "descent into humiliation" concentrating on the loss for man. For many readers the curve of the action is far too shattered into patterns of arcs, spirals, and parallels to bear the weight of a central theme. Stein found "the harsh immediacies of time mitigated by the known promise of eternity." But Stein subordinated theological to human meanings in the poem. As the emphasis in reading *Paradise Lost* shifts to the poet's theology, the tragic tensions dissolve. William Madsen ("Earth the Shadow of Heaven," *PMLA* 75, 1960) can say of the fall: "Only by an act of sin that destroyed the Garden could the Garden come to be seen as a type of the spiritual life." The Christian lesson of patience, the final teaching of *Paradise Lost,* is that no event reveals its meaning until the last age when "the righteous have entered into the state of 'perfect glorification.' " In 1955 Robert Martin Adams (*Ikon*) was protesting against Maud Bodkin and Zwi Werblowsky that "the fall of mankind is mankind's tragedy, not the devil's." In the newer perspective there is no tragedy: the split between the human and the divine actions has ended with the divine superimposed on the human, subordinating man's brief present to his eschatological destiny in God's *commedia.*

Theodicy or *Paideia*

The conviction that *Paradise Lost* ends happily with man's destiny assured stems in part from the conviction that the poem is a theodicy. That in turn stems in part from a new urgency about Milton's orthodoxy or heterodoxy, in part from a new emphasis on the central and final books, in part from a new scrutiny of the poem's structure.

Interest in *Paradise Lost* as a Christian poem is, of course, hardly new; but earlier commentators read it as a product of Milton's Christian humanism. Some, like Bowra, saw a conflict between the humanism and the Christianity; some, like C. S. Lewis, saw a fusion. The fusion might be read in many ways. Typically, for Jacques Blondel Milton subordinates his classical knowledge to a demonstration of the Christian *felix culpa,* at one with his time in seeing the world as the battle-ground of God and the devil. Milton, in characteristic seven-teenth-century vein, takes his doctrine from the Bible and makes original sin the crux of *Paradise Lost.* Yet dogma, as Blondel reads the poem, takes second place to the dramatic and epic plan which exploits man's natural grandeur and his Christian hope.

A different motive is at work in the pursuit of Milton's Christian doctrine in *Paradise Lost.* With Maurice Kelley's study of *De Doctrina Christiana* as a gloss on the poem (*This Great Argument,* 1941) Milton's orthodoxy or heterodoxy took on major importance. Sister Miriam Joseph (*Orthodoxy in Paradise Lost,* 1952), like C. S. Lewis earlier but to a far greater extent, stresses the correspondence between the poem and traditional Christianity. William B. Hunter, Jr. ("Milton's Arianism Reconsidered," *HTR* 52, 1959; "Milton on the In-carnation," *JHI* 21, 1960) argues that Milton was no Arian, but an orthodox subordinationist. Harry F. Robins (*If This Be Heresy,* 1962) finds his theological heresies most fully in accord with Origen's. To the whole question of Milton's rela-tion to orthodox belief, C. A. Patrides (*Milton and the Chris-tian Tradition,* 1966) has given exhaustive and definitive treatment, placing him unmistakably in the seventeenth-cen-tury Protestant tradition. The Christian thought of centuries is synthesized to provide the background for Milton's views on the Godhead, creation, nature, the fall, the redemption, love and grace, history and eschatology.

How much of *Paradise Lost* falls outside such studies de-pends, of course, on whether *Paradise Lost* is primarily theo-logical in its emphasis. Bowra too called it "the epic of

Protestantism," but thought the poet less involved in theology than in his humanist convictions about such matters as order, justice, and liberty as the goods man can attain. Not so George W. Whiting (*Milton and This Pendant World,* 1958), who concludes that the reader must come to terms with Milton's "orthodox Protestant opinions" and traditional Christian symbols to get at the spiritual truths of the poem. And not only those who look back to seventeenth-century contexts put first stress on Milton's justification of God's ways. Roland Frye, more concerned with contemporary than with traditional theology, reads *Paradise Lost* as a Christian existentialist acceptance of life in God.

That the Bible, specifically in the Authorized English version, provided the very tissue of Milton's diction can hardly be doubted after James H. Sims's work (*The Bible in Milton's Epics,* 1962). But what thought Milton poured into Biblical phrases and even into familiar Christian doctrine may remain a question. H. R. MacCallum ("Milton and the Figurative Interpretation of the Bible," *UTQ* 31, 1962) specifically warns against assuming that Milton used anything like allegorical interpretation of the Bible or the "traditional form of typology." Rather, in the vein of the Reformation, he distrusted "the order and coherence sought by the symbol-making imagination."

In addition to studies of Milton's Christian doctrine, a new concentration on the central and final books has produced much of the interpretation of the poem as a theodicy. The War in Heaven, proving God's omnipotence in the Son's victory; the Book of Creation, proving the benevolence that draws good from evil; and the forecast of human history till Doomsday, proving the divine grace that grants Adam a "Paradise within" attainable even now and an ultimate reunion with God as his assured destiny—these have preoccupied commentators in increasing numbers. Here too, common interest has not made for agreement. Mason Tung ("The Abdiel Episode," *SP* 62, 1965), for example, is not taking *Paradise Lost* as a theodicy when he argues that the Abdiel episode is central because it provides a model for both Eve and Adam of what each might have done in Book IX, a poetic example that proves the fall avoidable, a paradigm of the "one just man" more elaborate than those in Book XI and hence more illuminating of Milton's central thesis on God's justice. Priscilla St. George ("Psychomachia in V and VI of *Paradise Lost*," *MLQ* 27, 1966) reviews what others, chiefly theodicists, have said on the War in Heaven to fault them all for not recognizing in it a dramatization in Homeric terms of the "psychomachia of the Christian soul."

Books XI and XII have won even more attention. No longer "bleak and barren," as Rajan called them, a mere "insurance against sin" rather than a "basis for virtue," for E. N. S. Thompson ("For *Paradise Lost* XI–XII," *PQ* 22, 1943) they give a "concentrate of human experience" leading to the new era of Christ as climax, and thus fortify Adam by inducing a "calm and confident final acceptance," in which the reader shares. F. T. Prince ("On the Last Two Books of *Paradise Lost*," *Essays and Studies* 11, 1958) similarly finds the "series of far-sweeping visions" designed to produce an evolution in Adam's consciousness, and to all who observe a weariness of tone in the last books answers that the tone is there to "set the mood for what Milton has still to say." In even more affirmative vein Roland Frye reads them as a constant repetition of the "primary sin" and yet a pattern of salvation as Adam grows through successive submissions to God's will "until he has attained to the paradise within him." So too for Lawrence A. Sasek ("The Drama of *Paradise Lost*, Books XI–XII," *SERL,* 1962) and H. R. MacCallum ("Milton and Sacred History: Books XI and XII of *Paradise Lost*," *Essays . . . Presented to A. S. P. Woodhouse,* 1964) the last books successfully dramatize Adam's final development. Very much in the new vein, B. A. Wright (*Milton's Paradise Lost,* 1962) finds in Adam's speech in XII.561–573 his fulfillment "as the hero of the poem," and in XI–XII as a whole the completion not only of the structure but of the story. Specific passages too win elaborate defense: Barbara K. Lewalski ("Structure and the Symbolism of Vision in Michael's Prophecy," *PQ* 42, 1963) justifies the shift from visual to auditory imagery; Robert A. Bryan ("Adam's Tragic Vision in *Paradise Lost,*" *SP* 62, 1965) examines XI.385–411 as a condensed statement on the futility of human glory; Virginia R. Mollenkott ("The Cycle of Sins in *Paradise Lost* XI," *MLQ* 27, 1966) elaborates the series of visions in XI as a "microcosm of the whole epic."

The new concentration on these parts, formerly neglected or thought faulty, is in line with a new effort to understand Milton's purpose in revising his earlier ten books into the twelve-book version. Arthur Barker ("Structural Pattern in *Paradise Lost,*" *PQ* 28, 1949) argues that, whereas the earlier divisions suggested something like a five-act tragedy ending with the aftermath of the fall, the twelve books underscore a more Virgilian pattern culminating in "the Messianic prophecy of final victory" which restores Adam even while expelling him from the Garden. Like Barker, Summers takes the revised numbering of the books as structurally important. When Milton divided Book VII of the 1667 version into the present Books VII and VIII, and the last book into the present Books XI and XII, he gave a more victorious emphasis to the action: twice over, at the center and again at the end, destruction is resolved in creation. John Shawcross ("The Balanced Structure of *Paradise Lost,*" *SP* 62, 1965) presses the argument to make the triumph at the end of Book VI the highest point of the poem and the cause of what follows in VII–XII, so that all man's disaster becomes a means of showing God's love. The whole poem thus moves to the apocalyptic view of the human story, marked in the parallels between Books VI and XII.

But emphasis on Books V–VII and XI–XII or on the ten- and twelve-book structures need not prove the poem a theodicy. George Williamson ("The Education of Adam," *MP* 61, 1963) takes the central and final books as Adam's "moral preparation," subordinate to the action of the fall. In 1949, Ruth Mohl (*Studies in Spenser, Milton, and the Theory of Monarchy*) concentrated on the final books to read *Paradise Lost* as "the making of the greater man." Stein and Blondel take them as turning the reader toward the present world. Conversely, reading *Paradise Lost* as a theodicy does not necessarily make the final books successful for every reader. While Rosalie Colie thinks we end our reading sharing Adam's expectation of Doomsday in an optimistic frame of mind, Louis Martz (*The Paradise Within*, 1964), finding the theme of the poem in an "interior journey toward the center of the soul," thinks that Milton "lost touch" with his own conception in the last books and that *Paradise Lost* ends by sinking into pessimism where Milton intended piety.

The whole concern with Milton's relation to orthodoxy, the whole emphasis on *Paradise Lost* as a theodicy centered in the victories of the Son in Heaven and at Doomsday, even the emphasis on the regeneration of Adam as he learns the Christian meaning of his fall and redemption, may be symptomatic of the retreat from humanism that Miriam K. Starkman excoriated in "The Militant Miltonist" (*ELH* 26, 1959). If E. L. Marilla was right to name his essay "The Central Problem in *Paradise Lost:* the Fall of Man" (*Essays and Studies on English Language and Literature* 15, 1953) and find the constant point of reference in "the moral responsibility on which the welfare of humanity always depends"—if R. M. Adams was right to assert that by the end "all the supernatural persons are withdrawn or reduced to attendant, symbolic roles" so that "only man is left to carry on the story of history"—*Paradise Lost* may be more *paideia* than theodicy.

So Joseph Summers apparently reads it. The speech of the Son in Book III provides a paradigm for Eve's gestures of reconciliation in Book X. The sequence from Book VI to Book VII provides a paradigm for the resolution of the destruction of Book XI in the new dispensations of Book XII. Milton could not let his poem end with Adam and Eve in despair; as little could he provide them and his readers with factitious comfort. The human pair must leave Eden knowing the worst and nonetheless able to live their lives in expectation of blessedness. As Adam witnesses the movements of unredeemed human history in Book XI, constantly leading to death, he learns to avoid "false consolations" and rejoice in the covenant of God. Ready then for the typological patterns of Book XII, he hears with increasing joy the workings of divine Providence until he can finally accept and understand God's methods. Having discovered that his faith can be independent of society's progress or regress, having learned the meaning of grace, freedom, and the eternal inward Eden, Adam has still to live what he has learned, still to choose his way, still to gain his inner paradise through deeds. The end, both sorrowful and rejoicing, thus returns the reader with fallen—and renewed— Adam and Eve to the responsibilities of the life we know. So too Helen Gardner has come to see the cosmic theme of *Paradise Lost* as "framing and interpreting the human theme," which finally brings us "to life as we know it, where the triumph of good is matter for faith and future hope, not matter of experience."

It may be significant that those who scrutinize passages outside the War in Heaven and the prevision of human history find them justified by their human relevance: Frank L. Huntley, for example ("A Justification of Milton's 'Paradise of Fools,'" *ELH* 21, 1954), reads the Limbo of Vanities as exploring cause and effect in the involutions of sin with its violation of nature; and Mary Ann Radzinowicz ("Eve and Dalila: Renovation and the Hardening of the Heart," *Reason and the Imagination,* ed. J. A. Mazzeo, 1962) reads Eve's role in the latter part of Book X as demonstrating how regeneration can be won after the fall on terms not unlike the prelapsarian plan for man's upward refining.

Paradise Lost and the Epic Tradition

With so much stress on the renewal of Adam or the exaltation of God's providence in the final books of *Paradise Lost,* what has happened to the old concern with Satan as hero? Few readers any longer agree with A. J. A. Waldock or E. E. Stoll ("Give the Devil His Due," *RES* 20, 1944; "A Postscript," *PQ* 28, 1949) on Satan's heroism. Few would grant Mrs. MacCaffrey that he is joint hero with Adam in a mythic quest. Some might accept Helen Gardner's earlier thesis ("Milton's Satan and the Theme of Damnation in Elizabethan Tragedy," *E&S* 1, 1948) that he is a "heroic figure" through whom Milton explored the "fact of perversity." But in general Geoffrey Hartman's view of Satan's whole story as "Milton's Counterplot" (*ELH* 25, 1958) has won the day. The question has largely shifted to the relation of *Paradise Lost* to the heroic genre. For J. B. Broadbent the time for such a "genuinely Christian and heroic" poem as Milton wished to write had passed, so that at best he produced the last "significant redaction of the whole celestial cycle."

Interestingly enough, for the editor of *The Celestial Cycle* (1952), Watson Kirkconnell, what chiefly emerges is that Milton's is an epic poem, modeled on Homer and Virgil, not a hexameron. While it "includes more phases of the Celestial Cycle than any other epic," it subordinates all hexameral matter to epic narrative. Yet for Burton O. Kurth (*Milton and Christian Heroism,* 1959) it is a hexameron. And J. R. Watson ("Divine Providence and the Structure of *Paradise Lost,*" *Essays in Criticism* 14, 1964) castigates those who take for an epic "of action" concerned with man's fall what the whole structure proves an epic "of justification" centrally concerned with Divine Providence.

Much depends, of course, on what makes a poem epic. Bowra, who studied the genre, found *Paradise Lost* the last great literary epic, giving new life to all the traditional heroic themes by investing them with new meaning. Other scholars have marked Milton's conformity to the traditional norms of epic poetry, either those especially favored in the Renaissance or those that link the whole genre from Homer down. Thus Kester Svendsen ("Epic Address and Reference and the Principle of Decorum in *Paradise Lost,*" *PQ* 28, 1949) observed how precisely Milton kept epic decorum in his changing epithets for the agents; and John M. Steadman ("Recognition in the Fable of *Paradise Lost,*" *SN* 31, 1959; "Allegory and Verisimilitude in *Paradise Lost,*" *PMLA* 78, 1963) has worked with the applicability of Aristotelian and Renaissance canons of heroic poetry to the plot.

But the view that something strange overtook the heroic norms at Milton's hands dominates recent studies of *Paradise Lost* as epic poem. Where Gordon W. O'Brien (*Renaissance Poetics and the Problem of Power,* 1956) argued for the man-god philosophy of the Renaissance, "the intellectual movement . . . which sought to exalt man to the Godhead," as shaping Milton's epic of Christian humanism with all its celebration of active energy, Davis P. Harding (*The Club of Hercules,* 1962), concentrating on Milton's use of the *Aeneid,* finds him consistently transvaluing Virgil's themes as Virgil had transvalued Homer's. Thomas Greene (*The Descent from Heaven,* 1963) raises the question whether Mil-

ton's separation of energy from human heroism is possible
within the norms of epic poetry. The genre demands a hero
who does great deeds despite his mortality, a hero whose
importance to his community is defined through the dangers in
which he is tested. *Paradise Lost* then is an anomaly. Milton,
by internalizing the essential action, removes the very ground
that heroic poetry requires—individual excellence and the
hero's relation to the community. Indeed Christianity is in-
compatible with epic awe before human achievement, and
since science from the seventeenth century on has steadily
destroyed epic assurance, the modern era no longer can afford
heroic poetry its needed ground. Yet Greene finds a properly
heroic quality in Milton's verse, in his spacious imaginings
which fuse the classical and the Christian without strain.

Peter Hägin (*The Epic Hero and the Decline of Heroic
Poetry,* 1964) pushes an argument like Greene's still further:
"Milton rejected the very essence of heroic poetry" when he
abandoned Arthur as his epic hero and decided to treat instead
the fall of man. He was able to stave off the inevitable demise
of the genre in the modern world only by a strategic concealment of the central issue of his poem. His problem was to fuse
traditional epic matter with his unheroic theme of the tragedy
of the human soul. *Paradise Lost* is thus not only the first but
also inevitably the last example of a modern heroic poem.
Using epic scaffolding for a metaphysical argument, its apparent is far from being its real subject. The heroic treatment of
Satan is Milton's device for making the epic treatment of
Adam and Eve possible through a series of parallels between
the two falls: Satan gets reduced from the opponent of God to
become the opponent of man; Adam and Eve in turn get
exalted so that they may be his equals in the conflict. By such
strategies Milton raised an epic façade, behind which he
stripped man to the point where he could become the unheroic

hero of the eighteenth-century novel. Remove the façade and there in Milton's Adam is Tom Jones in the making.

Once thought of as the last stronghold of classical tradition, the consummate statement of Renaissance energies, the great European epic, *Paradise Lost* has become for many readers a celebration of God's ways through all his triumphs, and for at least one the precursor of the chief modern literary form, the realistic novel.

The Poem

After such a survey the natural sequel might be to consider out of what assumptions about poetry and poets—for that matter about life itself—commentators have been writing. But that would be to desert *Paradise Lost*. Most of the trends I have reviewed can be somehow supported from the text; many, if subordinated to its main plan, can profitably be read back into the poem. The richness of the parts need not distort the clear design; indeed it is because the large design is so firm that it can support local richness. My own assumption is that the work is an epic poem in tragic vein about the losing of Paradise, designed as a *paideia*. It starts at the beginning of its single action, in the midst of things, but not in the midst of the main, or even of a subordinate plot. It ends at the end of its single action. The beginning introduces a main agent bent on destroying what he can, the inhabitants of a newly created world; the end shows those inhabitants going into exile. His success has proved failure for him; but the concern of the poem is what it proves for man. And for man it proves tragic. The full aftermath of the tragedy is exploited, tempered only by the fact that the continuities of life surround every possible tragedy. There is always a future as there was always a past;

Paradise Lost is not alone in tragic literature in proclaiming that.

As epic mimesis, the poem largely represents its main action through the speeches and deeds of its main agents. The poet seldom intrudes, indeed enters only to redirect the reader to the action. Chiefly, what the agents say and do provides the poem's momentum. It moves—as narrative does—through scenes that produce a complication, ultimately resolved through recognitions and reversals with their attendant suffering. At the same time it steadily reveals the nature and mentality of the persons involved, exploring motives and values, psychology and ethics. Any mimesis tells what its author thinks desirable, what contemptible. *Paradise Lost,* as a mimesis specifically of man's conspiring to destroy his own happiness, inevitably speaks more immediately and obviously than most narratives on what man's happiness consists in, what maintains it, what ends it.

That indeed was the compelling attraction for Milton of the story he chose. More clearly and immediately than any other it offers in paradigm man's central story, speaks to man's central concerns. It therefore offers itself virtually without impediment to the function of *paideia.* By the time he wrote *Paradise Lost* Milton had given up the search for "the pattern of a Christian hero"—that could only be Christ—and concluded that the unity of an epic poem depends on its unified action. He had not given up the lifelong consuming interest in man's full development that had drawn him into the struggles of his time for liberty in church and state, in private life and public utterance. His object as poet was one with his object as statesman and educator: the realization of man's possible excellence, to which freedom is requisite. Tragic narrative, as it studies the relations between varieties of mistake and their consequences, may illuminate man's possibilities even more than exemplary patterns can. Like the story of the creation

Raphael tells Adam, shaped to reach its climax in the "master-work" man, *Paradise Lost* is shaped to encourage magnanimity and self-knowledge. The Renaissance humanist who wrote *Paradise Lost* retained the conviction that marks *Of Education:*

> These ways would try all their peculiar gifts of nature; and if there were any secret excellence among them would fetch it out and give it fair opportunities to advance itself by, which could not but mightily redound to the good of this nation, and bring into fashion again those old admired virtues and excellencies, with far more advantage now in this purity of Christian knowledge.

The ways of tragic narrative are necessarily different from the program of an academy; the end *Paradise Lost* aims at is the same—human excellence. Far from assigning the old admired Greek virtues to Hell, it exhalts them as enabling man to "correspond with Heaven." It uses Christian doctrine to the same end, not to formulate a theodicy, but to induce the love of excellence and the confidence in its possibility without which human energies frustrate themselves.

But the mimesis of *Paradise Lost* not only provides a *paideia,* as any deeply imaginative representation of human life does; it also contains a *paideia* twice over: for unfallen Adam in Books V–VIII and for fallen Adam in Books XI–XII. The proportions tell a good deal about the poem. Far from rushing Adam and Eve to the fall in order to establish some greater postlapsarian good, Milton thrusts off the fall by every available means. The instruction by Raphael constitutes a large part of the means. Together with the sequence that precedes, it exploits what Eden can contain. In addition to beauty, spontaneity, fertility, variety, intellectual and artistic activity, it can contain a nightmare, an understanding of evil, mistaken notions that need correction; nothing that can be the stuff of growth is alien to Eden. And hence the Edenic theme increases in assurance until the sudden reversal in Book IX. An Eve who recovers from her nightmare, an Adam who corrects his mistaken notions—a pair who have heard and thus imaginatively participated in the revolt of Satan, the independence of Abdiel, the prolonged struggle of the War in Heaven with its climactic ending, who have comprehended as well the chain of being and the splendors of the creation—have grown immensely in their natures and in their knowledge from the idyllic couple we first behold. This is no blank innocence that Milton celebrates, but the best possibilities of the life we know, spared no awareness of evil, rather protected by growing awareness.

Thus the whole sequence of Books V–VIII provides the antecedent of Book IX, not only as it answers every question Book IX can logically raise, but as it enlarges the life of Eden, pushing back every limitation that might seem imposed, erasing every motive that might have suggested itself for thinking the fall inevitable. Because we know the fatal event in advance we are not to suppose it necessary. We do not know how it happens until we see it happening, and the how is all-important to Milton's poem. Before Book IX we can guess nothing of the circumstances of the fall except that Satan intends to cause it, as we could guess nothing of Raphael's detailed instruction until he gives it, except its purpose of preventing the fall. We may also remark that if the War in Heaven were in any way central to Milton's plot, either because Satan's story formed a parallel subplot, or because the triumph of the Son of God or Abdiel constituted Milton's primary theme, it would not enter the poem as one among several parts of Adam's instruction. It would not be tied to the exposition of the chain of being before and the discussion of nature's supposed "disproportions" later. Nor would it be tied to the account of the creation that immediately follows. But again the resolution of destruction in creation cannot be a central theme. Neither Raphael's nor Milton's audience is to fancy that God needed Satan's rebellion as motive to the creation. Creation is not only greater than destruction but wholly independent of it. The account that Raphael gives is shaped by the clear purpose of supporting Adam's self-knowledge and magnanimity: *he* is the climax, surely not to be deluded into thinking he must break something in order to show his or someone else's skill at making repairs, but to be encouraged in the due self-esteem that would preserve Eden.

So too the sequence of Books X–XII contains the *paideia* of fallen Adam in a context that controls its meaning. When Adam and Eve have pulled themselves from the abyss of mutual recrimination and despair, they have still to face exile and death. As the instruction of Michael prepares them to confront the shattered world they have brought into being, it supplements, without superceding, the instruction of Raphael. It adds what Adam now needs to know: the full horror he has caused as evil begets evil, the thin thread of promise running through the tale of woes, and the full hope with which he may yet live his life. If Books XI–XII were in the poem for any other purpose, their proportions and emphases would be wrong. The woe preponderates too largely over the hope until too nearly the end. Even Adam's ecstatic relief when he learns of the redemption is too immediately and decidedly tempered by Michael with a reminder that he has still to earn his redemption. The whole forecast of human history is tied too closely to the enormous changes in the world that precede it and to the expulsion from Eden that immediately follows to resolve the tensions of the fall and its aftermath with an "O Altitudo!" The poem has not reached Doomsday; Adam has not yet attained his possible inner Paradise; the "brandisht sword of God" closes for ever the entrance to Eden, "so late their happy seat," now guarded with "dreadful faces . . . and fiery arms." And all history looms before Adam and Eve, no mere "parenthesis" in an eternity of bliss, but the long story of mankind to be lived through: "The world was all before them."

Milton did not choose the subject of *Paradise Lost* to give readers a happy ending or any facile comfort. The story of mankind is patently not a happy one and its end is not yet. It will not end in mankind's defeat; so much assurance Milton gives to the race. And every man need not choose the errors that stain man's tragic history. Indeed any man can add to the hope and the promise by renewing the Edenic life in himself. For reassurance the last book gives disproportionate emphasis to the weight of woe; for tragic aftermath its proportions are right. The mitigation of doom does not cancel the sense of loss with which a poem named *Paradise Lost* must end. If mercy turned "forbearance" into bland "acquittance," it would over-turn the whole action of the poem, make Eden a thing of too little account to preserve or regain, and remove from the "one easy prohibition" any function but as a lever to remove Adam to greater joys. That Doomsday is coming hardly makes *Paradise Lost* a *commedia*. As well say that *Hamlet* ends happily because flights of angels may indeed be singing the Prince to his rest. Whatever Milton was, he was no Pangloss.

The entire tragic mimesis of *Paradise Lost* can be a *paideia* because it evades nothing of the realities that test it. As in tragedy generally the preponderance of the terrifying and piti-ful may seem pessimistic. But like tragedy generally *Paradise Lost* is saved from pessimism by asserting in the very face of "all our woe" the values in terms of which life need not be a tissue of woes. Epic poetry is not distinguished from tragedy by requiring a happy ending. Nor is it distinguished by requir-ing a hero. If *Paradise Lost* asks to be compared with the *Iliad*, *Odyssey*, and *Aeneid*—as at point after point it clearly does —it is not in order to redefine heroism. Milton does that at just one point in his poem, and not in order to say that "true" heroism or "the better fortitude of patience and heroic martyrdom" is his subject, but to obviate just such criticism as those who search for heroes and heroics might make, that his central episode is inappropriate in a heroic poem. He asserts that the fall is a sufficiently important theme, and that epic poetry does not require what readers mistakenly suppose. Just as "patience and heroic martyrdom" are higher values than military prowess and princely luxury, Adam's "breach disloyal" is a higher argument than other epic themes. Man as man counts enough so that his story merits the loftiest vein of sustained narrative ever thought appropriate to work that deals with the most serious issues of human life.

Content that his theme is fit for epic treatment, Milton uses the array of epic conventions. He is not masking an unheroic theme in heroic trappings. What in fact was heroic about Achilles sulking in his tent? or about Odysseus detained in Calypso's isle? Homer, we may observe, never engaged to celebrate heroes. In a significant way, when Milton shifted from his Tassonian poetics of the 1640's to his later, more Aristotelian poetics, he shifted also from the Virgilian complexities of the epic hero who, the gods have decreed, is to found the great imperial city, back to Homeric simplicities, where story is of prime importance and the immediacies of life and death the main issues. Adam needs no special dedication to make his well-being significant to us; that he is man is enough. Satan need not enter the scene to give him importance; Raphael does that far better. Hell need not turn Eden into a battleground to provide it with epic dignity; Heaven has assured its dignity by creating the place. If the Son himself is to become man to suffer his heroic martyrdom, man needs none of the trappings "deemed heroic" to have his fortunes the subject of heroic treatment.

A narrative poem inevitably reveals the system of values it

involves. But the person who most fully illustrates those values need not be the central agent. So, too, intrinsic importance cannot determine the importance a narrative grants to any of its elements. Milton surely thought the calling of Abraham more intrinsically important than the murder of Abel or Noah's flood; yet he lavishes narrative and descriptive detail on these, reduces that to a brisk notation in the evolution of "the woman's Seed." Eternity in itself is doubtless a more beautiful as well as a more inclusive concept than time; but in *Paradise Lost* everything is subordinate to the temporal sequence of man's fall and its aftermath. Adam might like to contemplate a little longer the beyond "whose end no eye can reach"; Michael reminds him that "the hour precise/ Exacts [his] parting hence"—and hurries him from Eden.

The proportions and emphases the poem gives to various episodes and themes clearly show its focus. On some matters Milton is clear, precise, emphatic, even repetitious; some he deliberately blurs or scants. Those he blurs can hardly be of central importance. Thus *Paradise Lost* cannot turn on a doctrine of hierarchy as the central ordering principle of a universe in which everyone has a natural superior whom he must obey and a natural inferior whom he must rule. If Raphael, explaining the chain of being, loosely describes the higher orders of creation as "nearer to . . . [God] placed or nearer tending" and asserts that man and angel are more alike than different, if Milton himself assigns the sense of strict hierarchical superiority exclusively to Satan, the poem cannot hinge on just such a system as Milton's prose constantly denies. Abdiel is right to serve truth rather than his immediate overlord Satan. The crux of Book IX cannot be that Eve disobeys Adam or that he fails to rule her; indeed she does not precisely disobey him. At any rate, Milton still calls her innocent up to the precise moment at which she decides to break the one law of Eden. Presumably he invents the morning dispute between

Eve and Adam to distinguish trifling from fatal errors, as well as to provide a narrative sequence that makes the fatal error plausible.

Again, Milton blurs the structure of the universe. Evidently he did not think his poem primarily a cosmology. All the structures read into *Paradise Lost* to show the correspondence of its plan to the universe, all the patterns so elaborately collected to argue its meaning, turn the poem into a kind of Rorschach test: the explication of the blur tells us more about the explicator than about *Paradise Lost*. Satan has fallen an immense distance, three times the radius of the new cosmos, yet can behold that cosmos in its entirety as a pinpoint of light. Raphael answers Adam "doubtfully" about the structure of the universe and exhorts him "to search things more worthy of knowledge." We are neither given nor encouraged to work out any "severely structured universe" in the poem, but a sequence of linked episodes, as we generally are in a narrative.

Milton also blurs the future of his agents. Of Satan and his devils-turned-serpents "some say" one thing, some "tradition" another. As for Adam, he cannot know that the first scene of the future he beholds will involve his own two first-born sons, or how many of the evils he has foreseen his own life will witness, or even whether he will himself gain a "Paradise within." He knows only that he will have time enough to "add deeds" answerable to the instruction Michael has vouchsafed him. Michael has not taught him to regard human life *sub specie aeternitatis*. Indeed Milton specifically warns in his poem against man's attempt to take a superhuman view of space, and so too presumably of time—to take God's view as it were: only omniscience can. When humanity tries to, it merely baffles itself or distracts itself from its human concerns and opportunities. *Paradise Lost* directs us at every point to the living of our lives, as Raphael and Michael direct Adam to the living of his. Its paradox is not of time and eternity, but

> what cause
> Mov'd our Grand Parents in that happy State,
> Favor'd of Heav'n so highly, to fall off
> From thir Creator, and transgress his Will
> For one restraint, Lords of the World besides?

The paradox is of the fall—not of a fortunate fall, not of God's foreknowledge and man's free will, but that man, given all that he needs for joy, brings himself to misery. The reader, of course, comes to the poem knowing the story in Genesis 1–3. The whole issue of God's foreknowledge enters the action only to be excluded as not impinging on man's free will—or Satan's —or the Son's.

It is the doctrine of free will that the poem presses home, through emphatic repetition, through detailed argument, and especially through the fatal episode of Book IX.

Man's choices have consequences. That is the central thesis of the poem as it is the one law on which the action hinges. In the losing of Eden that law is writ large. As Eve makes her disastrous choice and Adam his, they transform themselves before our eyes from the "happy pair" to the flawed and wretched creatures of the familiar world. There are many ways in which the fall can be formulated, and the formulas hardly matter. We can say that Eve and later Adam think that they know what they do not know, she that the apple produced the serpent's power of speech, he that there is only one alternative to losing her. We can say that they think they do not know what they know very well, she that Eden provides her with a quite adequate sphere, he that he can at least try to make good the damage she has done. Innumerable other formulas suggest themselves: that both at critical moments lack a due self-esteem, that each proposes some false good worth destroying happiness for, that each takes magic as preferable to realities, that each inflates one motive in the self to the exclusion of all other possible motives. Any of these and any number of other formulas will serve, and none can capture the full dramatic complexity of the crisis in Book IX. The tensions brought to bear on the episode by all that precedes are more than matched by the tensions created in its enactment. All else fades into background as this central mimesis occurs, engaging a multiplicity of feelings, comments, recognitions, revulsions in the reader who participates, neither guiltless nor guilty like the falling pair, but wholly involved with them. This is how joy ends, how mankind reduces its perfections to rubble. It is all too immediate to us, played too close to our pulses, to be a mere illustration of any formula, ethical, cosmological, or pious.

Formulas can prepare for the scene, and formulas can supplement it. Other examples suggested in simile or allusion can illuminate its meanings, and other scenes clarify what this scene contains. Nothing in the poem compares with it as the moment of our deepest involvement. Every thread has drawn us to this center; every answer in the poem to every question it raised bore on this. The interpreters who pluck at our sleeves to assure us that we are misdirecting our attention sound like so many nags, eager no doubt to cheer us up for our own good, but self-deluding about just those depths of life that Milton has sounded.

Paradise Lost does not, of course, end with Book IX. Choices have their consequences in the large world and in the course of time as well as immediately in the human mind. Healings will prove possible; there will be a future. But it is no instantaneous healing Adam and Eve get. It takes the whole of Book X, moving back and forth through the universe to the broken pair, even to suggest what their destructive act will mean. As Adam wrestles with its import and Eve strains to restore their mutual love, new possibilities start, possibilities of endurance, of relief, of deeds with which to reshape their destiny, of everything but spontaneous joy in a world all theirs. That large ease that took Heaven itself as next-door neighbor and each new event as sure to increase delight has disappeared with a finality that every new hopeful motion only underscores.

Yet through it all, even as the wound spreads, the same values sound. Magnanimity and self-knowledge are still the great virtues; joy still the purpose for which man was designed. But to attain these will now be costly—of effort, of energy, of suffering, of life. The self that man will have to know is the Cain self, the lazar-house self, the self deluded by "the arts that polish life," the warring self, the embroiled self, the drowned self—as well as the Abel-Enoch-Noah self. The large-mindedness will have to include ways of coping with the ill-enduring body, the self-deceiving mind, the recalcitrant will, a society of enmities, a world of natural and even more of man-made calamities. And the joy will be wrested from pain, engaged in an endless salvage operation. The sheer diversion of energy from living to reconstructing the grounds of life speaks the impassable gap from Eden. Of course the "world of woe" is not the whole of Adam's future; that too would belie the fact. A great hope accompanies him into exile, and ground for faith in his ultimate salvation. The ecstasy of his *felix culpa* speech, however, stems too clearly from relief to bear scrutiny as a resolution of the poem's complexities. It supplies rather the resolution with which Adam may leave Eden, "though sorrowing, yet in peace," with Eve also comforted by her propitious dreams.

When we return from that end to the beginning to study the economy of the whole, the tragic design gains still greater clarity. Why so much time in Hell, so little in Heaven? The mood is properly set: this Hell is so immensely recognizable because the central action will introduce it into our world. If we are drawn into Satan's magnetic field in the opening books, we know better as the episode proceeds what we are to call Hell, so that we may experience proper relief when we get out of it. The tissue of self-contradicting lies, the obstinacy, vengefulness, envy, anger, thirst for domination, contempt for others except as they can be used, readiness to manipulate every impulse that may ensure preeminence, the propagandist's pretense that words can annihilate realities by calling disease health and health disease, the willingness to terrorize, and always the demand for adulation—all these we have known in our world. Some religions have even assigned just such a character to God. As Milton disentangles the whole web of mankind's idolatries from any least trace of benevolence, the poem defines the evil it strains against. So Heaven defines the good the poem strains toward: God is straightforward, undemanding, glad to exalt others, assertive only of objective laws and realities that hold for everyone, willing to allow every being the full free enactment of his own nature. The moral law of the universe *Paradise Lost* creates names generosity, love, compassion the fullest expression of harmony with itself. That is the source of the one edict in Paradise, this Being from whom all being issues. The word "obedience" gains its value from what is to be obeyed. To recognize what is worthy of love, trust, admiration *as* worthy is to remove the envy, suspicion, hate that build Hell.

By the time we arrive in Eden we know that to arrive there is not to leave Heaven behind, but to explore it further in human terms. This newest creation is "a Heaven on Earth," exalted by Heaven's concern to central importance in this action, as it has also been made central by Satan's purposes. If Eden did not matter centrally, "joy and love" would not matter, Heaven itself would not matter in this poem, or Satan's purposes, or anything else. When the Book of Eden opens with the cry "O for that warning voice," we echo the cry, even before we behold the place. The concentration with which the action has moved toward Eden, gathering in the universe on the way, focusing all regard, all expectation, on its inhabitants, is matched by the prolonged contemplation we are encouraged to give it when we arrive. Only in Book VII—the making of, climactically, Eden and man—will we be encouraged so to luxuriate in admiration. But there admiration will be subordinate to the attention we give Raphael's purpose in his account. Here our first attention is to the objects for admiration.

True, it is in the disturbing presence of Eden's threatener that we attend. The first voice we hear on earth is not the "warning voice" the poet cried out for, though it gives its warning. Satan, freed by solitude to speak so much truth as would-be omnipotence can face, brings his poison to the garden. As we imaginatively participate in his problem, we learn what to avoid in beholding this Eden. It is ours no more than his, except as what we delight in becomes ours. This malignance, confronting itself as the last court of appeal ("O then at last relent" is clearly Satan to Satan), cannot both change that "fixed mind" of which he boasted in Hell and retain it: the pre-eminence his whole nature craves finally involves, in spite of his obsessive self-pity, a pitilessness towards himself that can sustain itself only on self-delusion and the sound of its own lying voice. Not to belabor the mathematics that can divide infinity, we may observe the self-projection that decides for God what God must know, feel, think, and so thrusts him off into the role of "punisher." With this presence our companion in Eden, we concentrate all the more intensely on its joy, beauty, ease to restore our sense of normality. We have to hear his remarks on the scene, how he *"could* love," *"could* pity" what he gloats at the prospect of destroying, how he envies and scorns what cannot be his, congratulating himself that it will be no one else's for long; we want his voice silenced, his presence removed. At the end of Book IV they are, and that highly dramatic scene of recognitions and reversals should give us immense satisfaction as the bubble of arrogance, lies, pretensions is pricked.

The poem as a whole constantly gives such satisfactions dramatic and emotional—all the satisfactions it can without falsifying its central event. Of course, as soon as the intruder in Eden hears of something forbidden he begins to work up a delusive persuasion from its mere name. But then how carefully Books V–VIII make clear that knowledge is not forbidden, as Adam, formed "for contemplation and valor," gains new objects of contemplation. Even opportunity for valor is not wanting in Eden: Adam can reassure Eve about her nightmare, and can learn of danger loose in his world without fear, as he could fearlessly "dispute" with his creator. So too Eve's "softness and sweet attractive grace" in the Edenic books should give the reader pleasure. In assigning their distinctive virtues to each of the pair Milton is obviously not suggesting that Eve is a fool or Adam a boor, but surprisingly attributing to softness and gracefulness a high value, next only to contemplation and valor. The courtesies of his angels underscore that value. *Paradise Lost* says at least as much about gracefulness as about grace, speaks to the desire for beauty at least as much as to the desire for salvation.

On such matters we hear little from commentators. Milton thought them important: the hateful tone of Adam and Eve to each other at the end of Book IX is the clear proof of the fall. But Milton's concentration, as his invented episodes show, is always on human values: he equates with the glory of his maker whatever "infers" man happier. The cosmic and the human need not be weighed against each other in *Paradise Lost:* they affirm the same truth. The cosmos of this poem supplies in abundance fit objects of delight and requires of its inhabitants only that they use right reason to recognize them. The recognition is made easy for prelapsarian Eve and Adam; it comes infinitely harder to the postlapsarian pair.

It comes harder also to us. The poem must therefore elicit our normal responses to achieve its catharsis of our abnormalities. "Right reason obscured" needs all the help it can get. Not by chiding, but by using our disposition to wonder and delight, by tapping our repugnance for cruelty and ugliness, by assuming and encouraging reasonableness and *caritas* in us, Milton at once provides the experience of tragedy with its distinctive relief and reshapes our sense of the perfections we have seen shattered. As a *paideia Paradise Lost* invites readers to "repair the ruins of our first parents" in themselves and in their world.

If we are to get from the poem anything like the humanizing richness it contains, we need to come to it trained in reading the kind of literature Milton himself enjoyed. We can give less time to how he agreed or disagreed with the banal minds of his era: the formulas that represent such agreements or disagreements leave out of account what distinguishes *him*. For one thing, he was distinguished by a discriminating taste. Even for a valuable purpose he could hardly bear to steep himself in inferior writing. When he pauses in his *History of Britain* to exclaim "What labor is to be endured turning over volumes of rubbish," he consoles himself:

> This travail, rather than not know at once what may be known of our ancient story, sifted from fables and impertinences, I voluntarily undergo, and to save others, if they please, the like unpleasing labor, except those who take pleasure to be all their lifetime raking the foundations of old abbeys and cathedrals. (Col.X.180)

He had on the whole better uses for his time. The account of his habit while composing *Paradise Lost* tells of his "reading some choice poets . . . to store his fancy against morning." A great deal of the printed matter used to explicate *Paradise Lost* Milton would hardly have thought choice or poetic.

The Bible first, then Homer, Virgil, Ovid; Aeschylus, Sophocles, and Euripides; Plato, Augustine, and Dante; Chaucer, Spenser, Shakespeare—the great imaginative work he himself praised can best train us to perceive what he is doing in *Paradise Lost*. Great imaginative literature always addresses us as its "fit audience," always pays implicit tribute to our humanity. As it invites us mimetically to explore its variety of possible stances, feeling what they assume and recognizing what they lead to, poetry enlarges and refines our capacities. Milton's is a greatly enlarging poem, not because it takes as subject the largest terms anyone can think of—God, Man, Heaven, Hell—but because it pours into its subject the full riches of an imaginative, thoughtful, humane mind. The tale of the loss of Eden could be small, mean-minded, depressing. So could the tale of Achilles or Hamlet. If *Paradise Lost* increases self-knowledge and magnanimity, it is because this poet never ceased to occupy himself with the essential problems and the essential well-being of man. To pierce the shams that inflate themselves and clamor for attention, to exalt and engage in the efforts that might rid the world of barriers to man's fulfillment —these describe Milton's purposes throughout his life. They are his purposes in *Paradise Lost*. Those who cannot share his faith in God may have some translating to do before they make their way into the poem; it is only to those who cannot share his concern with humanity that the poem locks itself.

Paradise Lost is both unusually easy and unusually difficult to keep in mind as a whole. It presents no great problem in the main line of its story: no reader comes to it entirely unfamiliar with its chief persons and their chief deeds. Even given the poet's many additions and inventions, no reader can lose his way among the incidents, mistake the characters, fail at any moment to know where he is. In part the problems of reading stem from this very clarity. Readers may too quickly assume that they know what it will say: God is good, Satan evil, Eve and Adam are tempted and fall, Eden is lost. Then, recognizing complexities introduced into such simplicities, they assume they must somehow invert their first assumptions: perhaps Satan is good, God evil; perhaps Adam and Eve are not "tempted," do not fall; perhaps Paradise is not lost. Perhaps some hidden clue will reveal the reason for so much complexity. But the complexities of *Paradise Lost* are held fast within its simplicities: the professed subject *is* the subject; the action does not invert the obvious terms of the story. Only as it enlarges the enactment of its obvious terms, these reveal their complexity. What good can we conceive of fit to call God, what evil fit to call Satan, what native capacities fit to call man, what joys are worth naming Eden, what kind of testing does a temptation involve, what does loss mean? And as the mimesis explores its *données,* it takes in ever-increasing mental and emotional territory, not content to give simple answers. If it reaches out to the bounds of space and time, it is that it may reach in to the subtle questions the human condition poses. Through accumulation and simile, through effects of immediate juxtaposition and widely separated repetitions it probes deeper and deeper into its one chosen action, surprising us with unexpected vistas and reminding us of known fact to intensify the experience of its single paradigm.

To discuss the art of *Paradise Lost* without reference to the kind of purpose Milton habitually set himself is to lose his distinctive achievement. In poetics—as in politics, religion, and ethics—he was a radical conservative liberal. He no more wished to uproot man's heritage than to repeat old errors. Disentangled from time-honored misconceptions, tradition could liberate poetry—as well as church or state—to serve man. For himself Milton scorned mere games at "tic-tac" with phrases (V. 273), and dedicated his poetic along with his polemical gift to clarifying the issues that turn man's course to joy or woe. Almost any page of his prose reminds us that his purposes were never niggling. Perhaps a passage from his first

Defense may recall us to *his* aims and *his* concerns. Like *Paradise Lost* it sounds the authentic Miltonic note:

> Nature and laws would be in ill case if slavery were eloquent and liberty mute. . . . And it were deplorable indeed if the reason mankind is endowed with, which is God's gift, should not furnish more arguments for men's preservation, for their deliverance, and as much as the nature of the thing will bear, for their equality, than for their oppression and utter ruin. . . . Let me therefore enter upon this noble cause with cheerfulness grounded upon the assurance that . . . on my side are the light of truth and reason, and the practice and theory of the best historic ages.

INDEX